Winewoman

@Bergerac.France

Helen Gillespie-Peck

Published by

MELROSE BOOKS

An Imprint of Melrose Press Limited
St Thomas Place, Ely
Cambridgeshire
CB7 4GG, UK
www.melrosebooks.com

FIRST EDITION

Copyright © Helen Gillespie-Peck 2005

The Author asserts her moral right to
be identified as the author of this work

Cover designed by Ross Hilton

ISBN 0 9548480 9 8

Printed and bound in Great Britain by:
Cromwell Press Ltd., Aintree Avenue,
White Horse Business Park, Trowbridge,
Wiltshire, BA14 0XB, UK

The book is dedicated to my beloved husband, David

Foreword

This book has been compiled with an introduction of how I became interested in wine and how my life evolved in the world of wine.

I spent a lot of the time organising and accompanying wine tours so therefore it was necessary to prepare for each region – just as as a teacher does when preparing for lessons.

I turned to wine books, old and new, for my research and made copious notes – well over 1000 memoir cards, and these have helped me to write this book.

When I started teaching, it was in kindergarten, and I used the Froebel method. This was a method introduced to teach young children through play. Friedrich Froebel opened the first kindergarten in 1837 in Germany. I found this technique extremely successful. I suppose when I started teaching about wine – I used the same system.

I feel I have written the book in the same way, and those who read it will not only find it interesting and amusing, but will also learn something about wine and its history – a little education.... . After all, first and foremost, I am a wine educator!

I should like to thank the many authors who gave me much of the information, John Arlott and Christopher Fielden, AnthonyHogg, Michael Broadbent, Hugh Johnson, Lyn MacDonald, Edmund Pennington Rowsell, David Peppercorn, Cyril Ray, Anthony Rose, André Simon, Pamela Vandyke Price, and so many and many more.

Contents

Introduction

In 1970, my ex-husband and I, like many others came to the Dordogne to prepare for a retirement of the 'Good Life'. Unfortunately – like many of the others, we failed.

During our last few months of service in Singapore, we had read in *The Sunday Times* about the attractive barns being sold in the Dordogne at extremely reasonable prices. This interested my husband as we had saved one of our allowances and had a tidy sum to invest.

The first part of the Dordogne to be invaded by the Union Jack was Riberac and its environs. This is north of Bergerac and one of the first places you come to when you drive into the region.

We found out that a Mr Robinson, a 'fruit and veg' importer, had bought a barn south of Bergerac in Loubes Bernac, restored it very successfully and furnished it with local furniture, i.e. long heavy refectory table, benches on either side, etc. To make the property more attractive, he also had a swimming pool. He invited Brits looking for property to visit his home and naturally, they all fell for the idea – hook, line and sinker! It wasn't long before he became a well-known estate agent in France. Another estate agent in London had joined him and together they really got the business going. It was all conducted from a hotel in Saussignac, about 14 km south west of Bergerac, which had been newly built and was perfect for this new development of 'barn selling in the Dordogne'.

Saussignac 'was out in the wilds' – a small village with nothing ... except the hotel with 17 bedrooms, most with a small bathroom with shower and a few with a bath. About four of the bedrooms had only a washbasin. It was typical of the new style of hotel to be found in the region around the 1970s. The owners did a roaring trade looking after the Brits brought down to view properties. The two restaurants were full every evening – the money was pouring in … . The idea was that you arrived at the hotel during the evening. The following day, Mr Robinson collected you in the morning and the whole day was spent looking around the 'barns for sale'.

It was most probable that you would make a decision before leaving and, conveniently, there was a solicitor in Saussignac who would take on the sale. The 'barn' business was like 'the golden eagles landing' for the village solicitor, whose mundane little business until then had been looking after the farmers and their legal worries, wills, etc.

The 'boom' continued for a few years but eventually all the best barns had been sold; Mr Robinson and his associate in London had disassociated after quarrelling about more commission, etc. All of a sudden, we heard that Mr Robinson had moved to the Mediterranean and was never heard of again!

By this time Monsieur Rabat, the solicitor, was well established, dealing with all the sales of properties and other business, which was coming from the British residents.

It is at this point I should like to quote 'The English lost the Hundred Years War at Castillon La Bataille in the 15th century and now they seem to be taking it back – brick by brick!' I can't remember where I heard it but I thought it was so true.

So, off my ex-husband and I went like many others searching for this good life; we stayed at the Saussignac Hotel and toured around the area the whole weekend. There was a lot of rubbish being offered and I didn't really see anything I liked. We returned to Arundel.

My ex-husband was getting rather impatient; he said that most of the good properties would go very quickly and he returned to France the following weekend and found something.

It was a ruin, an oblong-shaped farmhouse – at least 300 years old – hence the name we gave the property, *Les Trois Siècles*. The owners were farmers nearby, who needed money to buy farm machinery and they used the ruin as collateral. You can guess what happened – they couldn't afford to repay the loan and the property was taken from them and put on the market. A move I'm sure they lived to regret.

I couldn't believe my eyes when I saw it and the state it was in! The best thing about it was the situation, an acre of ground, in a quiet corner, secluded garden and next to a vineyard.

From the construction, it had been built in three parts. The 'top end' was the original part, then a barn added and later, the third part. There was a room [I draw my breath at that grand description] at the 'top end' which had an old Basque fireplace. In the centre, the Basque sign had been cut out of the stone, on each side of the sign were two simple carvings – one had not been completed. A neighbour later told me that this room [and hole!] had probably been a cottage belonging to a shepherd, who came home in the evening and carved the fireplace. Unfortunately, he didn't live long enough to finish the second carving.

There are still lots of sheep around Bergerac, but the shepherds now have much better homes. I was often asked why lots of town names in the South-west end in 'ac'. According to old history books, it means something like 'land belonging to…' and this fits in perfectly with Bergerac – land of the shepherds.

The tiles on the floor were 'original' and badly cracked. I soon found out why because every time it rained the water came in through the wall and the tiles [laid directly on to the earth] started to, literally, float! It got worse.

We bought the house in August 1970 and the following Christmas, we told everyone 'we were spending Christmas in our French home'. How posh!

The only room we had to eat and sleep in was the one with the floating tiles!

On Christmas Eve we got into our camp beds with wellies neatly laid out at the side and, sure thing, on Christmas morning it had poured with rain. We were flooded and my daughter and I sat up, laughed and sang Christmas carols…. . My ex-husband wasn't amused.

There was no ceiling, only beams and the leaking roof above. I noticed that the walls above the beams were stained a beautiful blue and thought perhaps a little decorating had been done at one time…. . Later, I found some bags of powder resting on the beams and realised it was copper sulphate, used to spray vines for protection against mildew. It leaves a beautiful hue of blue on the vine leaves – same as the 'decorating'.

There were two doors, the side one led into a hole and when we shone the torch in here we found a tree growing. This had obviously been used for the loo! The other door led to the next level where there was a low-beamed barn, the difference in floor level at one end was about 24 inches from the other end! The rain came in on the right [at the high end], and ran through to the other!

Opposite, there was another little door, my word, these people must have been very small! Through this door was a room with a floor that had been crudely cemented; very cracked and the difference in floor level from one end to the other was about 12 inches, so it was impossible to put any furniture down.

The 'rural' way of living was laid out before me. Two rooms, one on each side of the barn, cows in the barn, *voilà*! Central heating … . There were three tiny electric lights in the whole place which were hanging by a feeble wire and you thought twice about switching any on because the switches were not secured to the wall and there seemed to be bare wires everywhere. [Water was available from the source down the road.]

At the end of the ruin, near the entrance to it all, was a wine press with two stone vats. Well, I thought … perhaps I would start making my own wine!

The plan was already agreed. It would be slowly restored so that in about 20 years time we would have a perfect home for retirement! What a dream!

I'll tell you now, I wasn't totally convinced… . 'Restored' was a ridiculous word to use – it needed to be *rebuilt*! From then on, every available free moment was spent in 'our country home'. Sometimes it meant crossing by ferry on the Thursday or Friday, driving down in our Renault 5, which then took about 12 hours as we didn't have the motorways there are today. On arrival, the whole place had to be opened up, water brought from the source, and linen taken out of the plastic cases – we couldn't leave it out as the mice would have had a feast!

I did the 'woman's work', setting up a kitchen – which had to be done each time because of the 'mice' problem and keeping the water buckets full for the kitchen. Toilet facilities were as for open air camping and the only way we were able to wash was with a bucket of cold water.

We worked non-stop, breaking through 3 feet thick walls, digging out mud, etc. for a couple of days or so then spent another day packing everything away and driving back to the ferry to return to UK. WE WERE MAD!

It was difficult for me at first, my ex-husband had become quite fluent in French as he had studied whilst abroad, but to say I was extremely limited in my understanding of French was no exaggeration.

We got on really well with the people of the village, as being the first Brits to move in, they seemed to enjoy having us around. We enjoyed the involvement, but it was getting to the stage where we were invited to everything going on in the community. [I put the stopper in when Bingo was suggested!].

The wedding of our neighbour's daughter was one of the memorable events.

Weddings start early in the day. Family and close friends meet for the civil part of it and this particular one was held in Bergerac in the Town Hall. Afterwards, it was off to the public gardens for photographs followed by a gastronomic lunch in a restaurant.

Everyone rested after this, but by six o'clock, they were all ready to go again and this is when *yours truly* joined in. We met at the village church where the wedding service was held and followed by a cocktail party in the church grounds. The drinking and chatting went on for nearly 2 hours!

Someone announced it was time for dinner and off we drove to the Saussignac Hotel where a huge banquet was served. By this time, the group had expanded from 'family and close friends' to 'family, close friends and friends', which included us … . Dinner took the usual 3–4 hours and it was then time to 'cut the cake' or, as they do in France, pull off the sticky choux pastries, which had been piled high and then covered with caramel. This was the time when everyone from the village joined in and the music started!

After being dragged around the floor by farmers with two 'left feet', then twirled round and round for what seemed ages [the idea being that the lady eventually fell over], I decided that enough was enough and made my 'farewells', got in the car and drove home. My bed, with white sheets, and beautiful bedspread sitting there in the middle of the barn on a none too even mud floor, under 300-year-old oak beams dripping with cobwebs was an absolute sight of paradise! I collapsed into it and fell asleep.

All of a sudden, I was awoken by shrieks of 'Helène' 'Helène'. I had to answer, and then the response came:

Helène, the wedding isn't over [it was around 3 am] and we have still to have the 'fertility soup' … . I felt like telling them what to do with the fertility soup but, being British, I got dressed and went up to the farmhouse. It was packed and, as I made my way to the hub of it all, the soup came into view … . It was a white soup, with garlic and yolks floating about on a surface of whites of eggs, which had been slowly poured into the soup and looked very stringy. Gosh, I thought, this is taking the 'British upper lip' a bit far…if they expect me to have some of this! 'Feeble Brit' succumbed, and it wasn't as bad as expected but then, at that hour of the morning and the way I felt, I probably didn't really taste it… .

A few of the guests were then pushed into the bedroom and there before us was the bridal couple in their pyjamas. It was explained to me that it was our job to turn the mattress over so that they fell out of bed! I crawled back to my palatial barn and collapsed for the second time.

After that, I managed to find excuses for not attending weddings.

John, a telephone engineer, and his wife and two children came down a few times. He enjoyed tinkering with electricity – we ended up with wires running everywhere and a few plugs here and there. We could switch on – this was really something. The only trouble was, we had a certain level of electricity coming into the house and, when you switched on the electric kettle, the trip switch reacted and you were left in darkness. These 'blackouts' were frequent as you can imagine and torches had to be left in strategic spots so that we could make our way to the 'box' [after we had switched off the kettle or the lights] to turn it on again.

Later, we rose to 'dizzy heights'. We were able to shower! Not a real shower, remember – we had no water… .

This was great, as I recall one night previously, a French couple had invited about ten of us to their home for dinner. We had managed to wash our hands and face but when you looked at our feet – it was embarrassing…covered in mud.

For the shower, a wine cubitainer [10-litre plastic wine container] was used. We fitted a pipe to the tap and a watering-can 'rose' on the other end of the pipe. The cubitainer was fitted to a branch of a tree and refilled from the source for each person.

The kitchen was moved regularly from one area to the other; this was to facilitate the work being done. I was becoming a *professional kitchen arranger*… but getting fed up with it. The shelves, i.e., planks of wood suspended from the beams with rope, to hold the food, were a bit dodgy to say the least. The wash bowl sat on another couple of planks, which rested both sides on bricks we were using for building.

My friends from 'Medicines Inspectorate' didn't go much on the hygiene. In fact, on one visit, they brought sterilisation tablets to put in the water brought from the well! A sample of the well water was taken back to UK for analysis and the report was dreadful! I was overjoyed when we later had mains water put in.... Of course, we never drank the water directly from the well – it was always boiled.

The same friends were appalled at the then farming conditions in the Dordogne. I would send them up to collect the milk for me it was wonderful.... I put it in a large pan, boiled it to sterilise, then let it simmer slowly. Cornish cream didn't have a look in.... I agreed completely, the barn was filthy but the people around didn't seem to suffer.

Every morning around 4 am, the lorries would come to collect the milk. It woke you up but it became so 'automatic' to fall asleep again immediately. The only nights I didn't sleep were just after they had taken away the calves. The cows would cry all night – for several nights; it was cruel and I sympathised with the animals.

When the *Marché Commune* started to take shape, all this ended. Small farms have gone out of existence.

It took only 10 years for my ex-husband, a naval officer, to become obsessed with the project and he planned his retirement before he was 40. In 1980, we took up residence in France – the move was mammoth!

We had a few friends in Bath who suggested their teenage sons should come down in the summer to give us a hand. First it was Stephen – son of a retired naval officer, I had taught him to read and write at kindergarten .... He brought his friend David, who at that time was rebelling against his parents and society, so much so that he had dyed his blonde hair black! His father [another naval officer] and mother, a teacher in a local school, must have gone through hell trying to cope with this outburst!

David was 17 years at the time, a pupil of King Edward's School in Bath and hadn't a clue which way he was going in life. His only ambition seemed to be to dress in black – to go with his new hair colour and to listen to 'Clash' on his cassette machine. Is it a coincidence that his name is David *Black*man?

The number of students grew. After all, Stephen has four brothers and then there were 'the friends'.

By this time, we had cleared the loft above the barn and laid a new floor, as the original was over 100 years old and extremely dangerous. I put down mattresses all over the place and the boys slept there. You can imagine what it was like with the shower facilities in the summer when we had 10 to 15 people staying at the same time! In the colder months, it wasn't possible to shower outside, so the cubitainer was brought in doors and put on a beam! We used a child's plastic pool to stand in.

Feeding them was a nightmare! Not that they were fussy about food – it was the amount. My two-burner gas cooker and little portable oven did very well. It was the organisation of the day that was most important. Up at seven and not in bed until after eleven – bearing in mind that we still had to bring the water up from the well and that was a continual job for me. ... When I wasn't doing that, I was baking pies and cakes, preparing vegetables, going for bread, etc. It was non-stop. I was making about three cheeses – onion and potato pies each week as this was the boys' favourite – with baked beans, of course!

Washing clothes and especially the boys' rugby shirts in the cooler weather was tough... . Because of the water problem, I had to – as the village people did – wash at the well, not forgetting to rub the clothes well on the stone surrounding the source as 'this is what really cleans clothes' I was told... .

My French friends thought I was mad and said that 'no French woman would work and put up with that way of life'. But then, I'm British and as my ex-husband kept telling me, as every penny we had went into this project, 'we must sacrifice for our future' and it was long before I began to realise who was doing the sacrificing!

I didn't regret the hard work looking after the boys. They worked from sun-up to sun-down and they enjoyed it, because they were working as a team in an organised environment. Each evening around seven, they would finish and start showering – each filling the cubitainer for the next one. I had cold beers ready for them, which they would drink and discuss the day's work and think up some 'brilliant' ideas for future work... . The talking went right through dinner – with a few glasses of the local wine. About 10.30, everyone went to bed and I finished clearing up.

My daughter, four years on, seemed to have lost interest in France, as she came over only once during the working period. Her life as an officer in the WRAF kept her pretty occupied and I don't think she relished the thought of having to work!

A girlfriend of mine from London arrived with her daughter and boyfriend. They had bought a ruin about 20 km from us. They stayed for dinner and she explained that, because of her busy life and her daughter's schooling – she was actually at college – they had to rush back to London, but could they leave the 'boyfriend' with us. The 'Bath Buns' [as I had nicknamed my boys] waited for my reply, which was 'yes', after all – what's another one? But – what 'another one'?!

The following night he informed me he was 'vegetarian'; I had already made the meal so with quick thinking, asked if he would like beans and something? 'That will be fine' was his reply. He ate the whole tin – with other things and my 'bath buns' were furious as baked beans were a luxury – not to be found in France and I could bring only one carton of tins with me in the Renault 5 but, as the boys pointed out, they would all go in no time if Eric lived on them!

I was tired that night, and went to bed earlier than usual, but the boys stayed for discussion with their new inmate.

The next morning, David was up before me – most unusual! Seemingly, Eric was also a Hare Krishna follower and the conversation of the evening got 'very deep' and unpleasant – upsetting one of Stephen's brothers very much – it almost led to blows … .

Well, I thought, my 'friend' had certainly landed me in it… .

One night, the 'bath buns' had noticed that Eric was having rather large helpings and seconds of the cheese and potato pie – as this was 'veggie'. This was not acceptable and when it came to the dessert – another favourite, rum and chocolate, three-tiered gateau, a great chunk was cut by him. That was the end … . Eric was told that there were eggs in the gateau and that was not 'veggie'. 'Ah,' Eric said 'That is no problem because when I go up to the old windmill to say my prayers, I shall ask for forgiveness'. I telephoned my friend and said she must arrange for him to leave immediately.

The boys got on really well together, I enjoyed having them around… . By the end of the holiday, they were all beautifully tanned [to pull the birds...] and David's hair was blonde with black tips!

The following year, they came down at the end of term and stayed until November. As the summer left and autumn came in, the boys kept their eyes on the temperature because I had promised that, when it got to a certain temperature, I would make porridge for breakfast – which they all seemed to enjoy.

Stephen was hoping to continue with his art studies and become an artist [which I am pleased to say he now is, living in Chelsea and New York – and rather wealthy…], he was at that time practising 'shading with oils'.

A shower room had been built in the 'hole' I referred to at the beginning of the chapter, and I suggested Stephen painted something in oil on one of the walls.

He suffered from acne and we had many talks about it. He asked me once, 'Why, at the most important time of my life when I want to meet girls, have I been blessed with acne?' I almost cried, because he was a good-looking chap, like his father, tall, blonde, slim and a beautiful smile. I was lost for words.

There was a girl he liked, very much, in Bath but she had little time for him because of the spots. It was this girl, dressed in jeans and white shirt, wearing sunglasses, which reflect the bathroom cabinet on the opposite wall, he painted on one of the walls. She's still there and often people washing their hands, look in the mirror above the washbasin, see her and think someone has come into the bathroom!

The boys would tease me from time to time, but on one particular occasion it wasn't funny. I was working in the garden and the boys were up above the barn, taking down a wall, which wasn't safe. All of a sudden, one of them ran out to tell me Paul had been hurt. For me, the worst nightmare had happened! Paul came down the ladders, covered in blood – my heart sank. I rushed for bandages and the boys laughed. Stephen had decorated him with red paint!

The locals, especially the young girls, loved having the boys around. They would come to call, practise their English … .

Stephen's younger brother, Robert, was extremely good looking. He upset the older boys quite a lot – so much so one time they pegged him out in the garden and said, if he didn't behave, they would plaster him with some of my homemade jam and leave him for the ants! We had a few tears from him but he did deserve a warning. With girls, he was very shy and when the local roof specialist's daughter [who spoke very good English] came to call to invite him to the house, he went mad! 'I'm not going round there,' he said, but his older brothers and friend said 'oh yes you are'. Later in the day, they took him to the source, washed him down and sprayed him with Fabergé... . He was ready when the girl and mother called to collect him.

The big event of the summer for the boys was the local fête held in August. They would get dressed in the latest gear [I believe it was frilly shirts that year] and up we would go to the village hall. Outside, the tables had been set with paper cups and plates and you had to take your own knives and forks.

The wine flowed for the aperitifs then we sat down to the crudités. After that, the 'Méchoui' [roasted lamb], brutally torn apart was put on your plate. I remember my cousin-in-law, a little fussy about hygiene, almost throwing up at the sight of this and commenting something like 'you would have to be paralytic to eat food like this!' By this time we had drunk so much wine – we were getting near the 'paralytic' stage, so we tucked in. This was followed by cheese and a tub of ice-cream. Not bad for 30 Fr!

A 'liqueur' with a base of Monbazillac was served and the music started. We always had a few of the French 'in a circle' type of dancing. Lady put in the centre, and whoever she presented the 'hankie' to, was 'her man' for the evening. My boys were being gobbled up!

Later, the pop music started and the boys were there showing off their talents as they all belonged to little groups in Bath. The 'Blue Suede Shoes' was the best effort. Haydon, who had a rather sad life as his mother suffered from MS, got on the drums and Stephen did the singing – the French were in raptures!

By this time, the house was becoming more habitable. Inside walls had been built, water had been laid on and we had three toilets, *en suite* in the main bedroom, at the top of the stairs, for guests and in the shower-room downstairs! The furniture we had brought from England was now in place in a library, dining room, kitchen and two bedrooms. Sounds great – and it was! At last it was coming together. My ex-husband was very good with wood and many of the wood features such as restored beams, etc. were his handiwork.

We were receiving lots of visitors, some were extremely helpful, but others wanted a holiday and I'm afraid 'Trois Siècles' was not ready for guests.

Among the visitors was a naval colleague we had met in Singapore. He became very 'attached' to us. I had met his wife once when they visited us in Arundel. They were both most helpful and soon they had decided that they would also like to live in the Dordogne and started looking for property. My ex-husband wasn't very pleased about this, as the relationship was really a bit of 'love/hate'. When John had finally found a piece of land to build on in the centre of the village, my ex-husband had mixed feelings.

We helped them with all the administration, etc. and they started coming down on a regular basis. John had decided to work on a little longer in order to secure a better pension – he was a few years older than us.

The shell of the house was soon built and John's family and friends came down to work on the interior. They all stayed with us, some had beds indoors and others in tents. John's wife, Pauline, wasn't really into cooking and such – she helped with the 'team' on the house. Each evening they would return and, after showers and 'drinks', dinner was served.

They had decided that, in advance of their move to use their caravan, as they were bringing more people down and it would be better to live 'on site'. The caravan filled with wood, machinery and tools, followed by a Landrover and three other cars came in convoy from Portsmouth. Some of the 'workers' had never driven in France before, so it was going to be a *slowish* journey.

They disembarked at Le Havre and it was pouring with rain. From there to Alençon the roads are pretty 'twisty' and very much so around Gacé. The convoy got as far as north of Gacé and the caravan swerved, overturned into a field and ended up in bits! The unfortunate thing was that John had taken it out of insurance as the caravan was never going to be on the road again after arrival at its destination, Cunèges.

John phoned us at 7.30 am asking if we could go up north to bring some of the contents back to the Dordogne. My ex-husband explained that this would be impossible as our car, although a decent size, was certainly not big enough to carry all that which had been stored in the caravan.

Fortunately, locals came to his help, in particular a garage owner from the centre of Gacé. John brought what he could cram into the other four vehicles and left the rest with the *garagiste*.

They arrived late that evening, soaked and very tired. Then out came everything that they had collected from the broken-up caravan. There was loads of bed linen, clothes, soft furnishings, etc. which had been stored in the drawers of the caravan. All was soaking wet and dirty! There was nothing to do other than lay it out on the grass in the back garden. If anyone had passed over in low flight, they would have wondered what was going on!

Without the caravan, they had nowhere to sleep, so for the next few days, I had beds and mattresses in every room!

It wasn't long after that John and his family movd to France permanently and the following year my ex-husband started talking about selling up and moving on – but I had no intention of moving – my moving days were over.

I had to learn French – at least enough to get by – so when friends phoned me from Britain asking if I could find good host families for their children to spend some time learning French, I decided to advertise in the local paper. This ended up quite a hoot! French parents would phone me and I, understanding very little of what they said, managed to get the name of the town/village and their phone number. After that it was a case of searching the directory [the French list numbers by town/village], with the village and most of the phone number, I contacted them and made a visit. Fortunately a lot of the parents spoke a little English and this helped me to discuss a 'learning holiday' in England for their children. Talking to them and later the students, as I accompanied them to stay with the families in UK, helped me to improve my French! I didn't arrange many exchanges, so the keen interest in wine and studying the subject continued.

Some time later, I wrote an article on how I would organise a wine tour in Bordeaux – this being only an hour away from where I live. This article was sent to a tour operator who contacted me and asked if I would take wine tours for him.

I was very pleased about this but with only about four tours each year and the poor fee offered, I knew I wasn't going to be earning much.

The Saussignac Hotel was eventually sold and, with the profit, the owners bought some land on the main road between Bergerac and Bordeaux and built a night club which has been, and still is, hugely successful. They also have a hotel on the route to Agen.

The Saussignac hotel never recovered. The next couple who took over, Maurice and his wife, were very good, lots of experience and she a Bon Chef de France. They had what was needed to run such a hotel but unfortunately there weren't so many people coming. Because of the pleasant atmosphere – and the good food, I regularly took small groups studying wine, to stay for a few days – and they loved it!

Maurice was much older than his wife and his health started to fail; he ended up carrying a machine to monitor his heartbeat. They had to sell the hotel.

They had a few offers – one from Germans and the locals were very anxious about this. Germans were not welcome in the Dordogne! There are too many memories of the Second World War: the Resistance men who were killed in Ste Foy La Grande nearby.

A local lady heard of the sale and her son was then working as a chef in Mantes le Jolie [between Paris and Le Havre]. His girlfriend had just finished her training in hotel management in Paris. Thierry and his partner took over the hotel.

I went along for dinner and was 'tepidly' welcomed by this Parisian-dressed young girl and taken into the restaurant, which *tout à coup* had lost its atmosphere. The locals didn't like the 'new look'; they don't accept change and, although very chic, very Parisien, etc. it was not what the locals wanted. Thierry was a super chef, but for me to take groups there we needed both atmosphere and good cooking – with some good down-to-earth Dordogne 'plates'. I found another hotel for my groups.

Before coming to France, I had worked in London with 'Medicines Division' of the Civil Service. In one of the Newsletters I noticed that there was a Wine Appreciation Group held every Wednesday at the DTI. I decided to join and am jolly glad I did – it changed my life! This was the serious start of Winewoman.

Each evening we had a different speaker from one of the wine houses in London and slowly I got even more involved as I became a member of The Sommeliers and then a member of The Cellarmasters.

Pamela Van Dyke Price, Cyril Ray and Hugh Johnson came into my life. Pamela was one of the top wine writers at that time and her work was truly original. Today, in her 80s, she is known as queen of wine writers and thoroughly deserves the title. Her books took me not only into wine but into the history of it. Cyril Ray has gone but has an honoured place in the Circle of Wine Writers. Hugh Johnson continues to be one of the best wine educators we have in Britain today.

I learnt a lot at the wine appreciation evenings – certainly about the different wines available in London, as we visited a few of the City wine cellars. One of the most enjoyable evenings was at the Café Royal in Regent Street; I can recall it was the group's task to taste wines of the 1930s, I can't remember whether we had six or eight, but I know that only one was worth drinking and I wouldn't have liked to pay much for it!

Another evening was held by the DTI. A Company in Argentina was introducing wines to the British supermarkets at extremely reasonable prices. They invited us along to make comments. I was most impressed by the reds, as they were rich and fruity and so easy to drink … the white wine wasn't nearly so good, but then the vinification of it wasn't controlled as it is today.

The Australian wine evenings were few and far between. They were just discovering Barrossa and the Shiraz grape. This 'weed' had something to offer and it wasn't long before the Australian wine-makers found out what exactly it was! Pre- the 'High Tec', their wines were quite different. I could always pick out an Australian Red because I could taste burnt grape skins. They have a lot of sun and it is so easy to pick just that little bit too late.

All this tasting was interesting and enjoyable but I had a hankering to learn more. I wanted to know how the wine got in the glass – from the grape.

A couple of years after settling in France I decided to take a course at the CIVRB [i.e. Conseil Interprofessionnel des Vins de la Région de Bergerac]. I joined a group of vignerons to increase my knowledge about the wines and vineyards of Bergerac.

The wine tastings were very enlightening. Not only did we taste wine but also the constituents of wine: tannin, acidity, sweetness and alcohol – all served in water!

The 'water' tasting didn't end there. One week, I arrived to learn that we would be tasting waters from different areas of Bergerac. I was absolutely lost! You can imagine my embarrassment as the other chaps had a full discussion of these waters and were able to identify the source! Later it dawned on me … all these different bottled waters in the supermarket – they drink so much of it and this is why they were able to recognise it! After that, I started drinking more bottled water and you would be amazed in the difference of taste from each source.

I knew our 'good life' wouldn't work after the type of life we have in the Royal Navy. We did the 'wining and dining' in the summer with friends who came to visit – and to give a hand with this mammoth project – but after the season, it was a case of getting on with it, working long hours and watching the pennies dwindle away on building materials.

Two years later, my ex-husband walked out and advised me to get out of the property because he had put it up for sale. It broke my heart to see our dream home advertised in the local estate agent's window in Bergerac.

Being a survivor and having spent my life moving from one house to the other, I decided that 'decision time' had come ... . Taking professional advice, I didn't move out and took the house as a settlement when I divorced him.

I thought of the years of saving, working and the effort that had to be put in to restore this barn; and here I was, abandoned in France, with no income, and speaking very little French.

Each day, I did a little more of the restoration with materials that had been left. I started by exercising in the morning to the music of Gloria Gaynor – 'I Will Survive'.

Realising that I couldn't go on without work, I turned to my 'passion' – wine.

For the next 2 years, I studied wine and its history – this helped to keep me 'sane' and recover from a traumatic experience! I managed to get a few little jobs in-between, but earning a living was a continual struggle.

Since then, I have been completely immersed in the subject – all facets – but the most important is wine education and writing.

Chapter 1
Immersed In Wine

Wine tours took me to over 32 wine regions of Europe and I have also visited those of Canada, California, Argentina and Chile. I have visited some of the most prestigious vineyards and met some of the top wine-makers.

The tour company I worked for went bust. I was quite pleased as, by that time, I had had enough of touring around in inferior coaches some of which, I later learned, didn't even have MOT Certificates – and I was taking them to the south of France! Tour operators often have problems getting the number of passengers for which they have *costed* into their budget. If they can't get the 'minimum number', they make the effort to run the tour by making cuts. The 'cuts' can vary, using a less expensive hotel, using a smaller coach or in one or two cases of specialised tours, using a not so specialised guide. The coach company may offer you a coach with a driver who hasn't been with the firm very long and therefore is not as popular – or so demanded. Most drivers are very good and, because of poor pay, they know that with 'extra effort' on tour they can do very well 'thank you'. Passengers appreciate being well looked after and getting into a spick and span coach every day.

It pays to drive for the 'more up-market' type of tour – tipping is much better, the coach is kept cleaner and the drivers are more appreciated. A good tour operator will make sure the driver is suitable for the tour but, of course, there are one or two who slide through the net and, although they have a record, manage to get on one of the 'better class' tours when tips are good. I have experienced only one such driver but that was enough! I had, as always, discussed the driver with the coach company and I knew who the driver for that particular tour would be. Unfortunately, the appointed driver's wife had run off with another man and the coach company sent the only one available and he was not at all suitable! At the end of the tour, I told the manager that I would refuse to take out a coach again driven by this individual.

He arrived on board, took off his shoes and proceeded to drive. I asked him to put his shoes back on his feet. Smoking didn't seem to bother him, but it did my passengers and my voice, so we had another little 'set to'.

On board a coach, your passengers come first and both driver and leader, as I always accompanied the tours, must accept the responsibility to make sure that everything is running smoothly.

You might think I'm a 'bossy boots' but on my tours, I'm in charge – some drivers wouldn't accept the fact that a woman who is in charge, knows a lot more about the roads and rules than they do.

One certainly didn't! I explained the routine, that on arrival at the hotel I expect him to look after the baggage and if anyone needed help it should be given 'with a smile'. I also pointed out that, because these tours are small in number and conducted more as a 'house party', the driver is expected to join the group for dinner and he should dress accordingly. At 8 pm he arrived for dinner, dressed in a scruffy T-shirt and jeans and, what was even worse, carrying a bottle of brown sauce! I just about died … I kept my calm until everyone was seated, then stood up and asked him to remove the bottle from the table. The rest of the week was hell!

But it's not only the staff who give problems of which, thank goodness, I haven't had many … . I once took a private club of very upmarket members on a wine tour. Everything went well until they started bickering amongst themselves. It ended up as two definite sides and I found the whole situation embarrassing. One chap stood up and tried to verbally undermine me, I forget what about, but I can remember he was extremely rude and very loud mouthed. I didn't say anything in return but waited my chance. It came the next evening.

At this particular village hotel where the food is superb, we always had a special dinner on the last night. We started with a *Plateau Royale Fruits de Mers* which included shellfish piled high on silver platters standing high on the table, followed by *foie gras, confit de canard*, cheese and a dessert decorated with loads of glitters. Gourmet at its best and I always wore a loose-fitting long dress! The gentleman in question insisted in ordering a bottle of Champagne to accompany the dish – and he let everyone know that he and his friends would be having 'champers'. [Actually, the Sauvignon, dry and zingy from Duras, was perfect with the royal fish dish.] The Champagne arrived and with true dexterity, or so he thought, he opened the bottle with a loud bang. Champagne went everywhere! He was very proud of making so much noise and started to pour what was left into the glasses. This was my moment. This was my chance so I stood up, projected my voice like an old school '*marm*' and said:

> This gives me a chance to explain how one opens a bottle of champagne. One removes the cage, carefully. The cork should be covered with a napkin and held very securely with one hand, making sure that the bottle top is pointing away from everyone. You should then turn the bottle firmly with the other hand, easing out the cork slowly. All that should be heard is a quiet 'phutt'. This shows experience.

> Loud bangs are made only by inexperienced Champagne drinkers.

Within a week of the company I worked for closing down, another from Bristol contacted me to say that they would be sending their representative to France the following week to discuss a contract. This was in October. The Director arrived and offered me a yearly retainer to work solely for them. It was agreed that unlike the last company who were only interested in 'bums on seats' [a horrible but acceptable term], they would upgrade the tours and be 'backed' by first-class marketing. I accepted.

Nothing happened and, by the following April, my clients had not received a brochure. In May I went to Bristol and closed the agreement.

My friend Jenny, who owned two off-licence stores in Devon, suggested I ran my own wine tours and used one of her shops as my business address. We both had the same accountant who advised us accordingly. This was quite ambitious as I had very little capital but after much thought went ahead.

Keeping the property going in France was becoming more difficult. The upkeep, maintenance [although I did a lot of it myself], rates, heating were costing too much and money was running out. I didn't want to sell it as I had given so much of me to keep it going, but things were bad so I put it on the market.

As well as the tours, I was able to get a little work in England but not enough to keep everything ticking over.

Working long hours, trying to get the tours operating, was a hard struggle especially battling with the *big boys* and being constantly degraded by the media because I wasn't a member of ABTA or similar. I pressed on not making much success or money – but I enjoyed every hour of work I put in to making each tour a success. I had a small group of clients who travelled with me every year – some covered 14 years!

I was never able to expand because of the media. No one would risk paying for my type of tour without insurance and not being a member of one of the 'protectors' made sure of that.

During this time I also started teaching at one of the catering colleges in Devon. A visiting lecturer told me of the Association of Wine Educators that had been formed in London. He was a 'founder member' and asked me if I would like to be considered for membership. A few months later, after the 'vetting', I received a letter to say I was accepted and invited to the next AGM.

I had also found an office in a 'low' area of Torquay, as Jenny was finding it difficult to answer the phone and run her business. I hated the office and 3 years later, after a hard struggle with Railtrack, took over one of the listed 'signal boxes' in Devon, a beautiful signal box. Railtrack refurbished it for me and decorated it with vertical, pale pink blinds and claret-coloured carpet. In this office I was able to pursue my vocation in wine education.

I had then set up Wine Associates Ltd and created L'Academie du Vin Devon, a place for wine enthusiasts to come and learn more about the subject. I took on 'business partners' for both and learned to regret it.

By this time, I had become an Accredited Tutor of the Wine and Spirit Education Trust and I have had great satisfaction in helping students to pass exams and set them on their way, following a career in wine.

I was getting known and starting to write articles in Devon magazines. I enjoyed this very much.

An article about me appeared in one of the Bergerac wine journals and, because of it, I had a call from two chaps, who had bought a vineyard quite near my home in France, asking me to come and taste their wines.

This was in 1997 and on 1 January 1998, I telephoned and went along the same afternoon, tasted the wines and gave my opinion. It was a coincidence as the owner of the property came from Edinburgh, my birthplace.

His 'business partner' and girlfriend had decided to pull out because they realised the work involved in getting this vineyard up to standard was going to be too much for them.

David Baxter, a financier from Newton Investment in London, had taken early retirement in order to find something interesting to do for the rest of his working life. His business colleague, a farmer, had suggested farming in France – but they ended up with a vineyard!

David hadn't a clue about vines – or wine, but found this a challenge and developed the vineyard.

He asked me to help him, acting as his consultant. I agreed but continued to work with students and take wine tours travelling excessively.

Chapter 2
Wine Associates Ltd

As I said, when I took over the wine tours, I set myself up in business and created Wine Associates Ltd in the Southwest of England. Sometimes I think it was a crazy idea, I now know that there really isn't the market in that region, but not having this type of experience I took on something which demanded a lot of hard work for very little monetary reward. To have done such a thing near London – or Manchester – or my home town, Edinburgh, it would have been a completely different story.

Pat was my 'backbone' in Wine Associates Ltd which covered all aspects of wine education, L'Academie du Vin Devon, wine tours, etc. and we were kept very busy. I coped with the administration and publicity but the accounts were all too much for me. Pat, my friend, came to the rescue for, without her help, there is no doubt that I should have been struggling.

I met Pat in the early 1990s. She was one of the first members of L'Academie du Vin Devon, which I had started so that wine enthusiasts in Devon had a chance to meet, discuss and learn something about wine.

She lived with her mother, sister and brother-in-law, niece and grand niece in the most beautiful cottage just outside Newton Abbot. Moss Cottage is a delightful place to visit, real Devon! Her family were keen gardeners of flowers, fruit and vegetables; her sister is an excellent cook and going to dinner – usually for Pat's birthday in January – was a real treat!

Pat and Neil Cole [my accountant] looked after the accounts and kept me on the straight and narrow and, although the 'accounting days' are finished, Pat and I still keep in touch.

I suppose choosing Torquay to start a wine school wasn't a good idea although the venue was the Palace Hotel and we couldn't have asked for more, as the management were extremely kind and offered every assistance possible. There were very few wine enthusiasts in the area and the numbers slowly dwindled. I later accepted the kind invitation from the Toorak Hotel to base the academy there. The idea was that we were permitted to hold our monthly tastings there and I would host their gastronomic evenings. The little dining room was perfect and the head chef was delighted to be doing something like this as he could exercise his prowess. The evenings we held were very good and very much appreciated by the guests but, alas, there weren't enough people interested – or willing to pay for this type of thing in Torquay.

Nick Borst-Smith was also very helpful with our accommodation problems. The Nobody Inn wasn't very busy on a Monday evening and there was a room we could use. This was a truly delightful setting and I did appreciate it but getting to it, down all the narrow Devon lanes, was a bit of a nightmare in the winter months.

It was at the Palace Hotel where I first met Lee, a 20-year-old who had just left Exeter University and had a mad passion to learn more about wine. His mother had noticed his keen interest and had contacted the Association of Wine Educators in London. They suggested he telephone my office and, as soon as he came to the Palace Hotel and took hold of his glass to taste the wines of the evening, I said to my colleague, this boy is going to go far in the wine world and as it has happened – he has!

His mother explained to me that he had tried to find work in the wine world and each time he was told that, without experience or knowledge, he could not be accepted for interview.

He took a job in a bank in Cornwall and very soon decided that it was not his scene. He started studying with me for the WSET Ordinary Certificate.

Just after he took the bank job, the 'New Deal' scheme came out in Cornwall. His mother went to find out more about the scheme, hoping that this would take Lee into the wine world. She explained to them that I was willing to take him on as an assistant and train him at the same time. The Job Centre said that this was not possible as Lee lived in Cornwall, the scheme was only being tried there and Lee would have to find the work in Cornwall. His mother said that there was no one him to train him in wine and in the end permission was given for Lee to work for me and be trained at the same time. He then studied and passed his WSET Advanced Course with distinction. We were delighted.

Whilst working with me during the day, he spent his evenings working in restaurants, serving at tables, washing dishes – whatever he could do to save some money for his wine studies because I suggested that he must get some experience in the 'New World'. I took him to the London World Wine Fair, where he had a chance to meet and talk to people about his future. He wrote and sent many letters and received only a few replies. But eventually, Philip Shaw contacted us to say that there would be a job for him in Rosemount – one of the most important Australian wineries. Lee was told that he would have to find his own fare and would earn very little but he would gain experience – and that was just what we wanted.

After only a short period, Philip Shaw saw what I had seen the first time I met Lee. He was a young 'Wineman' and it wasn't long before he was given more advanced work in the winery and Lee was very happy. His living conditions weren't the greatest whilst he was out there but that didn't matter, he came back to Britain a far wiser person. Rosemount had also shown their appreciation by refunding Lee his air fare. His father flew out to Australia to take Lee sightseeing before returning to UK.

I then suggested he went to California and that turned out to be quite a challenge. Letters were sent to all the wineries, but laws are strict in the States and he was unable to get work. Still determined to go there, he had saved enough for his fare and decided to hitch-hike around the vineyards. He saw most of Napa and was very fortunate to meet up with a family who had a son of the same age. Lee borrowed a bicycle from them which made getting around much easier.

His father joined him at the end of the 'training' period. With the hired car, Lee was then able to visit the vineyards of Sonoma in comfort.

That was it! On his return to the UK, Lee wrote for two or three jobs and had immediate replies and went to London to train as an apprentice winebroker. I didn't see much of him – except at the London Wine Fair, he was so busy. When he came to visit one of his clients in the Dordogne, he would come and stay with us.

Then one day, we had an email to say that he wouldn't be seeing us for a while as he had taken a job in Singapore. That didn't surprise me – Lee never surprises me…. . We kept in touch.

Later, my husband, David, and I went to the Far East to meet up with some friends and, by that time, Lee was setting up a wine shop in Kuala Lumpur. It was a small, exclusive wine shop with beautiful display cabinets, which showed only a few bottles. As I walked into the shop, Lee, with a cheeky grin on his face, said to me as he placed a second wine of one of the Premier Growths of Bordeaux in the cabinet, 'I know what you think of such second wines but the Malaysians go by the name, and the wines sell'. Well, there was no answer to that!

We went out to dinner and reminisced over Lee's learning period. His lady friend was quite amused with the stories, especially when we told her the one about being invited to London by Mr Blunkett.

Lee had been the first 'New Deal' applicant in Devon – and I think, Cornwall. Because of this we had been invited to a conference in London with similar people from the 'trial' areas of Britain; we were accompanied by a representative of the job centre, who had followed Lee's progress. We stayed in a very nice hotel which was close to Fortnum and Mason and Lee went out after dinner to look in the windows of his favourite food and wine store.

The next day, we were taken to the Conference by coach and, on arrival, were served coffee. After that, we were shown a film of the endeavours of the Government's new scheme and what it hoped to achieve. I laughed when I heard the theme music – it was that of "The Full Monty"! I might have laughed, but the next time I watched the film – and after the Conference – I saw the serious side of the film!

Around that time, I remembered speaking to some Americans on one of my tours, who had also seen the film and they had obviously appreciated the depth of the message in the film because I was quite surprised when they told me that the film was better than 'The Titanic' and should have received the Award. This surprised me, but I now know why.

Back to the Conference, I often digress, there is so much to talk about…

After the short film, we had a couple of talks from members of the government and were allowed to chat with them later. David Blunkett was truly interested in what Lee had achieved and said to me, 'It's a pity we don't have red wine in Britain'. Immediately I replied, 'Ah, but we do and a very good one is produced in the Southwest!' He laughed and his answer was 'When I retire, I am going to study wine with you!' There was great laughter from all around and the cameras flashed.

I have to admit that the best Academy venue was Exeter. Andy McLarin is a keen wine enthusiast and at the time was Assistant Manager at the Royal Clarence Hotel. I had met his Manager, David, many years before at another hotel where I gave a wine presentation and I shall never forget the dinner because the roast beef was so perfect! When I asked David how it had been cooked [I'm so nosey], he explained that the hotel had just invested in a very expensive oven, which cooked very, very slowly and after several hours the beef turned out pink and juicy in the centre and perfect on the outside.

The Royal Clarence was the most beautiful hotel in Exeter, set on a terrace of old buildings surrounding the grounds of Exeter Cathedral. I say 'was' because later it was sold and I think the word they used was 're-modernised'. The word I would use is 'hashed'. The bedrooms were left the same, but two of the ground-floor reception rooms were made into a coffee bar with a separate entrance, and the beautiful old-fashioned dining room, which overlooked the Cathedral grounds, had been completely stripped of all its glory [including the staff which included Richard whose experience and charm were welcomed by many clients] and re-designed in contemporary style – completely out of place in a property that stands on the ground where once stood the house of Sir Francis Drake! Oh dear! So, I have decided to live with the memories of how it was and the super times spent there educating the people of Exeter about wine.

Andy and I worked well together, he had the thirst for knowledge – which I could supply and this was done by holding wine courses, gastronomic dinners and specialised wine presentations. We were often fully booked and sometimes the management would squeeze another couple into the gastronomic dinner, which I objected to as I liked to be able to talk to everyone around the table and, when the table got bigger, it wasn't so easy!

Then disaster struck. For reasons we couldn't understand at that time, Andy was made redundant [this was just before the sale of the hotel – although we didn't know it was being sold]. He soon found work and as he was already qualified in hotel management (he had taken his WSET exam with me), he was then invited to run the wine courses in the Catering Department of the University.

We tried desperately to find another venue, Andy had lots of contacts in Exeter but none could offer us such a wonderful venue as the Royal Clarence. Clients who loved coming to the Clarence dwindled away, wine evenings continued at different venues – but it was never the same.

We were asked to start classes in Tiverton, but that turned out to be worse than Torquay. It was a 40-minute car drive from Torquay and in the winter it was hell, driving through the snow. Three of us, Pat, Paul and I, would meet at Newton Abbot, transfer all the material and wine into one car and drive to Tiverton. It was very difficult to get more than eight to attend, although there was promise of more. Again, the management of the hotel allowed us the room free – for a short time, but later asked for hire charges – and rightly so, but we couldn't afford it so it was goodbye to Tiverton. Actually, I was quite pleased because by that time Pat had found herself a boyfriend and was reluctant to sacrifice the evening of his presence.

Then we had good news, that the manager of the Southgate Hotel in the centre of Exeter agreed that, in exchange for me giving wine presentations to his business clients, I would be able to hold meetings of L'Académie du Vin Devon on a regular basis at the hotel.

This was an extremely generous offer which we did appreciate. We enjoyed our wine evenings there until I finally left Devon to work in France.

Paul worked in the office with me, what can I say? If I was asked to say in one word something about his attributes I would immediately answer loyalty – for he was and still is extremely loyal, but ask me about his work – well that's a different story. Paul worked very well as long as I was standing over him. It was so tiring sometimes; he was absolutely useless at filing, he repeatedly forgot to give me messages and he often missed deadlines for bills to be paid, but he was loyal! Apart from these failures, he was great at reading the 'small print', keeping the day-to-day accounts in order [although we could never find the invoices!] and he was always by my side at tastings and other presentations. You can never have it all ways.

He took the place of Debbie, who was very good but needed to earn more, as she had taken on a share of a flat in Totnes. As she was part-time with me, I suggested she found an afternoon job so we put an application letter together with a CV. It wasn't long afterwards that she came into the office one morning and said that the part-time job she had applied for turned out to be full-time and, in the midst of sobs, said she would like to take it. What could I say? I had trained her, prepared her for the WSET – which she had passed and with her fluent French, she was a positive asset but I couldn't afford to keep her full-time. She left reluctantly, but kept in touch. It was just as well it happened because a few months later she phoned with the news that she was pregnant!

Paul's father was the car-park attendant at the station, my office is the old signal box, one of the ten listed in Cornwall and Devon and, when he heard there was a job going for his son, he came in to see me. He explained that because Paul, ex-Torquay Grammar School boy, was so shy and timid, he had great difficulty getting a job and was stuck at home and this was becoming quite worrying as he had got into the habit of staying up very late at night and also getting up late in the morning. This habit soon changed when he came to work for me – he ended up exhausted in the evening and went to bed at a reasonable time. Getting into the office at the right time remained a problem – for a while.... . Of course, he has completely changed now, full of confidence, never stops talking – and knows a fair bit about wine. The filing problem still remains.

Well, I said at the beginning, there was no financial reward in this venture but the satisfaction of passing on my wine knowledge to so many, and some having benefited from that knowledge, the achievement in doing so is a great reward to me.

Chapter 3
What's In A Glass Of Wine?

At introduction classes, I'm often asked, 'What's in a glass of wine?'

When I look into a glass of wine and have a sniff, I think of the goodness in it, suitable food to accompany it, and who I'm going to invite to dinner…,

We are often told that wine is good for us, and I believe this to be true. It can help heart problems, ease stress, etc. Taken in moderation, it is a health attribute.

When I talk about drinking wine, I mean quality wine – not necessarily expensive, but wine that has been produced correctly.

One of the first lessons I learned about wine is that if you drink 'pure' wine you will add 10 years to your life – if not, you're likely to take 10 years off!

Wine can help you to relax, a glass before dinner is a good way to switch off after a hard day's work. This method of relaxation is much better than depending on prescribed drugs to which you become addicted.

Dry white wine is good for patients in convalescence – it titillates the taste buds and revives the appetite, which often goes into hibernation after an illness.

Red wine has many treatments to offer, it helps digestion of food, breaks up fatty tissue and gives your body minerals – one of the reasons it is sold in *pichets* in French restaurant at reasonable prices – or is sometimes included with the menu.

I read an article last year written recently on a report by environmental campaigners. This referred to chemicals used in red wine production that caused all sorts of problems. Pesticides used in the vineyards were blamed but I am pleased to know that these are being used less and less in modern-day viticulture. No evidence directly linking health problems with drinking organic wine was found.

Whether this is true or not, I cannot say; I have no experience in this field but I don't know of anyone who has suffered by drinking red wine in moderation.

It is possible that breathing in sulphates can trigger breathlessness [especially in those suffering from asthma]. On the other hand, I am told that, if you suffer from a cold, it can be cleared with a good sniff of sulphur in the chais during the barrel-cleaning time, when they burn sulphur tablets in the barrel at the final stage.

In a recent conversation with the queen of wine writers, Pamela Vandyke-Price, whose books weaned me into the world of wine, at a recent lunch in London, I asked her what she thought of all this controversy about wine and health. She shrugged, adding, 'My charming girl, I am very nearly 80 years old and drink a bottle of red wine every day – no fortified wines or spirits but ... and I emphasise, I also drink at least eight glasses of water each day!'

When you consider our social life and most of us have one, wine is an important factor.

When friends call, opening a bottle of wine and offering a glass of wine is always a very good idea and for those of us who are wine enthusiasts, a delightful evening can be spent discussing wines and introducing those that are different and not so well known.

It helps tremendously when giving those sometimes difficult dinner parties – when you don't know everyone and as a good host/ess want to make your *invited* as welcome as possible as soon as possible. Just put a bottle of wine on the table and start talking about it. This soon gets the conversation going.

Of course, it helps to have a little wine education – to which I am dedicated. Educating yourself can be done in many ways by reading and tasting. Belonging to a wine society where a variety of wine enthusiasts [some with very little knowledge and others with more] meet to discuss and taste wine gives a more practical experience to relate when talking on the subject.

Wine puts fun into cooking. You think of a menu, then you decide which wines will accompany the meal. Wine can enhance food and again a little education helps. It is <u>not</u> essential to have red wine with red meat, dry white wine with fish or sweet wine with a pudding.

I would describe the former statement as a simple guide but, as with my belief that wine is a *personal choice*, I also believe choosing wine with food is as personal – apart from a few nos.

For instance, to drink wine with a salad or a dish with vinaigrette is sacrilege. All wines have acidity of different levels and the two don't go together.

Red wine with some fish dishes can leave a metallic taste on the palate. Contrary to this, I was recently contacted by a very well-known restaurateur in Torquay to say that she had prepared my favourite fish dish for the lunchtime menu and if I had time I could join her for a late lunch. What an offer!

With the Bouillabaisse, a Mediterranean soup of different fish, she served a bottle of Beaujolais Villages Morgon which went perfectly with this gastronomic delight. The compatibility of the wine was with the soup – rather than with the fish.

Yet another *fishy* story – a couple of years ago, I was invited with other wine educators to a Champagne seminar held in one of London's top restaurants. I looked forward to this with great anticipation because lunch was included! The menu displayed looked marvellous…. We tasted and discussed several Champagnes and were brought up to date with recent vintages. Imagine my surprise when I found out lunch was traditional fish and chips ….

Well, there's 'fish and chips' and 'fish and chips' but this particular dish was something very special – it was 'designer' presented – even to the mushy peas! We were then given the challenge of matching Champagne with food. This exercise was so enlightening that it prompted me to arrange a similar evening in Torquay!

A sparkling wine or rosé as well as certain dry wines go well with fresh salmon. A lightly oaked dry white is most suitable with smoked salmon.

I adore shellfish and one of my favourite dishes is *Plateau Royale*: shellfish of all sorts piled high on two tiers. Dry white wine is most appropriate but there is no need to go for the very expensive type. One of my favourites is a young Gros Plant from the Atlantic Loire region and is very cheap. It is most important that it is young as it loses its freshness very quickly.

As with fish dishes, the sauce of meat dishes can be the dominating factor. For instance, white wine as well as red wine goes very well with chicken – especially Riesling or Champagne and more so if the chicken has been prepared with the wine!

When it comes to *coq au vin* or *boeuf bourguignon*, etc., a red wine is recommended, again, preferably the same type of wine used in the preparation.

Certain whites, rosés or lighter red wines are excellent with lamb. The wine should be of a drier style, as the acidity 'cuts' into the fattiness of the meat.

Game can take the heavy reds from Italy quite easily and it's almost the same story with other red meat such as steaks, which need a full bodied red.

When it comes to cheese, this is where that special bottle can be opened: a red wine with character, slightly older and full bodied. This is also the chance to experiment because, if you enjoy blue cheeses, some of the 'liquid golds' of Sauternes, Monbazillac or Quarts de Chaume are excellent accompaniments.

For lighter desserts, such as fruit, try fruit salad, which has been soaked in a Moelleux [lighter sweet wine] in the morning and served in the evening – absolutely delicious. Such a simple dish to prepare and served with a small glass of similar wine makes an excellent *finalé* to dinner. Another favourite is pears poached in red wine – or prunes which have been preserved in red wine – the latter with *crème fraiche* is superb.

Assessing what's in a glass of wine can take a long time … .

Chapter 4
In The Vineyard

It seems no time since we were harvesting and the vinification is still going on but autumn and winter have almost gone and spring is peeping its head around the corner. The wonderful glow of autumn colours in the vineyards doesn't last long; the leaves soon dry up and are quickly blown away by the winds. The vineyard looks bare and sad, but nature helps because the frost comes along and 'decorates' the vines.

Some think that this is the end of the work in the vineyards until next spring – but not at all, the work that is done in November through to April is very important.

In November, it is necessary to break up the soil. Buttage is also carried out and this means taking the soil right up to the trunk of the vines to protect them from frost. A European vine root will survive to about $-18°$ C.

Stage one of the pruning starts.

The vines are pruned – similarly to raspberry canes, and are then 'trained' to a certain style. Training is done for better production. In France, the most popular is 'Guyot'. This 'training' was created by Professor Guyot, a wine man at the University of Montpellier in southern France. The 'Simple Guyot' has only one branch to attach and is used most commonly for young vines. Other vines are trained to 'Double Guyot' with two branches to tie. The Guyot method allows the grapes, as they ripen, to hang below the foliage, which is given a regular 'short back and sides' cut during the season, to ensure the grapes capture maximum sun – thus increasing the sugar content.

There are several methods of 'training', for instance, in California where they have more sun, they use a 'bush'-type as it protects the grapes from the hot sun. In parts of Italy they use 'Trellis' – to protect the grapes from the heat from the ground. All clever stuff!

Vine branch or branches then have to be attached [tied] to the wires. In days gone by, tying used to be done with 'withy', which was soaked for a couple of days before using it in the vineyards. The ladies often did the 'tying' and carried the strands of withy in their apron by pinning the bottom of the apron to the waist and making a 'sling'. Nowadays, the 'ties' are often made of plastic.

The canes [branches] must be burned – it is a way of killing diseases that branches may carry, which could ruin the next crop. The burning is often in portable braziers, which are moved around the vineyard as the pruning is done. This continues until the middle of January and around St Vincent's day [22nd] the main pruning starts. It is one of the worst jobs as, mixed with the lovely bright days we have in January and February, we also have a lot of rain, and standing in a vineyard cutting vines – with your wellies deep in mud – is not much fun.

Grafting must be carried out. A European vine cannot be put straight into the ground. This rule was made after the vineyard disaster at the end of the 19th century, when vines carrying a louse were brought over from the States. They carried a bug called *Phylloxera*. USA vine species are immune to this bug but not the European *Vitis vinifera*. *Phylloxera* means 'devastator' and that's just what it did. The louse attacked the roots and devastated nearly all the vines in Europe. Every method to get rid of the disease was used – even using raised platforms and then flooding the vineyards. There was no alternative other than to dig up the vines. A lot of vineyards were never replanted because of the cost involved. Since then, only grafted vines have been used. Very few vineyards survived; only those with very sandy soil had a chance because *Phylloxera* can't live in sand!

Now, the European vine is grafted on to American rootstock. The latter is put into the soil and the European roots are exposed and eventually die. Most vignerons buy new vines that have already been grafted. These are called 'pieds' and are propagated in specialised nurseries.

In March, fertilisers [if required] are used and the pruning and training ends. The sap of the vine begins to rise – a new vintage!

New vines prepared the previous year are put into the ground in around April. Many of you may think that vignerons go along with a measuring tape and spade to do this but not at all – it's all done by machine. First the machine will put the holes in the ground at exact intervals, then another machine will pop the new vines into the holes – simple!

These new vines must be protected – especially from rabbits, which thoroughly enjoy nibbling the young shoots. Popping a plastic tube on to each vine gives it the protection required. Fruit from new vines cannot be used for wine production until the vine is 5 years old. At this age the juice will be thin and only suitable for blending and 'second' wines of lesser quality.

In April, the soil, which has been 'butted' will be loosened. This is called 'debuttage'. Hoeing will then aerate the soil and, if herbicides have to be sprayed, it is usually done in April. The first buds will appear.

May is quite a busy month because things are happening in the vineyard and, as well as spraying, suckers have to be removed from the vines and the lower wires are lifted to hold the foliage high.

In June the flowers [floraison] appear. They're very small and this is a guide as 100 days after the flowering is roughly the time of harvest.

There have been many changes in harvesting and winemaking over recent years. The biggest change was the introduction of machine-picking. It is not done everywhere – but the majority of vineyards now harvest in this way.

To me, this 'Introduction' was like finding out that there wasn't a Father Christmas – totally devastating! Later, I watched vines being uprooted and new vines planted in rows with enough space to take these machines.

In former times the smaller space between each row had fruit trees and small salad patches. There was an abundance of pear, apple, plum, cherry, peach and fig trees growing in and around the vineyards.

Harvesting by hand still exists. It is a *romantic* time, when vineyard owners and *village* people look forward to the return of regular pickers and newcomers to help. In the past, when harvests were unusually early and pickers hadn't arrived in time, soldiers had to be called in. This is serious work!

The majority of hand-picking is done in prestigious red wine regions, in sweet wine regions such as Sauternes and Monbazillac or in vineyards which are 'organic' or where machine picking would be impossible – such as the Rhine/Mosel, northern areas of Côtes du Rhône and the Douro Valley.

Accommodation is organised and the meals planned – after all, pickers are employed for periods of 2 to 3 weeks. Everyone participates but, if you are tall, they may suggest other work, as continually bending is backbreaking. Don't let anyone tell you differently. In regions where clay is predominant in the soil – it's even worse! When it rains, the mud clings to your *wellies* and you feel you are carrying twice the weight on your boots!

The days are long and by the time you return to your lodgings, a shower and period of relaxation is very much appreciated before dinner. The food is good and there is no shortage of local wine. The evening ends with a few songs, which is an excellent way to improve your French!

It is not as easy to find such work today, as the introduction of machine-picking has reduced the massive influx of students and agricultural workers required.

Harvesting by hand is becoming an expensive business. Pickers no longer work for a small payment – making a holiday of it. Paying the *'minimum wage'* as well as providing lodging for pickers can dig deep into a proprietor's pocket.

Machines harvest at great speed. Vineyards that had once taken 3 weeks to harvest by hand now take only 3 days! Hiring a machine for 3 days or less can be an excellent alternative.

The advantages of machine-picking apply mainly to larger producing vineyards. The importance of getting the grapes from the vineyard into the winery in the shortest possible time is a vital aspect in modern wine production.

It should be noted also that machines only 'knock off' ripe bunches; hand-picked bunches will include unripened grapes, and another important factor is picking at the most opportune time. Machines give more freedom to pick at any time of the day. White grapes for dry wine should be harvested during the coolest part of the day and red grapes should be harvested when it's nice and warm. Rolling *wine tanks* can be heard thundering in the vineyards in the very early hours – the favourite time for white grapes is around 3 am!

Economists did not advise 'owning your own machine', as prices were expected to come down in time – or at least become more affordable. Sadly, this has not happened. The design has become more advanced, the machine more streamlined and efficient but the price still remains high. Hiring machines has disadvantages, it can lead to problems of picking at the right time – or it may rain on *your* day.

There are many 'for and against' discussions regarding machine-picking, such as snakes, snails, caterpillars, etc. being included with the pick-up! I agree that all this is possible, but what about all the insects hiding in other fruit? When ripe bunches of grapes are taken to the winery after picking, they're checked before being transferred to the vat or pressoir. Leaves, *snails and snakes* are removed by hand as the bunches pass by on a conveyor belt. Just remember that fermented grape juice is alcohol – a wonderful disinfectant!

You may wonder how these machines operate. It's a very simple procedure. They straddle the vine and the paddles gently knock the ripe grapes [similar to a horseman jumping on a horse and giving it a gentle kick at each side] on to a conveyor belt, which lifts and transfers the grapes into the two containers on the sides of the machine. As soon as these containers are full, they are emptied into a larger container on a tractor in the vineyard and are transported to the winery [or chai]. The latest machines have *destalkers* fitted. [A *destalker* is a machine that removes the grapes from the stalks.]

VINIFICATION PROCESS

Red Wine	White Wine
Grapes	Grapes
Selecting	Selecting
Fermentation	Destalking
Malolactic fermentation	Pressing
Draw first wine	Wine into vats
Pressing	Fermentation
Maturing	Clarification
Clarifying	Bottling
Blending	
Bottling	
Ageing	

Chapter 5
Vinification

This varies enormously from vineyard to vineyard and region to region so what I am going to explain to you is fundamental fermentation in wine-making.

First, we shall cover white dry wine.

The grapes are picked at the coolest part of the day – if possible – after which they are brought to the winery. Speed is the major factor. They are put on to trays or a conveyor belt, inspected and any foreign bits are removed.

The grapes are then fed into a destalking machine, an oblong container with a huge screw lying lengthwise on the bottom. This separates the grapes from the stalks and feeds the grapes into the pressoir.

The juice then runs off into a tray, which feeds it along tubes and into the vat to start fermentation.

When the fermentation is finished, the clear wine is then run off into another vat to mature before it is clarified – which can be done in several ways. After a few months, it is bottled.

Cool fermentation is when the grapes are cooled down to very low temperatures before being processed.

Red wine fermentation is much more complicated.

Red grapes can be picked when it is warm – they benefit from this. With great swiftness, they are brought into the winery and are selected and destalked as for the white grapes; then the procedure changes.

They don't go into the pressoir, but instead, straight into the vats. It won't be long before fermentation starts and the skins start floating to the top and the sediment to the bottom of the tank. The skins on the top are called the *chapeau* [French word for hat] and once the skins get up there – they could dry out – this must not happen or the fermentation will stop. The answer to this is to pump the wine over the chapeau continually – and this is called 'remontage'. The skins give the wine colour and tannin – the latter is important for ageing; so at regular intervals, remontage takes place.

Eventually, the fermentation will finish naturally and then the skins are allowed to float to the top and the sediment continues to sink to the bottom of the tank or vat. We're left with a clear wine in the middle and this is carefully run off into another vat. So the chapeau is now on top of the sediment. Are you following me?

Now we are left with a load of valuable mush because in it we have still lots of colour and tannin which has to be removed. How is this done?

There's a door at the bottom of the vat and this is opened and the mush is fed from here into the pressoir. The wine from the pressing is fed into another vat and will be blended later with the clear wine.

A second fermentation takes place and that is the malolactic fermentation. Malic acid tastes like the acidity you find in green apples; as the grapes ripen, this acidity decreases and the bacteria in the wine transform it into lactic acid, which is much softer.

The wine is then left to mature for a few months and later it will be clarified, blended and either put into barrels for ageing, or bottled.

Chapter 6
What's On A Label?

The main problem 'Jo Bloggs' has when buying a bottle of wine is to comprehend what's on the label, so being able to understand one is a very important part of 'wine education'. The wine label not only gives us information about the contents but, in itself, it is what sells the wine.

Wine producers know that that the label is the selling point of the wine. The quality of a wine is often judged by its label and a vast amount of money is spent on design presentation and printing of the label.

Colour and the size and shape of the label is very important, it has to 'catch the eye' – as does the design. A cluttered label will confuse the buyer, who will most likely turn to something easier to read. Sometimes more than one label goes on the front of the bottle.

This may sound ridiculous, but bottles with labels higher up sell better than labels placed lower on the bottle! Why, I don't know. Perhaps we are a little lazy or in a hurry and find that the higher placed labels are easier and quicker to read.

The information on the label is very important. Firstly, you will read of the quality of the wine and whether or not it has been bottled on the premises. Wine can be susceptible to movement – not being able to 'travel' very well. Wines affected can deteriorate slightly and therefore reduce the quality of the wine or can take several weeks to 'recover' from the *move*.

You will also know the alcohol content of the wine, which can vary considerably. This is a good guide for those who don't like heavy alcohol or for those who prefer a lighter wine.

German labels are very much more complicated to read and recently this problem has been discussed with a view to making it easier for the consumer to read. French wines are much easier and I hope to explain in a *general and easy to understand* way, what the label is all about. So what's on a label?

A wine can be either a quality wine or a table wine and this is the difference:

A quality French wine is expressed in terms of abbreviations such as AOC and is controlled by the regional wine board. The 'quality and control' of wine production are governed by regional authorities.

This is a full control of production and I am referring to the moment when the vine is planted. There is a restriction on the number of vines per hectare, that amount of wine produced from each hectare, the method of vinification [wine making] and the alcohol content. All this is checked regularly throughout the production and if, at any time, the oenologue is not happy with the results of the tests he carries out, adjustments will be made where possible.

It could be that, at the end of this period, the wine does not come up to the accepted quality. It is possible that your wine will fail to gain its 'AOC' the first time round, but you have two chances. If it fails twice, it is downgraded. This is not only disheartening; it means a loss in income because there is quite a difference in the price of AOC and VSDQ. It should be noted that not all wine regions have 'AOC' status.

The average age of a vine is around 30 years. Up to this age, the production gives quality and quantity – after this, the quantity diminishes but the quality improves, producing better wines which are more expensive.

1. Style of the wine

This can be a general description, i.e. vin blanc, vin rouge or grape variety [as in Alsace].

2. Quality of the wine

Wines are divided into two categories, table and quality wines. The two categories are split yet again. In France; the *table wine* can also be a *vin de pays* which is a table wine with special characteristics of the region.

The quality wine can be **AC** – Appellation d'Origine Contrôlée or **VDQS** – Vin Délimité de Qualité Supérieure [VDQS is a lesser quality than the AC].

3. Vintage or year
It is not recorded on all wines.

4. Contents
The amount of wine in the bottle which is commonly 75 cl. Next to this, you will see the letter *'e'* and this is very important as it tells us that the contents are guaranteed by competent authorities in the producing country within the European country.

5. Registered trade name
Such as 'Domaine du Costa' or 'Château Monplaisir'.

6. Name of the producer
This is often recorded but not essential.

7. Address and postcode of where the wine has been bottled
This is an item that should be looked at carefully because, if there is no indication that the wine has been bottled on the premises at the Château or Domaine, i.e., *mis en bouteille au château* [or domaine], it can give you a rough idea where it has been bottled [if you are familiar with French postcodes!].

8. Country of origin
This is a *must*, and you will see, usually at the top of the label, e.g., 'Produce of France'.

9. Alcohol content
This must be recorded and you may be interested to know that there is a minimum and maximum alcohol content for every style of wine in each region.

10. Registration number
This is not to be found on all wines. Registration numbers are usually given to particular wines and could be applicable to wines that have been produced in small quantities.

The next time you buy wine, have a look at the label – you will be truly surprised how much information is given.

Chapter 7
So You Want To Start A Wine Cellar

I am often asked about storing wine and I never mind advising people as it is most important to know how to do this and more important to know how to buy wine for storing.

Going to a supermarket and buying the 'special offers' is very rarely the answer; you could make a mistake. Most supermarkets wines are for drinking now or in the near future and, although offers may be genuine, there are occasions when the wine is getting near maturity and the store prefers to sell it than to keep it.

Unless you have sufficient wine knowledge, you can still make a mistake. It is best to take the advice of the professionals.

The answer is to buy from the specialist or better still from a vineyard. When I say 'specialist', I mean independent wine merchants or a store – such as Oddbins, Majestic, etc. where the staff are trained and know something about the wines in the store.

Once you have collected a few wines, what's the next step? You may be considering a wine cellar. This needs organising. Temperature is most important; it should be constant and around 13 °C.

Light is also important. Very little is needed, one low wattage bulb is sufficient. Too much can age wine too rapidly and can damage the colour.

Some of you may have a suitable spare corner for doing this and others are not so lucky. Most people aim for the garage and, if this is your chosen place, try to find the coolest corner. Northeast walls are very good.

A bottle of wine that has lost its label is of no value and the bottles should be prepared beforehand for storage. The label must be protected against dampness, etc. One excellent tip given to me was to spray the label with hairspray lacquer. Dampness won't get through and mice don't include lacquer in their daily diet!

If possible, an old chest of drawers could come in very handy. Wrap each bottle of wine in newspaper, this can help to keep it cooler in the summer or a little warmer in cold weather. Never place your wine near a fridge or freezer, the vibration could damage the wine. Just imagine your bed moving all the time – you wouldn't sleep, and lack of sleep would make you ill!

Under the stairs can be another idea, with the door closed all the time, the temperature stays pretty constant. The more fortunate of us may have a barn or even a real wine cellar!

The bottle should always be laid down with the label upright. There is a reason for this – especially for wines that will be kept for a long period. As wine ages, it can throw off a sediment and, if you have laid the wine down on its label, you may have difficulty seeing this at first… because of the label.

When you have sorted all this out, the next thing to think about is how you are actually going to store the bottles and whilst considering this, you must also take into account how records are going to be kept. Your 'Record Book' can be one of the many you can buy or you can create record sheets on your computer – to match your personal needs. Sheets kept on file might be the better bet.

The chest of drawers can have a 'white wine' drawer and a 'red wine' drawer and don't forget to label each of the bottles. If you have a third drawer, keep the wines in it that need more ageing, as this drawer needn't be opened as often – thus saving movement.

If you put your wine on shelves, I recommend, what I call, the 'alpha/number' method. The idea is that the horizontal rows are alphabetical and the vertical rows are numbered. Your wines can then be recorded as A5, B6, K15, etc.

As recalled when visiting a port house in the Douro Valley, the owner took a liking to our small group and, after the visit, invited us to his social house on one of the highest mountains in the valley. The house was round with four floors and the ground floor was his wine cellar, where bottles were kept in 'pigeon-holes' all around the wall. He proudly boasted that he knew where every bottle of wine was – so we put him to the test. He didn't fail once – I wish I had a memory like that!

Of course, very few of us can achieve this, so it is no good plonking your wine on the shelves and then forgetting where you have put each bottle. Also, it is not always convenient to keep 12 places free for each carton you buy; as you drink it, the spaces are left empty. You may end up with a lot of empty spaces and cartons of wine you are not able to store.

With the 'alpha/number' method, this will not happen. When you take a bottle from the shelves, replace it with another and don't forget to record it in your book!

The problem of knowing when to drink it is the most difficult to answer. Every wine is different as is everyone's palate, but this is what I do. I buy my wines from vineyards in cases of three, six, or twelve. When the wine has settled for a few months, or years with the more complex wines, I try a bottle. If it's not ready, I leave the rest for a few months or even longer, tasting a bottle on occasions. When the wine is right for me, I drink the lot, not all in the same night!

Wine is like a human being! It grows up, matures and rests on a plateau for a few years, as we do. Then the ageing process steps in, structure changes, we develop certain deficiencies. We have to face it, we're not as good as we used to be… and neither is the wine!

Chapter 8
Tasting Wine

My greatest satisfaction when teaching young children at kindergarten was teaching them to write numbers – relating the numbers to certain items such as No. 2 and a swan. Then there was recognising words, aeroplane was the favourite – it was such a long word compared to Janet, John, dog and tree.

Now I get the same pleasure from teaching students how to taste wine.

It's heart-breaking to see so many people down a glass of wine – which maybe so special – but because of their lack of knowledge, and inability to taste correctly, they have not been able to fully appreciate it.

If you want to taste seriously, do it in daylight, stay clear of smokers and females wearing perfume and, if you are a female, go easy with the lipstick!

The best place is a room with lots of natural light and a table that is either white or with a white tablecloth.

The wine should be poured into an ISO glass [these are standard tasting glasses that narrow at the top, therefore trapping the bouquet/aroma]. The first glass should be poured to yourself as there might be bits of cork in the wine.

We have four senses for tasting, sight, smell, taste and feel. Hearing is also very important at certain times –when you open a bottle of wine. I always tell my students to use a sixth sense – common sense!

Let's look at 'sight'. The wine can be several colours, but we shall stick to white, rosé and red.

White wine can be pale or deeper. Dry wine is usually very pale or greeny pale [excuse newly created words – I feel they are more descriptive!] Chardonnay can be slightly deeper. Sweeter wines are likely to be more golden, although some sweet wine producers try for a paler colour. As sweet wine ages, the colour deepens and can be described as *maderising*. So this gives you some idea of what you are looking for when you evaluate colour.

We now think about *clarity*. A dry white wine should be crystal clear – even a little sparkle within. The sweet wine won't be quite as clear and will look heavier in the glass.

Now you must 'open' the wine and you do this by swirling the wine inside the glass. Some wines have to be opened up more than others and this is why a Claret glass is a different shape to a Burgundy glass – the latter needs more 'opening'.

At this point, I mention 'legs' or 'tears', whichever term you wish to use. After you swirl the wine, drops of wine will slide down the inside of the glass – sometimes thin and sometimes more oily. This gives us an idea of the structure of the wine and the alcohol content.

Now is the time to smell. Your 'smell' and 'taste' senses are judged in the olfactory region. Now we are getting clinical, but I think the explanation will help you to understand. This region is a tiny square patch, situated at the top of the nose – the nerves of this moist patch send messages to the brain which, like a computer, can interpret distinctive aromas.

Once you stick your nose into a glass of wine, things start to happen. It's a two-way system, you smell something – you're not sure what it is – the nerves take the smell to the olfactory then relate it to something you have smelt before, e.g. a Sauvignon wine can be related to gooseberries. You may never have tasted Sauvignon before but, the next time you do, you might recognise it because of the smell of gooseberries. All clever stuff!

When we talk about 'Aroma' and 'bouquet' we are talking about two different things. The aroma is related to the fruit smells, the bouquet describes the smells which develop after vinification.

We have 3000 tastebuds on our tongue and no two tongues are alike! [this is why some of us like sweet wine and others prefer dry]. They're all grouped in different sizes but the groups are as follows.

On the very front of the tongue, you have the group for tasting *sweetness*, next to it, there are the *acidity* groups, two of them – one at the front and one further back, nearer the middle. At the side of the tongue, there's a patch for saltiness and at the back there's a patch that will give you the taste of bitterness that may be in the wine.

When it comes to 'tactile' – the feel of the wine, I will give you two examples. The first is when you taste a very good, matured Sauternes, it slips over the 'touch' sense in the middle of your mouth like velvet. This is why Sauternes can be referred to as 'liquid gold'. The other example of 'feel' is with a good-quality young red wine.

As you take this in your mouth, your lips may pucker and you will feel a roughness coating the back of your teeth. As well as this, you may make statements such as 'This wine is terrible'. Don't you believe it…. . This is what I would expect to find! It comes from the *tannin* in the wine, which is necessary if the wine is going to age.

So the sequence of tasting a glass of wine is:

Look at the wine
Swirl it
Smell it
Take some in your mouth, draw in air through your lips
Impregnate your mouth with the wine – making sure all your little tastebuds get covered.
Slowly let it go down and let it talk to you!

It sounds insane, but it's true. For instance, if the taste lingers on the back of your mouth, this is what we call a 'long finish' and that's a good sign. If it has a short finish – don't buy any more!

The logo of the Association of Wine Educators is a square divided into four pictures of the sequence of tasting, i.e., sniff, swirl, slurp and spit.

Chapter 9
Wine and Health

There has been a lot of discussion recently about wine and health.

These discussions go back a lot further to when one of the kings of France, who were then Burgundy drinkers, sent a messenger to Bordeaux. This messenger suffering from a cold, drank the wine of Bordeaux, suddenly, his cold improved and he couldn't wait to get back to Paris to tell of the *new cure*. It was because of this that wines from Aquitaine were introduced to the Court in Paris.

Then we had the introduction of Champagne to the Court in Versailles. The ladies were responsible for making this so popular. Madame Pompadour found it particularly pleasing as it didn't make your cheeks pink!

According to a recent BBC programme, wine being good for the heart seems to be a fallacy. I'm not a doctor, so unable to comment on this, but the following information may be of some help to you.

Comments had been made about the French living longer and in the past this had been related to wine being good for the heart. I don't know about this connection but what I do know is that when you visit a French bistro or little restaurant, a carafe of red wine is usually included with the meal. It is most unusual to be given white wine and the reason for this is that red wine, usually brought in from local vineyards, has minerals and vitamins that are good for you. It also helps the digestive system and breaks up fatty tissue. The other point to bear in mind is that, psychologically, it makes you relax as you digest. Surely this is good for your health?

Some years ago, two articles on wine and health gave me 'food for thought' – or *wine* in this case.

The first was a report from the University of San Francisco. It stated that dry, white wine was good for those convalescing and, in moderation, could be drunk by diabetics. I have no reason to doubt this as dry white wine is often drunk as an aperitif and you find, after a glass or two, that you are quite hungry. The wine is obviously titillating the taste buds and encouraging you to eat, which must help those in convalescence who haven't yet regained their appetites.

This was confirmed only recently, when a colleague of mine came on tour with me and we were tasting white wines one morning. During our discussion about the wines, he said: 'Do you know, Helen, drinking dry white wine in the morning gives me a huge appetite for lunch.'

Regarding diabetics, again – I know nothing of diabetes – except that you must control sugar intake. The only conclusion I can come to is that dry white wine is produced by fermenting all the sugar into alcohol. Some of these wines have a low alcohol content and this may be the type of wine to which they are referring.

Another report was from the World Health Organisation (WHO) on the high cost of drugs to the Health Service. I can't remember all the details as it was some time ago, but it made reference to those patients under stress and being prescribed expensive drugs. It claimed that, if more people came home in the evening, sat down to relax with a glass of wine, then had a glass of wine or beer with dinner, fewer would be dependent on these drugs – some of which were addictive and costing the country a fortune.

This makes a lot of sense to me, knowledgeable of wine but lacking in medical science.

The way I see it is this. People who are stressed out usually have little time to eat, therefore they are not having the right nourishment. Their health suffers and this doesn't help the stress symptoms. As I said earlier, drinking wine with food helps you to relax and the WHO remedy seems justified.

Of course, there are those who will say that you could become an alcoholic! I don't entirely agree with this. There are usually much more profound reasons for alcoholism.

Wine is to enjoy – not abuse, so to all wine drinkers I say

À vôtre santé!

Chapter 10
Bergerac

When I first came to live in France, I was still making my own wine. Getting the *must* to the right temperature was no problem in the warmer climate, the fermentation started and kept going – with a little stir each day.

My Italian neighbours watched on in amazement. The incredible British! They were mesmerised by the hanging marrow, the potatoes rotting happily and the airlocks on the demijohns … . Well, that called for a photograph or two!

It was a morning, during the vendange, when I opened the back door and found a large rubbish bin full of grapes that I realised they were not so much amazed by my adroitness, but sympathetic as I had no vines in my garden! Needless to say that was the end of my wine-making – but on hindsight, it may have been the time when I should have bought a few hectares!

There are many Italians in the Dordogne. Monsieur and Madame Lorenzon, teenage farmers – with many others came over when France had heavy losses of lives during the First World War. The Dordogne had suffered badly and there were very few men left to look after the land. The Government invited Italian farmers to come to the region to look after the land and the land they looked after became theirs.

At one time, this was much resented by the French agriculture people, some Frenchmen became quite jealous of the progress the Italians were making and the better lifestyle they enjoyed because of this. It was silly really because the Italians worked extremely hard and all hours. Some children suffered at school, being called 'macaroni', etc.

When I first met the Lorenzons, one of the barns they owned had been made into a house for the parents. One of the two sons, already married, lived in another barn nearby which was extremely primitive. At that time they had cows and fields and this was their livelihood – apart from money made by the father who was a 'faith healer'. This annoyed the neighbours especially when more people arrived in the village for the 'cure' – but the faith healer was good and certainly helped me much later when touring the Bergerac region with a group, I damaged my hand and later needed treatment for a twisted ankle.

Not long after I met the family, the sons decided to turn some of the fields into vineyards. Their first effort was undrinkable – a sparkling wine. The idea was soon put on the shelf!

After this disaster, they concentrated on dry white and red wine. They struggled to get it all going and, because of lack of cash, were unable to publicise the wines. Fortunately, as the sons were the right age, they were able to get grants from the government to help with the cost of machinery.

In 1983, I received a phone call from one of the sons to say that they family had got enough money together for him to share a stand at the Agricultural Fair in Paris and that the red wine presented had won a Gold Medal!

It all changed after that although living in peace with the neighbours never happened. I asked once why they never spoke to their neighbour Monsieur Dubrieul. The mother told me that when her sons were little boys they went into his cowshed and hit the cows – the owner never spoke to the family after that!

Another neighbour made a point of being on the village council for one reason only and that was to stop the Italian family having a lane which divided their house from a ruin next door. Once a year, the miserable neighbour would walk down the lane – to prove that it was 'used by the public'! I am pleased to say that recently the lane in question was handed over to the Italian family and they are now able to complete their garden.

I have concentrated on the Dordogne and the wines of Bergerac for over 30 years and feel part of the history of recent years. I became terribly frustrated, and still am, regarding the poor effort made over the years to promote the wines.

Until recently, the only Bergerac wines to be found in supermarkets were of poorer quality or were bottled by the supermarket to be sold in the lower price range. Very few of the quality wines reached the shelves in Britain.

I was continually writing to negotiants asking them to refrain from categorising Bergerac wines as 'country wines' but gave up in the end.

It was only to be expected that the British wine drinkers would look down on Bergerac wines when no publicity was given by the Conseil Professionnel des Vins de la Région de Bergerac (CIVRB) to contradict this opinion. Thank goodness for Henry Ryman!

I felt that CIVRB could have done a lot more to publicise the wines of Bergerac. When you know how much money is poured into it by the vignerons of Bergerac and how little most of them get out of it – it is very disheartening. There are the 'chosen few' and this is very plain to · see on occasions when publicity events take place. Many of the other vineyards have been discovered with the advent of flocks of tourists into Bergerac via cheap flights and I'm happy to say the reputation in Britain of the wines of Bergerac is improving.

To give you some idea of the confusion, the 'Route des Vin' is a list of vineyards where you will be made welcome. It is organised by the CIVRB.

If you want to be included, the first thing you do is apply to join. You are then sent an application form, which must be completed and returned with a case of a selection of your wines. On being 'accepted', an obligatory board will be erected outside your vineyard and, by this sign, visitors know that they can visit, taste and buy your wines.

My husband, David, bought Château Monplaisir in 1997 – both the house and the vineyards were in a dreadful state! The previous French owner had let the vineyards go to ruin. It took 2 years and a huge amount of money to get the vineyard back into condition. At this point my husband was invited to join the Route des Vin.

He completed the application and took a case of his wines to CIVRB. He never heard another thing and after a year, when he made enquiries, he was told that the form had been lost and he would need to apply again.

We didn't apply until 2002 and, to my surprise, a young man – in his very early 20s came to inspect the property. He told us that he had been with CIVRB for only a few months! We gave him a case of a selection of our wines and completed the necessary forms.

Several weeks later we had a letter to say that our vineyard had not been accepted. No reason given – and we assumed our wines were not good enough. We couldn't understand this as compared with some of the wines of the vineyards on the list – our wines were far superior! We have Gold medals, an award from Hachette, etc. We challenged this result only to find out that it was nothing to do with our wine.

On the form you have to state whether visitors can just 'turn up' or must they make an appointment. We can't offer 'open all hours' as we are not here all the time – so we stated 'by appointment' and this, we were told, is why we were not accepted! My reply to all this was 'Why give us the choice?'

We were invited to apply again but after finding out the cost of the board, and the erection of it, which came to a tidy sum of hundreds of euros – and the cost of the administration – we decided not to bother.

Château Monplaisir produces some of the best wines in Bergerac, which can be found in many of the prestigious restaurants in the area. The château stands high on hills clad with vineyards and from its terrace you have wonderful panoramic views of the Dordogne Valley – a delightful place to visit, with the added interest of a plum orchard – 1500 trees in all, which are picked and dried in ovens on the estate.

We have many visitors, and the school where I can help people to better understand wine production and the Bergerac Region is something I look forward to in the summer months.

This year, I prepared my own brochure for my wine school and handed a few to the tourist office in Bergerac. I was quite surprised and thrilled to receive a telephone call to say that my school was going to be advertised in the summer activities publication of 'What's on in Bergerac'.

Later in the day, I received another phone call from the tourist office. The lady sounded most upset and said that she regretted very much that they were not permitted to advertise my school because … Château Monplaisir is not on the Route des Vin! This was incredible.

The French wine industry has suffered terribly because of New World competition and all efforts should be made to improve the situation. CIVRB must come into the 21st century!

Each regional wine board has its own Confrèrie [a brotherhood – similar to the Freemasons] and at the annual gathering, it is usual for someone who has been involved in the promotion of the region's wine – or a visiting celebrity to be *intronised*. This is a very colourful evening with a true Perigourdin gastronomic menu.

Bergerac wines have never had the right publicity in Britain. They are categorised as 'country wines' and CIVRB may be partly to blame for this. Each year the vignerons of Bergerac pay handsome sums for their wines to be administered, publicised, etc. As mentioned before, very little seems to have been used for publicity and only a handful of the 'quality wines' are known in Britain. There are the 'chosen few' but this has been because the producers have held 'high place' in CIVRB, had contacts in UK, or speak English well enough to get into the market.

Until recently, when Bergerac exhibited its wines at the London Wine Trade Fair, the stand was generally situated away from the 'hub' of Wines of France – which didn't help at all. It was the same situation at 'Vinexpo 2001' [an exhibition which is held once every 2 years in Bordeaux] the Bergerac wine stand was not in the main hall and didn't seem to have that *je ne sais quoi*! There seems to be a loose link in the organisation.

I think part of the trouble is that there are too many *change-arounds* with staff and many are young and inexperienced.

Now let me tell you something of this wonderful place. The Dordogne is one of the largest and principal gastronomic regions of France. Oyler, an author of one of the many books written about the Dordogne, stated: 'it is the richest and poorest region of France'.

Over the last 2 years, thousands of people have visited Bergerac because of the opening of the small airport to low-priced air carriers. This event has stunned the majority of this once described, 'sleepy market town'. I can assure you that it is no longer… .

Many years ago when Ryanair first started in Britain, I wrote to Mr O'Leary asking if he knew that there were 25,000 ex-pats living in the south west of France and a service such as his would be much appreciated. He never answered.

Buzz was the first airline to come in. They had been considering the area for a long time before – then took the plunge. They were amazed how much business they were doing and decided to expand by carrying the wine to UK for passengers, They contacted an acquaintance of mine, who phoned me asking for help, as they wanted to discuss a subject of which she knew very little.

We met for dinner in one of my favourite Bergerac restaurants, *L'Imparfait*, and soon got into discussion. I had the answers the Buzz team were looking for and a meeting was arranged at Château Monplaisir.

The idea was for visitors to come to Bergerac and visit the vineyards. They could buy as much wine as they wanted and BUZZ would ship it to their home address. Of course, there were problems to overcome – the biggest being Customs and Excise but after a few meetings with the BUZZ team, the way was clear. BUZZ explained that KLM had transport continually moving all over Britain and there was ample space to carry wine.

This was a great breakthrough. Transporting wine was always a nightmare for those who travelled by air. I couldn't wait to get involved and get the service off the ground.

Order forms, waybills, advertising matter were printed and sent out to the châteaux involved. Now we just had to wait for the holiday season to start... .

A few weeks later, we read in the newspapers that BUZZ had been sold to Ryanair. This was a dream that collapsed!

The next shock was to find out that Ryanair didn't intend to keep open the service between Bergerac and London. It was unbelievable... .

Committees were set up to try and resolve the situation, other low fare air companies were contacted – something must be done to give us back the convenience of travelling to the UK, to which we had become accustomed. Then one day, when I was visiting the airport, one of the staff asked me if I knew of 'Flybeeeeee' because she had heard that they were interested.

After that we heard that Ryanair and Bordeaux Airport couldn't come to an agreement on terms for flights for Stansted to Bordeaux – so Ryanair scrapped the idea of flying into Bordeaux and moved into Bergerac. Such joy – two flights every day, and not long after that we were told of yet another.

Unfortunately, the airlines don't seem to be interested in carrying wine.

Bergerac is an agricultural region, which can boast not only wine production but also excellent growing area for fruit, vegetables, nuts and even tobacco!

The majority of people in the area are employed in the wine industry and agriculture and, although the average wage is very low, the 'Bergeracois' live and eat exceptionally well!

The climate is similar to Britain but warmer. There is certainly more sun and 'summer days' start earlier and finish later in the year – sometimes into early November, making winter shorter and more bearable. The average rainfall is a little less than UK and this is what makes the Dordogne Valley so lusciously green. When I have brought wine enthusiasts to study the region, the same comment has arisen many times, 'It's so much like parts of Devon'.

There are 13 AOCs of Bergerac wine and six of these are direct Bergerac ACs.

The CIVRB controls production of wine from the time when the vine is planted in the ground to the bottling of the wine. Bergerac alcohol control is:

Wine	Min. alc.	Max. alc.	Residual sugar
Bergerac Sec	10%	13%	4 grams
Bergerac Rosé	10%		
Bergerac Rouge	10%	13%	2 grams
Côtes de Bergerac	11%	13%	4–17 grams
Moelleux	12%	16%	17–35 grams
Liquoreux	12%	18%	>54 grams

Bergerac is the wine-growing capital of the Dordogne, and there are around 93 villages with approximately 12600 hectares under vine. A 'Wine Fair' for holidaymakers is held each year in Sigoules [about 10 miles south of Bergerac]. It lasts the whole weekend and includes a dinner dance in the village square plus a 'Spectacular' on the Saturday evening. It gives the visitors a chance to taste some of the huge variety of wines available.

Monbazillac Château is surely the most popular visit in Bergerac. Since 1980 I have been a regular visitor – either by accompanying small groups or just taking my friends. It has changed a lot in recent years.

The first Château Monbazillac was built by the Catholics and it wasn't long after that it was burned down and then rebuilt by the Protestants. It then became a Protestant stronghold and was very much involved in the War of Religions. Since then, peace has prevailed and this beautiful château stands proudly on the hills overlooking the Dordogne Valley.

Until around 1960, the château was owned privately. It was then sold to the Co-operative of Monbazillac who furnished it with help from people in the houses nearby – many had collections of bibles, coins and maps which they handed over for the 'museum'.

The visits at that time were interesting; there seemed to be more to see and this gave you a very good idea how Bergerac and its environs had originated. For example, there was a room full of old maps and, from these, you could see how small Bergerac was in comparison to Monbazillac and La Calevie nearby. It was no wonder that, when the monks of the monastery of Bergerac went to see the Pope in Rome and were asked where they had come from, their reply was 'Bergerac, a small village outside Monbazillac'! This room had a door into one of the towers and the small area was used as a prison in times of war. It has a small window and stone seat where the prisoner was left to die. Such cruel times!

The two reception rooms give you an excellent example of the furniture made and the wood available in the region. The floor of one is laid with four different woods and the beams have flowers and other designs painted on them.

The religious room has a fantastic collection of Calvin bibles and literature of the period as well as a fair collection of coins that have been found on the land around. Some of these coins are extremely valuable and, because of this, the originals were taken to Paris and only copies remain in the château.

From this room, you go through a small door leading into part of the tower. In this room there is a 'family tree' painted on the walls. The name Rudel appears in the early part of the château's existence and he may well have been one of the first troubadours during the period of Eleanor of Aquitaine.

I was once told – and whether it is true I'm not sure – that he wrote a song about his love who was 'far away'. Eleanor took it to be a song about her and he was favoured to travel with her to the Holy lands.

Later it was discovered that he did have a far-away lover – but it wasn't Eleanor!

Before going upstairs, there is a room where you will find machinery used in trades of the past and this includes rope-making, clog-making and barrel-making.

One room upstairs is laid out as a dining room, which was furnished with very heavy furniture of the Baroque period, which had been given 'on loan' to the château by Monet Sully the Perigordin 'Shakespeare' actor. The family never asked for it to be returned – probably because it was so difficult to clean.

The room displaying photographs and models of châteaux in the Dordogne was just as interesting because it showed visitors that there are probably more châteaux on the Dordogne than on the Loire. The difference is that the Dordogne châteaux were built for war. Many of the villages in the surrounding Dordogne were called Bastides and these were held by either the Protestants or the Catholics – some actually changed from one religion to the other.

The lady's bedroom is furnished in local furniture of different styles; in particular, the incomplete prayer desk is of Italian style. The bed is very small, but seemingly they preferred to sleep in a sitting-up position!

The last room on this floor is devoted to the Perigordin Painter Sem, who lived at the same time as Toulouse Lautrec and they were friends. It is obvious from Sem's work that he was a great admirer of his friend's work, as Sem's work characterises the very well-known thin men and fat ladies of Paris. It never ceases to amaze me why the château has never made copies of his work for the public to buy – especially the one done for Maxim's in Paris where Sem frequented.

Down in the cellar is the kitchen, this to me was one of the most interesting visits. Apart from the many pots for storing walnut oil, pork fat, etc. which had been donated by those living around the château, everything else was original. There is a door leading from the kitchen into the lower part of one of the towers, this was the fridge. The water would drip in and settle on the floor and freeze and food could be stored in here. In the kitchen itself, there was a well – so they were never without water. Bread was baked in this kitchen, the oven with its concave ceiling of red bricks is worth looking into – once the fire was lit, it became very hot. Outside the oven there are two holes one on each side, which have been filled in with large stones. These holes were for storing salt and keeping it dry. Salt was a valuable commodity – especially during the time of Louis XIV. In order for him to get more money to pay for his armies, he put a tax on salt!

Next to the kitchen is a cellar where the famous Monbazillac sweet wine was produced, then stored for many years in the next cellar.

As we were guided through the château, we were shown a photograph of the Queen Mother when she visited the château. The guide told us that she had come to Bergerac to order some Monbazillac. This joke possible arose from the time when the sweet wine of Sauternes went to the Tsars of Russia, and the Monbazillac to the Royal household in London.

The lady who looks after the château is Italian. She no longer takes groups on tour through the château. The last time I saw her she was sitting at the reception desk in the entrance hall. She told me that she would be retiring shortly.

Up until the 1970s Bergerac was a poor market town but wine has always been produced here since the Middle Ages. Bergerac had its own appellation 'Grand Cru', up to the early 1930s before the 'AC' we know today was introduced in 1936. You can see such 'Grand Cru' bottles in Château Monbazillac.

The first thing you notice about a good Monbazillac is the colour – as gold as the sun; this colour is enhanced as it deepens with age. Monbazillac can reach 15% alcohol content quite easily, I've witnessed 18%.

I agree that the majority of Bergerac wine in the 1970s was poor. The only decent white wine was 'Monbazillac', but times have changed. It is interesting to note that Monbazillac wine is older than the wines of Sauternes, which date only from the period of the Second Empire. Monbazillac can be traced back to the Renaissance.

There is a story of a group of monks visiting Rome and when asked from where they had come, the monks said 'Monbazillac'. Immediately, the Pope's face lit up; he raised his hand in blessing, murmuring as he did so 'Ah! Monbazillac – an excellent wine'.

Until the 1930s, Bergerac wines were predominantly either red or sweet white. The reds from Pecharmant were so tannic you had to wait ages before they were drinkable, and by that time most of the fruit had disappeared!

The red wine from Pecharmant [meaning charming hill] is on the right side of the Dordogne, where the soil has more sand in it. Pecharmant had so much tannin that, by the time it was ready for drinking, the fruit had gone. I always refer to the original wine producers of Pecharmant as the 'Widows of Bergerac' – similar to those in Champagne. When they took over after their husbands' death they insisted on making the wine in the same traditional way, i.e., everything going in the pot. The juice stayed in contact with the skins, stalks, etc., for far too long. We use the term 'mouth puckering' in tasting, and tasting Pecharmant was *mouth puckering* in the extreme!

As the widows got older, their sons took over the production. Slowly and surreptitiously, they moved away from this method and introduced modern wine-making. Discussing this with Francois Xavier of Château Tirgand whilst preparing a radio programme for Devon, he said, 'but you know Hélène, my mother still has the final say in deciding the final selection of the different blends to be used for the vintage'.

The white wines were sweet, mainly produced around Monbazillac, but in 1932 when a farmer [Monsieur Becker] from the north of France moved to the Dordogne all this changed.

Château Panniseau built around the 13th century, and notably the home of Grimmoard Panisseaud, is situated near the villages of Cuneges, Thenac and Sigoules, an important wine-growing area of Bergerac. The land is set back from the Dordogne on one of the highest points of the left bank of the river.

Monsieur Becker wasn't a sweet wine drinker and it didn't take him long to start producing dry white wine which was unheard of in this region – until Mr Becker arrived in 1932. He couldn't drink the sweet Monbazillac wine, it was far too sweet for his palate and so he tried his hand at making dry white wine. It was a great success, simply because the soil of the left bank of the Dordogne is made up of clay and limestone and the Sauvignon and Semillon grapes thrive in it. A few years ago this family-run Château Pannisseau was sold to the group ISM SA. and is still producing white dry wines of high quality.

Château Pannisseau was one of the châteaux considered by Henry Ryman, a man I much admire. Henry liked the château, and the vineyards, but did not like the other buildings so much. If he had bought it, we would have been neighbours!

He later bought Château de La Jaubertie, a château built by the French King Henry for his mistress.

In my opinion, Henry Ryman gave Bergerac wines 'respectability' about 25 years ago. He fulfilled his dream by selling off his stationery stores in and around London and bought Château La Jaubertie, near Monbazillac, in Bergerac.

An astute businessman, he arrived with wife Anne and family, cars and animals, not knowing a thing about vines and set out to find himself a local vineyard manager who, with other workers, started work, replanting where necessary.

Henry invested a great deal of money in machinery and equipment – so much so that it left his finances quite low and, when it came to ageing some of his wines in barrels, the problem of 'how to pay for the costly barrels' arose. [New barrels at the moment are priced at around £300 each!]

A prominent nightclub owner in London came to the rescue. The money was borrowed on an agreement that the first wines bottled from the barrels were sold to the Club. Other 'deals' with business people, wine buyers and enthusiasts helped with the funding to get the winery going. It wasn't long before 'Ryman Wines' were in the British off licences, restaurants and bars.

He had tremendous publicity, and wine writers were continually arriving at the château built for one of the 'royal mistresses' in the 17th century.

When Henry's son, Hugh, returned from Australia where he had continued his wine studies after Bordeaux University, he became the wine-maker. The wines improved, being produced using New World methods.

Bergerac wines were at last on the British market – although there were two types, i.e. 'Ryman's' and 'others', that didn't matter. When I made presentations of these wines, it was no longer necessary to explain to my audience that *Bergerac was not in Jersey but in south-west France!*

It wasn't long before his son, Hugh, married and went to live in Bordeaux. His place was taken over by Charles Martin who had spent time in South Africa and certainly produced some excellent wines for Henry Ryman. Later, Henry was forced to sell Jaubertie to his son, Hugh.

Charles was asked to leave and that was when he bought 'La Colline'. He phoned me and said that it had always been his ambition to make Bergerac wines in the traditional way – but finer, and this he has done. His wines are now in demand.

Being one of the few Brits here in the 1980s, I was often asked to find a holiday home and one of my favourites was near the peacock farm on the way to Saussignac. It was owned by one of the many Italians in the regions, whose families had been invited by the French government to come and look after land in the Dordogne because of the great number of Frenchmen lost in the war. They were given the land free. This particular Italian produced very good traditional wine in his small vineyard but I think he made more profit from letting out his gîte in latter years. On retirement, the property was sold to Richard Doughty, and his French mother and British father live in the gîte.

Richard Doughty is an organic wine-maker and, because of this, his wines are highly priced. He also looked after the vineyard of Kiri Te Kanawa, Opera Singer, who had bought a house and vineyards nearby. Naturally she didn't have time to be involved with wine-making, so Richard was asked to be responsible. The involvement didn't last too long because Kiri divorced and sold up.

I took a group to taste Richard's wines and we were quite impressed. He has a very good range and a good selection chosen for tasting – especially the non-filtered sweet wine. The passengers bought a few cases – as was the normal procedure [it was not unknown for around 700 bottles to be bought among 12-15 passengers!]. Being small groups – we kept in touch, and later I was quite surprised to hear that some of the non-filtered wine didn't age well.

There are pockets of iron deposits scattered around Bergerac and this is evident by the village name of Gageac et Rouillac, *rouille* being the French word for rust. As mentioned before, I'm often asked what the 'ac' at the end of the word means. I can tell you that it means 'belonging to' and Rouillac is a perfect example – land belonging to rust!

Gageac et Rouillac is in the region of Saussignac. There are several British wine-growers here, such as Patricia Atkinson, who specialises in sweet wine as well as Richard Doughty.

Patricia Atkinson was introduced on a TV documentary, which I didn't consider painted a true picture of the Dordogne's ex-pats. It dwelt on newcomers, who were truly struggling and never mentioned those who had settleed well into the community since the 'boom' started in the late 60's. With lots of help from both British and French wine producers, Patricia survived.

David Baxter, my husband, is the latest and his arrival [1997] can be compared to Henry Ryman's. A financial analyst from London, who knew absolutely nothing about wine – buying a truly neglected vineyard, which needed terrific investment. Both Henry and David were fortunate in finding suitable employees to help. Château Monplaisir was even more neglected, but commands some of the best views in Bergerac of the Dordogne Valley.

It was in the Saussignac Hotel that I first met Henry Stewart, a Texan who had just bought a vineyard nearby. He and his wife joined the group – being quite relieved to speak 'English'. They bought 'Champagne for everyone', which cost a hefty sum by the look on his face when he received *l'addition*. Henry doesn't live here permanently but you always know when he's at home because he hangs the Texas flag over the balcony! He has done a lot for Bergerac wines as they are now sold one of the Texan airlines.

Bergerac wine is always being compared with Bordeaux. The grape varieties are the same but the percentages of each vary from region to region. The main difference is the soil.

Bergerac had the chance but refused to be included in the Bordeaux AC when it was formed in 1936.

Because of more recognition, the wine production in Bergerac is continually improving. The wines no longer lie in the 'shadows of the great cousin, Bordeaux' but can now compete healthily with many of the 'Bordeaux Superiors'. In fact, some, aged in oak are comparable with St Emilion!

Bergerac Sec [blend] and Bergerac Sauvignon are very popular in France and are exported in huge quantities to Holland, Belgium, Britain and the States. Bergerac Sec is a blend of Sauvignon and Semillon and has a delicate citrus aroma with a touch of tropical fruit on the nose and fresh and crisp on the palate. The level of acidity is slightly softer and pleasant in the mouth. Although a dry wine, there are delicate hints of honey and tropical fruits in the taste and finish.

Bergerac Sauvignon is dry with a nose reminiscent of gooseberries. It has a good level of acidity and is fresh, crisp, with zingy citrus flavours on the palate – ideal as an aperitif.

Bergerac Rosé is delicious. It is softer on the palate than most Rosés of Bordeaux and permeates strawberries to the nose and lingers right through to the finish. A 'definite' for Wimbledon, as well as for accompanying summer salads of chicken or salmon while holidaying in the Dordogne.

The reds vary tremendously with lovely aromas of blackcurrants, black cherries, raspberries and blackberries. The grapes, Cabernet Sauvignon, Cabernet Franc, Merlot and Malbec are the same variety of grapes as used in Bordeaux, the only difference being the percentage of each used. There are the lighter fruity reds which are perfect for picnics and lunch, to the slightly more tannic and fruity wines. At the top of the range, you have the rich in fruit, more tannic and often complex, Côtes de Bergerac and Pecharmant. Most wines are drinkable at 2 years and can age for 5 to 8 years – or even longer! It is a great pity that very few of the 'quality' reds get onto the British market.

At one time there was a vast difference between Côtes de Bergerac and Pecharmant. The latter was always the more complex, ageing extremely well. Pecharmant is still of this quality, but nowadays there are several Côtes de Bergerac of similar quality.

Bergerac red wines are rich and colourful without excessive tannin. At one time, they were at their best at 4–5 years but now some will age quite well for 10 years! Like St Emilion and Pomerol, these wines have lots of minerals and are particularly good for the digestive system.

The sweet wines are produced on the left bank of the Dordogne. They offer a choice of the 'not too sweet' Moelleux and the heavier, sweeter, creamier Liquoreux, which is produced in Monbazillac [a similar type can be found in Saussignac and its surrounding villages].

Moelleux is a lighter, not nearly as sweet, thinner wine. Ideal on its own, or by adding a little cassis, framboise, etc., as an aperitif.

The best Monbazillacs are produced as Sauternes wines. The grapes are affected by noble rot and are left on the vine for as long as possible – sometimes until November. The grapes are then picked by hand and taken to the winery for vinification.

Only certain vintages will have a harvest good enough to produce a true Monbazillac, which has a nose of honey and acacia. The word 'tactile' in one of our senses is not often used but, in the case of this quality of Monbazillac, it comes immediately to mind as the wine, creamy and deliciously sweet slips gently over the palate, leaving a lingering finish in the mouth.

The wines of Bergerac have come a long way during the last 25 years.

Chapter 11
Duras And The Lot Et Garonne

Duras is a smaller wine region just south of Bergerac where some very good wine is produced. This is where a lot of the wine came from that was shipped to England in the Middle Ages. So much went on there in the 14th and 15th centuries.

Every tour I brought to this region included a visit to the co-operative 'Berticot' at Duras. We were always made most welcome and the staff did all they possibly could to help me make people more aware of the wines of this area. Another big bonus of the co-op was that the Cellarmaster and wine-maker is Monsieur Devaux – one of the last students of Professor Peynaud, who was in charge of the oenology department at Bordeaux University. I sincerely admired this man to whom wine-makers of south-west France and other wine regions are greatly indebted. When he retired from the University, he became the consultant to Châteaux Margaux until arthritis forced him to stop working.

Monsieur Devaux is a very good wine-maker and put the wines of Duras on the British market. Right from the start, his Sauvignon Blanc was superb and, a few years ago, Berticot received an order for as much of this wine as they made. Unfortunately, during that summer, a tornado hit the region and the vines as well as the telephone and electricity constructions of Duras were hurled into the air and all was lost. The amazing thing was that no one was killed!

The vineyards around had to be replanted and it took several years to get back to normal.

Duras is typical of the 'bastide' towns of the Dordogne. They were either Protestant or Catholic during the wars and Duras was a Protestant bastide. Most of these towns are built strategically high on a hill so that the enemy could be viewed several miles away. The streets were planned on a 'grid system' as this made easy access for the soldiers.

The château is the most dominant feature and what a history it has… . When I first saw it in the 1970s it was a complete ruin. My daughter and I did a little searching in the rubble and found some kitchen tiles [looking very much like delph and a stone pot probably used for storing walnut oil]. I don't suppose they are very old, but I keep them as treasures.

By the 1980s, it had started to improve and later when I took the groups to Duras I found it was possible to have a guided tour. Things had improved! Monsieur Blanche, a man who was truly dedicated to his work, showed us around, where possible. We were taken into the main hall at ground level and told a little of the history of the château.

Bertrand de Goth who owned the vineyard Château Pape Clement in Bordeaux built the château in Duras in 1304. Most of the wine being shipped to the northern countries came from this area and he planted vineyards around Duras. He then built the Château which stands high and is surrounded by vineyards – his at the time.

It wasn't long after this that the Pope moved from Rome to Avignon and Bertrand de Goth joined him – becoming the first Pope of Avignon, Pape Clément V. The château was left and was involved in the wars that followed. Eventually it was ransacked and papers and furniture were destroyed by a fire, which burned outside the château, we were told, for a week.

The château remained in ruins and was a disgrace to the town. Just before the Second World War an American arrived and stated that there must be some connection because his name was Duras! Have I heard this sort of statement before? He was extremely rich and, on finding a builder, he commissioned him to restore it … leaving him a huge amount of money to cover the cost. Well, you can imagine, this poor village chap had probably never had more than a few francs in his pocket… . The temptation was too great … . He, his family and the money disappeared!

The American returned and was most upset to find that nothing had been done to the château and that the money had gone! Not being one to turn his back on his 'namesake', he found another person and left money in safe hands for the work to be carried out, after which he left to return to the States. He was never heard of after that, and the people of Duras made enquiries as the work got to the stage where more money was required. Seemingly, the boat he returned on was sunk by attack at the beginning of the War.

A definite effort was made to find relatives and, in the end, his wife was found in a mental hospital in Britain and died soon afterwards.

The château was left to ruin, but Paris agreed that it would be restored as it is part of the French heritage. The trouble was that France has so many châteaux in need of repair, and Duras was forgotten. The people of the town then offered to buy it and they got it for a pittance.

Most of the château was still in ruins but museums had been created in one or two of the rooms, a collection of farm tools and machinery, furniture, clothes of late the 19th and early 20th century, some Roman coins and pot which had been dug up around Duras. There were postcards galore of yester-year and a pair of long white lace knickers stole the prize in the clothes collection. There was also the centrepiece of an old wine press, and Monsieur Blanche told me that, when he first went to buy it for the museum, the lady was using it for a lampstand! When she went off on holiday, the husband contacted Monsieur Blanche and sold it to him – because he didn't like it! Later, we were shown the banqueting hall, which was difficult to get to because the staircase is in one of the towers and was extremely fragile. The hall had been renovated and it was explained that they let it out for weddings, meetings, etc. and this helped to pay for the restoration work. The ceiling is outstanding! Just like the hull of a wooden ship turned upside-down – and so it was! In days gone by, oak was needed for shipbuilding so, when it came to putting oak beams in a place such as this, the old wood from the ships had to be used. The little windows set in alcoves overlooking the town were all along the wall and at the end of the hall was a space, which you could just walk into. There you could find a seat with two holes – this was the toilet.

A narrow twisting staircase led you down to the cellars. The first thing we saw was the centre of 'plumbing' … . This was a well where the water was continually drawn off by animals that spent the whole day tied to the centrepiece, tramping around the well and pulling up the buckets of water. The water was then poured into gullies, which supplied the kitchen, stables, etc. I know we're more sophisticated today but it is still the same system.

The kitchen was massive and at the end of the room there was a huge fireplace with a spit on which they roasted the animals.

There is a large room near the kitchen, called the 'Whispering room'. Nearly all the staff suffered from disease and the only way the priest would visit and listen to their 'sins' was for this room to be used. You could stand in one corner and whisper to another person in the opposite corner and no contact between the two persons was made. This was all possible because of the shape of the ceiling.

There was only one more place to see down here and that was the guardroom and definitely the most gruesome. It is situated under one of the terraces. Just off the main room was the cell for the prisoners and, if you looked up to the ceiling, you could see a hole. Below the hole was a large spike and we were told that prisoners – mainly Protestants – were pushed in here from the terrace!

It was a relief to get away from here and back to a room on ground level, which is used for the meetings of the 'Commanderie of Duras', which controls the wines of Duras.

In the beginning, I wondered why Monsieur Blanche was so dedicated to his work. Having dinner with some friends in Saussignac one evening, they told me that his family lived in one of the cellars of the château – he was born in it and he felt it was his home.

The Lot et Garonne is sandwiched between the Dordogne and Gers [Armagnac country] and suffered severely when *Phylloxera* devastated the vineyards of France at the end of the 19th century.

The Côtes du Marmandais, within the region, like a few of the other poorer wine regions, invested so much in trying to prevent rather than actually trying to get rid of the disease. When the time came for replanting – which was the only solution – the wine producers couldn't afford to do so and this is when they turned to market gardening.

Slowly and surely, some vineyards were replanted but the wine production was on a much smaller scale for many years. The wines remained in the VDQS classification until 1990, when the region was elevated to full AC classification.

The co-operative wineries are now producing some exciting wines. Some of the wines in the cheaper range are extremely good value and are perfect for picnics, summer lunches and general 'quaffing'.

The whites vary considerably: one or two are a little 'flabby' but there are some '*WOWs*' with lovely citrus aromas, a well-balanced level of acidity and a 'zing' on the palate.

The 'quality' reds are *big* and juicy, penetrating the palate with flavours of dark, rich red fruit. They have a reasonable 'long finish' in the mouth and these wines are capable of ageing for a few years.

There are several very good co-operatives in the Lot et Garonne. The co-operative at Buzet is a 'must' for anyone with an interest in wine. It is the largest co-operative in France! The selection of wines is huge and, what is most unusual, is that all the wine is fermented in oak! I had heard about this winery but had never imagined it to be on such a large scale.

Chapter 12
Bordeaux

I can't say that I am attracted to the City of Bordeaux. I enjoy visiting the wine stores and other shops and for eating out in the evening – it is a treasure. I don't find it as interesting as other places for general tourism – but it is a *majestic* city. When it comes to the history related to the wine trade, I then get quite excited because so much went on there in the Middle Ages.

My pleasure is to walk along the Quai des Chartrons on the river Garonne, past the beautiful houses that once belonged to wine merchants. Two outstanding features about Bordeaux are the rooftops and the doors. The doors have been made from wonderful heavy woods. Bordeaux imported a lot of wood from Africa but unfortunately it wasn't treated and termites, which have lain dormant for years, have now devastated many properties in the city.

Below these houses and the quay were the cellars where some of the wines were stored. My imagination goes wild! It must have been an extremely busy port at one time. Boats bringing in wine from the wine villages of the Dordogne and lower Garonne, then it being loaded on to larger boats for the trip up the Gironde [the Dordogne and Garonne rivers join near Château Margaux in the Medoc] and out into the Bay of Biscay on its way to England.

People don't realise that, in the Middle Ages, *Claret* as we know it came mainly from the regions south of Bergerac, i.e. Duras and westwards to Libourne. In the 1300s more wine from this region was exported to England than ever before or ever again. ['Claret' with its many spellings was said to be the name of one of the English members of court of that time.]

Bertrand de Goth, who built Château Pape Clément in the centre of Bordeaux in 1300, needed more land to expand and this was why he built the Château of Duras in 1304. He didn't live there very long as, when the Papal Palace moved to Avignon in 1306, he took up residence there as the first Pope, Clement V.

In the Middle Ages, the wines of this region were better known in England than in France. In Paris, Burgundy was the only wine. That was until the 18th century when Marechal Richelieu, Governor of Guyenne and great friend of Louis XV, informed the King that his 'miraculous recovery to health was entirely due to imbibing the wine of Bordeaux!'

Bordeaux wine is said to be good for longevity and, to prove it, a celebration was given at St Julian in 1937 for the old people of the Medoc who had been married for over 50 years. Four hundred and seven old couples turned up!

Bordeaux became a truly a thriving city and the prosperity was due not only to its geographical position but to the labours of high Protestant families, such as the Cruses, Lawtons, Bartons, Johnsons, Lunchs and O'Brians. 'Trade' meant the WINE TRADE. The first wines were shipped to Bristol in the 14th century, and Chaucer mentions the shipman on the Madelaine, who drank all the wine onboard before it arrived in Bristol during that time.

The port of Bordeaux must have been a mass of little boats after the harvest and when the wine had been put into barrels. You couldn't get many barrels on those small boats. The voyage up to England took many months. In fact, some captains and crew managed to drink the lot before arriving in Bristol!

As time went on, there was the problem of pirates. They used to 'hang out' in La Rochelle and wait for the boats to come into view. The situation became quite serious because they were commandeering more and more wine. That was when the King of England gave an order that all boats transporting wine from Bordeaux should carry arms – the start of the Royal Navy!

History stretches back to Gallo-Roman times. It was a show place for the Roman Empire, who named it Burdigale – capital of Aquitaine [Land of Waters] [Scanty ruins of the palaces and temples can still be seen]. This is where the Roman officers would rest during the wars.

In AD 276 it was destroyed by the Germans [and they had another go in 1940!] after which it was rebuilt in a modest way, only to be destroyed yet again by the Visigoths, Francs and Saracens who all occupied the city at different times. The Vikings left the place in ruins and it was rebuilt in the 10th century.

For three centuries it was an English possession and it benefited greatly. It was the favourite residence of the Black Prince [son of Edward III of England]. The Black Prince's son, Richard II was born here.

Bordeaux's economy was ruined by Napoleon and Nelson's blockade, and remained depressed until after World War II.

The Place des Quinconces is the largest Square in Europe – an esplanade of 30 acres built in 1818–1828 on the site of Château Trompette, a 15th century fortress. I have an interesting tale to tell about it... .

When I first came to the region, I visited Bordeaux on several occasions. The Girondin Column of Peace which stands on the northern edge of the Place interested me. I was told that there were once iron prancing horses [*Les Chevaux des Girondins*] surrounding the statue but, during the Second World War, these had been removed and hidden in a cave by a group of the Resistance. Unfortunately, those involved were killed, so it was thought that the horses were lost forever – or taken to Germany without anyone knowing about it.

Then one day in the late 1980s early 1990s, I can't remember, on a visit to the Maison du Vin which is near the Place des Quinconces, I looked at one of my favourite sites and there, lo and behold, were the horses! I rushed into the tourist office which is opposite the Maison de Vin and asked where they came from. The girls couldn't tell me anything... .

I was having lunch with a French friend who lives near the Centre and could not wait to find out about it. She told me that, when excavating to lay the foundations for a new supermarket, the horses were found. There was great rejoicing and a special parade was arranged to put the horses back *in situ*. The local newspapers had covered it well. The parade went by the tourist office – and no one had taken any notice!

The Monument des Girondins is a 140 ft column with a bronze statue of Liberty on the top. When you think of the Girondins – and know Bordeaux, it is possible you will think of the football team. The team took the name from the political party formed at the time of Robispierre – after the French revolution. They called themselves the Girondins because members came from the Basin of the Gironde and thought they would be able to save Bordeaux. They dominated the Assembly in 1792 but, in 1794, Robespierre and his pack of Jacobins intimidated every member of the National Assembly to voting for the arrest of the 29 Girondins; they were found guilty. As they were led out, they cried 'we die on the day the people lost their reason. You [Robespierre] will die on the day they find it again.' They spent the last night in the Concierge prison and went to be beheaded by *Mme Guillotine* singing 'The Marseillaise'. The monument is to commemorate what they fought for... Liberty.

And so be it. Not long after, this wicked man was taken to the guillotine.

The guillotine was introduced to France by Dr Guillotine, egalitarian and humane person, who supported the use of it as a swift, relatively painless way of removing any head. The mechanical beheading device had been known in Sparta and reached Italy by the 13th century and Edinburgh by the 15th century. It was always well favoured for removing heads of the well born!

There are also other monuments in the Place, one to Montesquieu and the other to Montaigne.

Montesquieu, 1689–1755, an eminent philosopher and writer, had vineyards in La Brede, south of Bordeaux. He was an anglophile and designed a park in the 'English style'.... He spent most of his time at La Brede, looking after his estates and selling wine to the English, He said, 'I like being at La Brede because there my money is under my feet'! The château still belongs to his descendants and, until the euro was introduced, he was still connected to the money of France, as his head was printed on the 200 franc note. There are no longer vineyards at La Brede, instead you will find beautiful gardens – well worth a visit.

Montaigne's tomb is in the vestibule of the University Faculties of Science and Letters. He was the first Mayor of Bordeaux and lived east of the city near Castillon La Bataille. The tower still stands and can be visited.

From Roman times you can see the remains of the Palais Gallien, one entrance has survived. The Roman amphitheatre [3rd century] was 436 by 364 ft and could hold 15,000 spectators.

The Pont de Pierre was built in 1813–1821. This spans the river with 17 arches, and between each arch is carved Napoleon's Roman crown.

St Michel's Church in the student quartier is worth a visit. It's 16th century and pure Gothic. The spire is separate from the church and stands 374 ft high – the highest in the south-west of France. By ascending the 228 steps, you can get a fine view of the city. At one time, it was possible to see the mummified bodies in the crypt of the church!

St Andrew's Cathedral where Eleanor married Louis is one of the finest buildings in Bordeaux. It's in Romanesque style and was built in the 11th century. The large nave, which is 60 ft wide and 75 ft high, is 12th century and represents early Gothic structure. It has a detached bell tower [Pey Berland] with the largest bell weighing nearly 10 tonnes, which was built in the 15th century and is similar to the Italian style and very elegant.

As you walk along the quay from the Place des Quinconces you will come to the Place de Bourse, built in 1728–1755. Here you will find some very beautiful architecture, the Palais de Bourse, Customs House and the Maritime museum. In the centre is the statue of the 'Three Graces'.

The Grande Theatre stands majestically in the centre of Bordeaux. It was designed by the Parisian architect, Victor Louis, and built in 1773–80. The façade is most imposing, with Corinthian columns supporting a balustraded entablature with 12 statues of beautiful ladies.

The great stairway was modelled on the one in The Paris Grand Opera House and the chandelier in the theatre weighs 6160 lbs or 2¾ tons – if you ever visit the theatre – especially during the music season in May – make sure you get a seat away from the chandelier – you never know, accidents can happen!

Around the old city you will see what remains of the gate towers. These were gates in the walls that controlled entrance into the City. Bordeaux was very popular and people came in their hundreds, forming camps outside each gate – hoping that one day they would gain entry. This is why some of the Portes are named after the tribes who camped outside the gates.

The Grosse Cloche, built in the 16th century, still stands. Originally it was a 13th century gate tower. It once possessed six towers but now only two remain. The bell weighs nearly 9 tonnes and it took 14 pairs of oxen to bring the bell to the tower,

Of course, to write about Bordeaux and not mention Eleanor would be like having dinner without wine in France! She must be the woman I most admire in French history and I have read many interesting pieces on her life. The following is my version of the life of a very omnipotent woman.

Long before Alison Weir wrote her book on the *Plantagenet Queen*, I had studied this woman in connection with the wine trade of the 13th century.

From my findings, I gather that Eleanor was born somewhere around Belin Beliet which is south of Bordeaux. Her mother died during childbirth and her father William IX, the first troubadour of France, ruined his motherless daughter. She grew up wanting for nothing and was continually serenaded by the many young troubadours following in her father's footsteps.

William died at La Compostella on Good Friday 1137 and was buried under the High Altar. His pilgrimage had been for forgiveness, he had taken a young girl as a lover and locked her in a tower – for his pleasure!

La Compostella is in north-west Spain and it was here where Saint James who Christianized Spain was buried. Even after his death, it is said that he appeared on a white horse and terrorized the Moors and put them to flight!

He became a popular Saint, and pilgrimages were made in his name. Routes were marked out by the church. The Knights Templar guarded and guaranteed the safety of the pilgrims on the roads, which were marked with milestones known as *montjores*. The monks of Cluny built resting places *en route*, hospitals, etc., but one had to have suitable *bone fides* in one's possession – such as a letter of authority from one's bishop. He also had to be attired in suitable uniform. Jacgots [as the pilgrims were called] wore a large scallop shell because this had been adopted as the emblem of St Jacques [James in English]. That and a cloak were *obligatoire*. They travelled in groups. I suppose this is the origin of Cocquilles St Jacques.

Eleanor was tall, had light brown hair, blue eyes and was very beautiful – so we are told. Her greatest achievement was being able to speak *langue d'Oc*, language of the south and the language of the north of France.

Before continuing with the life of Eleanor, we have to go back to the time of Charlemagne [Charles the Magnificent]. He was King of the Franks ruling the lands of France, Belgium, etc. – as we know them today. When he died, his lands were shared equally between his many sons One son had Normandy [as we know it today], another had Aquitaine, another the Anjou … and so on. France was tiny in size, just around Paris and this is where the Ile d'France originated. So the King of France owned very little of France – just an island!

Paris was poor in comparison to Bordeaux – none of the palatial dwellings of the south where there was more sunshine… and wine.

The King of France, Louis VI, had heard about the beautiful Eleanor and wanted Aquitaine under his realm. There was only one way to get it and that was by arranging a marriage between his son who would later be Louis VII, and this beauty of the Land of Waters.

[It was actually Louis VII who introduced the tall, thin Cyprus tree to France from his trips to the Holy Lands.]

Son Louis didn't want to marry, he had chosen to be a monk and to travel with his 'friends' to the holy lands. He at first refused but later agreed to the wishes of his father.

On the other hand, Eleanor didn't want to live in Paris, life was great in Bordeaux, terrific social life, lovely sunshine – she had heard such awful tales of Paris….. But the marriage was agreed.

They were married in the Cathedral of St Andrew in the centre of Bordeaux on 25 July 1137. Eleanor reluctantly moved to Paris to start her married life and she was crowned Queen of France the following Christmas Day.

During her time with Louis VII, she bore him two daughters: Marie who was later Countess of Champagne and Alice, Countess of Blois.

She was a dutiful wife and, when her husband planned his visit to the Holy Land, there was no question that she would not accompany him. The brave woman! She suffered with discomfort and disease and was truly bored during the time spent there. She sighed with relief on their return to Paris.

There had to be some changes when the next visit was arranged. One addition was to take Uncle Raymond, Count of Toulouse with them. He was a troubadour and could entertain her.

Louis became very jealous of the relationship, accusing them of being more than 'good friends' and, on their return to Paris, Louis had made up his mind that they should be divorced. St Bernard and the church tried in every way to reverse his decision. In an effort to end their estrangement, the Pope elaborately decorated a double bed.

Eleanor said her husband had the morals of a monk. Also, he did not please her sexually.

St Bernard was extremely distressed with Louis VII over this divorce and it was not until they met much later in St Denis, the first Gothic church in France, that they were reconciled.

It wasn't long before Eleanor made her way back to Bordeaux, travelling by night to ensure her safety.

During their marriage, Louis VII had tried to add the region of Anjou to his realm.

The lands of Anjou were ruled by Geoffrey Plantagenet. Geoffrey had red hair and was therefore known as Geoffrey the Redhead. He was a very contented man and enjoyed riding through his lands – occasionally stopping to pick a piece of broom to put in his hat. It was because of this, the name Plantagenet originated. The French word for Broom is *Plant de Genêt.*

Louis VII invited Geoffrey to visit Paris and Geoffrey agreed – taking his son Henry who was just 11 years of age. This was during the time that Louis was married to Eleanor. They arrived in Paris safely for this audience with Louis – during which time Eleanor had passed by and admired the son, Henry.

Geoffrey refused the deal and Father and son made their way back to Anjou.

Geoffrey died later by drowning in the Loire River.

Henry II must have seen [and liked] Eleanor, because it wasn't long after Eleanor's return to Bordeaux that they were married in St Pierre at Poitiers on Whit Sunday 1152, only 8 weeks after the annulment.

This marriage made Henry a very powerful man, ruling the lands of Anjou and Aquitaine. It is said that Henry was one of the best kings Britain ever had.

[At this time, most upper class in commerce, courts, etc. spoke French.]

Eleanor must have enjoyed the marriage to Henry in the beginning because she had seven children by him: Henry, Richard, Geoffrey, John, Matilda, Eleanor and Joanne.

Henry [born in Le Mans] in 1133 was the son of Matilda who, if we hadn't had the Salic law, would have been Queen of England. Stephen was given the throne. The Salic law was made by the Salian Franks tribes. It came to be applied to a law that no woman may succeed to a throne. He was one of the most desirable, eligible bachelors in France.

Big, stocky, enormous energy, deep barrel chest and bandy legs of a horseman... .

He had a large round head with square freckled face, bulging, blue grey eyes and close cropped red hair and beard. He was always carelessly dressed, unceremonious in manner, energetic, restless as well as moody.

Matilda was the daughter of Henry I. A widow of the Emperor of Germany, she later married Geoffrey V [who was 11 years younger than her] in 1128 and it is strange that Eleanor was also 11 years older than Henry II. Perhaps this was the first era of *'toyboys'*!

Before Stephen died, there were many confrontations between Henry and himself and, in the end, it was agreed that, as Stephen didn't have an heir, the throne of England would be given to Henry. You can imagine this added even more power to his realm – owning the lands from the Pyrenees to the Southern Uplands of Scotland. Eleanor had taken note and she too became more powerful as queen of England. [There's more about Stephen in the Loire chapter.]

The last son they had was John – big, bad John as seen in the Robin Hood tale. They had given so much land to the other children, there was nothing left for him – hence the name John Lackland. Actually, he wasn't as bad as portrayed with the Sheriff of Nottingham. He was, in fact, a brilliant administrator and it was he who gave St Emilion the Charter date in 1199.

Of course, Eleanor's favourite was Richard, who preferred to be with his male friends than to get married. This worried Eleanor as she was planning to get rid of Henry so that Richard could become king.

The Abbey of Fontevraud was founded by Eleanor; it is said to be the first home for badly treated wives. It is here that you will find the tombs of the Plantagenets.

It is wrong for the English Royals to rest in France and Queen Victoria, who was very friendly with Eugenie and Napoleon III, almost persuaded them to return the tombs to London. Unfortunately, it was at the start of the Prussian War and the move never took place.

The Court that followed Henry to England missed the warmth of France and also the wine and it was simply because of this that the wine trade started between Bordeaux and England.

After Eleanor had passed child-bearing age, Henry started his long affair with Rosamund Clifford in 1167. She was a genuine rival to the queen. Where did Rosamund get her name from? It has been suggested that

Rosa-mundi = Rose of the world
Rosa immundi = Rose of unchastity

Henry's mother, Matilda, died in 1167. Her epitaph was 'Here lies Henry's daughter, wife and mother. Great by birth, greater by marriage but greatest by motherhood.' I suppose they could have used the same one for Eleanor!

When Henry II returned to England in 1161 it was to crush a rising in South Wales, which he did by dragging Prince Rhys of Deheubarth out of his mountain lair and, in 1163, Welsh princes paid homage to the King at Woodstock.

In 1173 Eleanor's sons, Henry, Richard and Geoffrey, were old enough and capable of leading her revolt against Henry II. At first, Henry suspected nothing but in 1174 Eleanor was shipped to England and confined first in Winchester and then in Old Sarum castle. She also spent time jailed in Berkshire, Buckinghamshire and Nottinghamshire and in 1179 she was taken to Aquitaine, where she publicly renounced the Duchy in favour of Richard – then returned to England and captivity.

In the same year, when Eleanor was nearly 70 years of age, she rode to Pamplona via Bordeaux and the Pyrenees. On Richard's behalf, she asked for the hand of Berengaria because Eleanor never wanted Richard to marry Alice of France. She then rode with Berengaria to Cyprus for the marriage to Richard – staying long enough to witness the marriage. Unfortunately, the 'Lion' didn't inherit his mama's healthy sensuality! On 3 September 1191, Richard I was crowned king at Westminster. No women or Jews were allowed to attend the banquet which followed.

We all look upon Richard the Lionheart as a good friend to Robin and Maid Marion – but I know differently. Although there were rumours... he had an illegitimate child named Philip and was known to have had very little affection for England. How could he, when he didn't speak English? The English knew nothing of his immorality, lack of scruples, sexual deviations, and devotion to the weirder ideas of chivalry, reckless violence and brutality.

Eleanor went to live in Fontevraud Abbey; she died when she was 82 years of age. She reigned first as a queen of France, then queen of

England for a total of 67 years That's what you call longevity! Perhaps it was the red wine of Bordeaux!

She arranged the marriage of her grand-daughter, Blanche of Castille, with Louis [son of Louis XII], who later became King and was such a good King that he was eventually canonised as St Louis. Eleanor became the Grandmother of a Saint!

Chapter 13
Wine Regions of Bordeaux

There are several wine regions around Bordeaux, which have the AOC Bordeaux, and I should like to concentrate on the main ones.

The main grapes used for wine production are the same in Bordeaux as in all the rest of south-west France. For the red, you have the Cabernet Sauvignon, Cabernet Franc, Merlot and Petit Verdot; for the white, there is the Sauvignon, Semillon and Muscadelle. There are others under the AOC. The difference between each region is the percentage of each used. For example, a lot more Merlot is used in St Emilion and Pomerol than in Medoc.

The 1855 Classification was introduced when the Syndicate des Courtiers de Bordeaux set up a committee of Bordeaux brokers to classify the wines of the Medoc and Sauternes at the Universal Exposition of Paris.

The classification was based on prices paid by Bordeaux merchants over the previous century, and wines from 62 vineyards were selected and arranged into five grades.

- 4 vineyards for the first growth and premier crus.
- 15 vineyards for the second cru
- 14 vineyards for the third cru
- 11 vineyards for the fourth cru
- 18 vineyards for the fifth cru.

I don't think this would ever be allowed today and many look upon the 1855 Classification as the most unfair classification, but it can't be changed now. A change was made in 1973 when Mouton Rothschild was moved from the 1st of the Second Growth to last of the 1st

Growths which include Lafite, Margaux, Latour [Medoc], Haut Brion [Graves] and Yquem in the Sauternes.

Château Haut Brion is France's oldest wine estate and probably the most senior of the premier crus. In the 1980s there was a special 'sale of the century' to mark the occasion of the 50th anniversary of the acquisition of Haut Brion by Clarence Dillon, the American Banker. To celebrate the occasion, a dinner was held at Brooke's Club for 40 of Britain's most respected wine experts.

In 1932 another Classification was brought in, the 'Bourgeois Classification', i.e., Bourgeois Superior Exceptional, Cru Bourgeois Superior and Cru Bourgeois.

It's all very complicated and I don't want my book to be complicated! For those of you who wish to delve further, you will find loads of books on the subject.

The main grapes used in the region are described as follows:

For the red wine,
   Cabernet Sauvignon: Thick skins, loads of tannin gives a wine longevity
   Cabernet Franc: Lighter than the Caberner Sauvignon, not so much tannin and fruitier
   Merlot: Fruity and gives a wine body. Excellent for blending with Cabernet Savignon
   Petit Verdot: the 'pepper and salt' giving the finishing touch to the wine.

For the white wine:
   Sauvignon Blanc: Very aromatic and gives wine 'zingyness' [my own word!].
   Semillon: This grape is susceptible to noble rot and has lovely tones of honey, tropical fruit, etc.
   Muscadelle: Blended with Sauvignon Blanc and Semillon to give the wine a distinct aroma.

It was the Dutch who were responsible for draining the Medoc, a triangular piece of land washed on one side by the Atlantic and on the other by the Gironde. It's roughly 45 miles long and 7 miles wide at its widest point. It is sheltered by pine forests from the Atlantic and the trees filter the salt air – a very important factor for the most important red wine region in France; before this, it was just swamp land. It was done very carefully, dividing parcels of land with little streams.

There are eight appellations for red wine, i.e., Haut Medoc, Margaux, Moulis, Listrac, St Julian, Pauillac, St Estephe and Medoc.

The wines from the south have more delicacy and less body than those from the north. Wines nearer the river have more finesse, wines further inland are more robust. Everything in the Medoc depends on depth of gravel and good drainage. The fertile alluvial palus next to the river is not suitable for vines.

When you approach the wine area, the first feeling you have is disappointment. The land seems so flat, the vines are trained low with very little space between each row. The soil is usually very dry and is covered with stones not much bigger than pebbles. Just keep driving on because, in a very short time, you will be able to feast your eyes on beautiful châteaux with magnificently kept gardens – this is an area of great affluence where negotiants travel from Bordeaux by helicopter to visit the vineyards – or to buy wine.

A few years ago, French television did a programme on the Medoc – covering all the prestigious vineyards and the families associated. The background music was the theme music from 'Dallas' – I thought then – how appropriate!

On your first stop, you will realise how silly it was to be disappointed because, as soon as you stand in the middle of the vineyard, you will observe the gentle sloping so vital to the production of this wine.

The vines are planted close together, so that the roots have to compete/struggle to find water. With deep gravel and poor subsoil, the roots have to go down into the bedrock and search. Isn't nature wonderful? By doing this, the roots bring up the minerals from the rock as well as the water to the vine…. . Although the vine looks short compared with those in other wine regions, the roots go down very deep because the vines are much older in this region.

It's all a case of economics. Vineyard proprietors in most other regions sell their wine at very low prices [compared to the Medoc and Bourgogne] and they have to sell all their stock as soon as possible in order to survive. They depend on vines producing quantity – as well as good quality and vines will produce well for about 30 years, after which quantity will decrease but quality will increase. Vines in the Medoc are much older, therefore the quality is much better and the wines will age longer, making the price of a bottle of wine much more expensive. Only recently, while on a visit with a student to Lafitte Rothschild, I was given a vine which had just been dug up – it was around 100 years of age!

I have visited many of the châteaux of the Medoc and some are very dear to me – simply because of the history attached, the most romantic of these being Château Palmer [pronounced 'pal mer']with its pointed turrets – typical of the region's châteaux built in 1856. The vineyards join those of Château Margaux.

The original owner was a young man who married and lived very happily until he, still quite young, became ill and died. The young wife had no other option than to sell the property. To do this she had to go to Paris, which meant a long journey by coach from Bordeaux. She sat on the coach sobbing, not only had she lost her husband but she was going to lose her home as well. On board the coach was an English army general who was going on leave and, during the journey, she told him the whole story. Need I say any more? By the time they reached Paris, he had asked her to marry him and they returned to the property in the Medoc. The officer's name was Palmer!

Beychevelle has the most wonderful gardens and, as you turn the corner, the distinguished château comes into view. It was another militaire who owned this and each day, when the boats went by, they would lower their sails in respect and this is how it got its name. To lower your sails in French is *baisser la voile.*

Then there's the magnificent château of Pichon Longueville – well actually there are two… . The original belongs to the sisters of the family and the modern one belongs to the brother. This may sound odd but, when the parents died, the children couldn't agree on the inheritance and, in the end, the sisters and brother went their own way. The brother decided to build 'Baron de Pichon Longueville' and the sisters kept 'Pichon Longueville Contesse le Lalande', now known as 'Pichon Lalande'. There was ill feeling for many years, but all was resolved and they lived happily together. The Baron is well worth a visit, not only for the beautiful site, but you will also see one of the most up-to-date, high tech methods of production in the region.

One of the most unusual châteaux is Cos d' Estournel, where one of my favourite wines is produced. It is on a hill on the opposite side of the road, just past Lafitte Rothschild. Seemingly, before it was built, the owner visited the place and stood on a small hill overlooking Lafitte and it was then he decided that this was the site for his winery

[Cos = hill]. Monsieur Estournel spent some time in the East and with pleasant eccentricity built his chais in eastern style, surmounted by pagoda roofs. This magnificent building never ceases to enthuse me.

Many years ago, one of my favourite wine writers, Cyril Ray, wrote a book on Lafitte Rothschild. I read it over and over again. It illustrated how the five Rothschilds went their separate ways, two buying vineyards in the Medoc [Mouton Rothschild and Lafitte Rothschild]. Mouton is easy to visit, and here you will find the famous labels – including the one of the naked lady, which I think is very charming. Château Lafitte Rothschild was bought at an auction in Paris in 1868 for 4,400,000 Fr [about £200,000] The original owner went to the guillotine and the estate was then sold by the government to a Dutch company. It is more difficult and, only by writing to their office in Paris, will you be allowed to visit this picturesque château with a pink painted building where the barrels are stored. The château set in beautiful gardens is itself quite unique and the five arrows with heads [representing each of the sons] joined at the middle, fanning out from the weathercock on a little pepper-pot clock-tower. Quite a remarkable story of how five brothers set out from a Frankfurt ghetto during the time of Napoleon, each going to a different country to make their fortune.

In the museum, you can see a bottle of 1797 [this was the year of the Battle of the Nile – Nelson and Napoleon]. This wine was the first Claret to be laid down for ageing.

Regal and splendid, the most important wine château in the world, Margaux where visitors are welcomed by the warm friendly Norwegian chatelaine who over the years has become a friend. Whenever I phone to arrange a rendezvous which isn't very often, she recognizes my voice. It is wonderful that this giant of a château doesn't shun visitors as some others do. The only time you have difficulty is during the trade fair in Bordeaux, when the Château has the chance to entertain their clients from all over the world.

One of my major disappointments of visits to the Medoc was with the Priory de Lichine, I had read quite a bit about Alexis Lichine, the American war correspondent stationed in Paris [like Hemingway], who made his way down to Bordeaux, fell in love with the region and bought the Priory. He was an instigator in the Bordeaux wine trade with the States. He had a wonderful collection of antique fire backs, which were displayed in the gardens surrounding the Priory. I visited often and, on one particular visit, I said to the staff that I hoped one day to meet Alexis Lichine. It was arranged and I looked forward to the meeting. A few days before that meeting, I read in the newspapers that he had died of a heart attack.

Château de Preuillac is the most recent château that I have added to my huge list of 'châteaux visited'. May I say from the start that it is one of the most difficult to find! The château is owned by Jean Christophe, the son of Yvon Mau, one of the most respected negotiants in Bordeaux. The visit – which was, in fact, a weekend – was arranged for me by one of our Masters of Wine, who actually runs wine courses at the château as well as being Jean-Christophe's consultant.

As a member of the Association of Wine Educators, spreading the good word, it is vital that we are kept up to date with what is going on in regions where we have an interest. My main interest is the south-west of France, and a chance to refresh my knowledge is most welcome – after all, the wine world is changing all the time. We had an excellent weekend – not only finding out more about the new methods of vinification that Jean Christophe had introduced but also about other vineyards and economic changes which had occurred.

There are many other châteaux I could write about – the list is long but this book is about all the wine regions I have visited.

Before leaving the Medoc, I should like to finish with an amusing little story about yet another château and this time I won't publish the name... .

An American asked me to arrange a visit to this particular château as it is very popular in the States. We were there immediately after lunch and were shown around by the owner. He was charming and most eager to practise his English as he had spent happy times over there. The American and I began to realise that we were going to have difficulty getting away and noted he was being very friendly towards me... . He told me that he had lost his wife. We insisted on ending the meeting and ordered several cases of wine. The proprietor told us that unfortunately he hadn't any wine ready in cartons but would arrange this and suggested that *I* went to his home in Bordeaux for lunch to collect the wines. The wines were never collected!

Chapter 14
St Emilion

Before we leave Bordeaux, a mention of the graves, which gets their name from the word 'gravel'. There was a lot of expansion in this area which includes Chaucer's 'Ho Brion' as well as 'Pape Clement'. It seemed to be spreading out further and further and in …….. Pessac Leognan was created. This split the original 'Graves' into two and now the Grave area is well south of Bordeaux, while the new Pessac Leognan takes in Bordeaux and the immediate south of the city.

The dry white wines from here were poor in quality a few years ago. They were flabby and uninteresting. Now you have white wines of quality and the reds are superb. The price reflects this…. .

Driving east from Bordeaux, you eventually arrive in Libourne [it's about 20 minutes by car or train]. The town gets its name from Roger of Leyburn, an English Vassal who planned it and built it in 1270. His name is to be found in on a coloured glass window in one of the churches in Kent.

It was a prime site with tremendous fortification – so massive that you can see part of it today as you drive from Bordeaux east in the direction of Bergerac. The Tour de Grand Port, one of the main gates with its tower can be seen from the road. This is where, during the 15th century, ships arrived with the tide.

This town was built because of its geographical position – the confluence of the two rivers, Dordogne and L'Isle [from Perigueux]. As I have explained in one of the other chapters, most of the wine for Bordeaux came from this region and it was carried on boats. Wood for making the piquets [stakes] for the vineyards was transported from Perigueux, then the boat returned with wine, etc. Libourne became the Administration Centre of the Region.

Pomerol is just a little further on from here. This is where the wines have the nickname 'The Burgundies of Bordeaux' – and I know why…. They are rich, plumy wines with a deeper, more rounded flavour than those of St Emilion.

There is an unbelievable calmness in Pomerol; when you drive around, you feel that you must do it quietly. The top soil is is very gravelly and the subsoil is rich in iron oxide, which lends its distinction and character to its wines.

You may have heard of Château Le Pin from where young wine is sold at outrageous prices. I went out to find it – not with a group but with individual students who were preparing for the WSET Advanced Certificate. We drove around for ages, stopping on several occasions in order to ask directions. In the end, we seemed to be going round and round and there wasn't a sign to be seen! At last, one kind lady pointed us down an unassuming lane; at the end there was a small house surrounded by vines – this was Château Le Pin. 'Well, what do you make of this?' I said to myself.

By the time we arrived, I knew that lunch would almost be over so I walked up the stairs to the main door, which was open, and asked the small group who were obviously the vineyard workers if they could possibly tell me more about Le Pin. One chappie very kindly accompanied me downstairs to where my two students were standing and told us more about this 1 square hectare vineyard. The land the house was standing on – which wasn't very much, is worth several times the value of the house!

The second time I visited was with yet another Advanced WSET student. This time I noticed that the doors to the winery under the house were open. Approaching the door, I called in my best French, Is there anyone there – like 'Allo', back came the reply 'Allo'. We went in, passed the pressoir and into the chai. There the owner stood amidst pipes galore, racking the wine. He immediately said 'Don't come any closer – I can't afford to lose a drop of this!' He then asked me who I was. With pride I said, 'I'm Helen Gillespie-Peck, member of the Association of Wine Educators.' 'Ah', he replied, 'You must know my wife, Fiona – she's an MW [Master of Wine] and a Scot….' I told him that I knew of Fiona. It's a small world.

I must take a moment to explain 'racking'. This is when the wine is ageing in the barrels – usually for 1 year to 18 months. The sediment [lees] falls to the bottom of the barrel and every 3 months the wine is drawn from the sediment, put into another clean barrel and topped up with the same wine to start over again.

The dominant grape of Pomerol [and St Emilion] is the Merlot. It ripens early and give s a gorgeous, succulent, minty, honeyed, blackcurrant or plum-flavoured wine – which explains why Pomerol and St Emilion take less effort to enjoy than the Medocs. The only problem is that the wines don't age as well as the ones from the Medoc.

We're now on our way to St Emilion, a couple of kilometres along the road.

Each time I visit St Emilion, I look at the gently sloping hills which seem to fold into one another therefore protecting the vines from the wind. I have often said God has blessed these vines with a wonderful location and, although I don't believe in re-incarnation, if I did come back to this earth, I would like to come back as a Cabernet Savignon grape and rest in these hills. The reason I would choose to be a Cab Sauv – rather than a Merlot is because the Cabernet Sauvignon takes about 3 weeks longer to ripen therefore I would rest – fully dressed in the sunshine for just that little bit longer!

The soil here is variegated, chiefly clay mixed with limestone but with silica in places. The hills are sandy, gravelly and chalky. The plains have sandy soil.

St Emilion can be described as the most beautiful wine town in France or an archaeological gem – depending where your interests lie. It has been described as a city resting in an amphitheatre, which lies in a dip between vine clad hills overlooked by a church bell tower.

The narrow streets are paved with large Cornish stone, which was brought in English boats as ballast on the outward journey when merchants came to ship wine from Libourne.

There are remains of Gallo Roman villas and we do know that Decimus Magnus Ausonius who was born and lived in Bordeaux during the 4th century also lived in St Emilion.

He was a scholar famous throughout the Empire and one of the greatest poets of his time. He was eventually made a Prefect of Gaul.

Later he went to live in the Emperor's Court in Trier and in AD 386, in his work 'Mosella', praised Germany's first wine region in glowing terms. Because the poet's home was in Bordeaux, the Moselle locals and their neighbours claimed that French wine could not compare with theirs. After all, Ausonius had emigrated from France to remain on the

Moselle because he had learned to appreciate good wine. He was the first to compose poetry about the Moselle and also the first Consul of Rome.

In the 8th century, *Semilione* founded the hermitage and the town soon grew around it. You can visit the Hermitage. It is in the centre of the town. There you will find a stone seat, coffin/bed and the Saint's altar. They say that the fountain is endowed with special powers.

The town was involved in many wars. Apart from the 100 years' war, we can go a little more recent to the period of the Revolution when the well owner of the King's Castle built in the 13 century during the reign of Louis III in 1224, hid his friend in the dungeon from the henchman, Robespierre.

The Monolithic church is well worth a mention. It is the most singular in France – unique in Europe. The steeple was built in the 12th, 15th and 16th centuries. The church was actually dug out of the rock by the monks. The church itself is supported by ten pillars of the original rock.

The Jurade of St Emilion parade through the street dressed in white ermine-lined scarlet robes. This is a procession to the Monolithic church for mass. It happens twice a year – to call the banns for the vintage and for thanksgiving at the end of the harvest.

The original *Jurat* was elected when Richard the Lionheart ruled Gascony. The Charter, conferring the powers to 24 jurors of the magistrates and the local council, was signed by King John [the enemy of Robin Hood] in 1199. These jurors were obliged to see that the King's laws were enforced. Their 'seal' was affixed to every cask of St Emilion wine, which went from Libourne to the Anglo Flemish and Northern German ports for 600 years until the Revolution, when the Jurade disappeared.

The Seal used by the Jurade guaranteed the production of quality of wine and held the 'fire blanc', an enormous iron seal of the arms of the town. The seal was applied by the Grand Vinetier to those casks which were to cross the frontier.

In the 1990s I noticed that several of the vineyards had the same type of 'nameplate' and that the number has been increasing. On a closer look, I realised that this is a copy of the 'fire blanc', which obviously signifies quality.

After the First World War, chaos gave birth to Appellation Controlée, which improved standards – defined boundaries as a method of control, but they could not guarantee the quality. Neglect and despair set in. It wasn't until 1948 that the Jurade as we know it today was re-introduced and this revived tasting and approval and high standards returned.

It is a good idea to view the Jurade in September [Sunday nearest 20th] when, from the 13th century tower, they issue call for the ban de vendanges. The banquet heralds the start of the vendange and there are always a few dignitaries present from Paris to enjoy the celebrations.

I have already explained the Classification of Bordeaux, which was introduced in 1855. Exactly 100 years later in 1955, a similar classification was introduced to St Emilion, the Premier Grand Cru Classe and the Grand Cru. Classification is based on the quality of the wine, climate, soil and surface exposure of vineyards – which do not change. The difference is that the St Emilion Classification is subject to revision every 10 years. Now, I ask myself, 'Is this a good or bad thing?'

On chatting to the locals, there are mixed feelings – such as, 'Well it makes sure the wine is of a good quality' then others who have said that it's a case of who you are… etc. Well I have a little story which may give you some idea what's going on … .

My visits to St Emilion started in the early 1980s, when my friends in Bordeaux invited me to lunch. The wine was served in a pichet and I was asked if I knew where it came from. The aroma was obvious – 'St Emilion' I said. Then they explained that every year they visited a private little vineyard where they were able to buy wine of this quality at a very reasonable price. I asked my friends if it was possible to take a small group there and the answer was that this was most unlikely. Anyway, I liked the wine and decided to pursue it.

My first stop was at the Maison du Vin in the centre of St Emilion. When I asked where I could find this vineyard, no one knew. They asked me why I wanted to go there and, silly me, I admitted I was considering taking a small group there. Immediately, I was told of other more suitable vineyards – probably on *their lists*. I politely said no thank you and went off to look for Château Guadet Plaissance. It took a little time, but there in St Christophe des Barde, I found it.

The house was typical St Emilion, square, cream-coloured stone, lots of windows and a door in the centre. I rang the bell, Mme Deson answered the door, she didn't look too well [I later found out she had kidney trouble] but had a lovely smile on her face – just the type of smile to welcome visitors. I explained who I was and what I was looking for

– a small family-run vineyard to bring my groups to. At first, she said it would not be possible but when I suggested that I helped her with the visit, she agreed. That was 20 years ago and I still go there to buy wine – superb quality and at a reasonably price.

Mme Deson was Jean-Paul Deson's 'backbone'. I was amazed at the amount of work she did in the winery. After all, there were only the two of them, as their sons had been sent to university. Jean-Paul's work was the vineyard and Mme Deson did everything else, from sticking labels on the bottles with an antiquated machine, sealing the 'capsule', which covers the cork and is a form of tax paid by vignerons to looking after the administration and visitors. Non stop!

Jean-Paul had converted one of the bedrooms into a little 'treatment room' for Mme Deson. She had her own dialysis machine and other equipment. Some days when I went to visit, I would sit with her in this room, I shall always remember her dark brown curly hair and very pretty smiling face which most times had an unhealthy yellow tinge.

As I write this, I am thinking very deeply of the happy memories I have of group visits to Château Gaudet Plaissance because it was only a few days ago that I heard that Mme Deson had passed away.

I went to visit Jean-Paul to offer my condolences, I found a very sad man. Neighbours told me that, although he knew she was very ill – for such a long time, he has taken her death extremely badly. He was sitting at his desk, and when he saw me at the door, a lovely smile came to his face. We talked of Madame and tears came to his eyes. I said how sorry I was to hear the news, but the wonderful memories of such happy visits will stay with me forever.

There are over 500,000 hectares of vineyards divided into nine communes: St Emilion, Sable St Emilion, St Christophe des Bardes St Etienne de Lisse, St Sulpice de Faleyrans, St Hippolyte, St Pey d'Armens, Viognet and St Laurent des Combes.

The wines of St Emilion can be described as wines that have body, generosity, colour with an agreeable savour and a distinctive bouquet. The tannin is hidden by a deep concentration of fruit. Premier Grande Cru Classe has a great deal of body, splendid finesse and is distinguished by an almost regal elegance.

The colour is brilliant, deep and velvety. You'll find a slight touch of bitterness on the younger ones, but the majority of these wines will age quite easily for 10–20 years.

The top châteaux are as follows.

Château Ausone gets its name from Ausonius. The vineyards are on steep slopes. It would be impossible to use a machine on such slopes so a horse and plough do the work.

Cheval Blanc was built as an Inn by Roger Leyburn in 1269 and this is where some of the best wines of St Emilion are produced. In 1945, the wine in Cheval Blanc was allowed to get too warm – half the crop had to be pasteurised.

Château Pavie is the largest of the Premiers Grands Crus – 35/36 hectares. The vines are on gentle hill slopes and like several of the top wineries, the cliffs underneath have been tunnelled and the caves are used for the vinification as well as storage. I think of St Emilion as being similar to the Rock of Gibralter [in a different way] – just really a shell!

Château Soutard is a beautiful château, just out of the centre of the town – owned by a charming family, the Comtes des Ligneris. I have visited it often with groups and on one occasion I had the most pleasant surprise. After the Comte had taken us through the winery and answered our many questions, we went out into the courtyard to taste the wine, but we didn't only taste the wine. The Comte had arranged for the wine to be accompanied with barbecued sausages and guess who did the barbecuing? The Comte! He has now retired and his son is also the 'perfect host', taking time to explain everything to you in a language you could understand. I find that on occasions, the hosts of some wineries forget that people in such groups come on tour to learn – and some know very little about wine, so to use technical terms is sometimes too much for the poor novice. We have had the sausages again, but his son has opened a super bistro restaurant in the town – just down the road from the tourist office.

During the Middle Ages, St Emilion was a leper colony and this is where Château Gaffelière got its name. Gaffelière means leper and the hospital where these poor people were treated is part of the château.

We mustn't leave St Emilion without talking about the Macaroons. They are referred to as the 'third glory of the city' and there are only five makers of them! They are best produced by Mme Blanchez – or her descendants. Her mother bought the only authentic recipe dating from 1620 from the nuns in the presence of a lawyer – which may give you some idea of the seriousness of the business. There's a great silence about the business but thousands of boxes of 2 dozen in a box are sold every year to tourists.

Chapter 15
Sweet Wines of Bordeaux

There are three areas of sweet wine in the region, the first is Sauternes on the left bank of the Garonne, then Loupiac and last, but not least, St Croix du Mont on the right bank.

The vines were brought to Bordeaux by the Romans – probably in about Julius Caesar's time. Ausonius, mentioned earlier, was said to be the owner of the original vineyard at Château Ausone; St Emilion is also said to have had vineyards in Loupiac.

Whenever I think of Loupiac, I think of my dear friends, Shirley and Simon.

They had explained to me on the very first tour that they weren't interested in wine, but loved travelling around France. They were bird-watchers and could identify every one we saw *en route*!

As time went on, they became interested in wine, sweet wine, and that of Château Mazarin in Loupiac. We did find others that pleased Simon's palette but Mazarin was his great love.

Every trip was booked well in advance so that they could ask to sit in the front seat of the coach in order to see more. For each tour they would arrive with binoculars, notebooks and maps, and sit crammed together on the front seat. I think it is the worst seat on the coach because you have very little room for your legs.

In the end, Simon became my navigator and was known as 'Simon the Navigator'. They travelled with me twice a year and sometimes I did only two or three tours a year, so I left the map-reading to him and we went wrong very rarely – unfortunately, when we did it was usually a 'big wrong' but, with a careful study of the map, we soon got back on track.

In, 1453, at the end of the 100 Years' War, the English trade fell away and, with the growth of Calvinism, trade between Protestant Huguenots and Hanseatic states developed in its place. The new markets favoured sweet wines and, because of this, the Graves area switched from the traditional red to white.

The estates of the region were very small until the 17th century. They were worked by peasants or small tenant farmers who shared the crops. In the 17th century, a new merchant class arose, Bordeaux Parliament families became increasingly wealthy and, during the 40 years or so before the Revolution, the poor tenants got into debt and sold out – this increased the size of the estates.

To give you some idea of the size of the Sauternes region, it is only seven by four miles, and the yield is about 300 bottles an acre.

Before this, in the 1870s, an attempt was made by Normandin et Cie to make sparkling wine. Experienced wine-makers from Epernay were employed to use the Champagne method. The wine won a Gold Medal in Angouleme in 1877 – but the success didn't last.

After the General Slump at the end of the 19th century [the *Phyloxera* period], an association was formed of Sauternes and Barsac producers. In 1935 the Association acquired the standards for AOC.

The wine was always a great favourite of the Russian archdukes. Quantities of it went to the Russian Courts while the English Court couldn't get enough of the Monbazillac.

How is this sweet white wine made? Well, here is a recipe I found many years ago which may give you some idea.

For a classic Sauternes take

- ⅔ Sémillon, ⅓ Sauvignon, press five times [NO STALKS]
- Wild yeasts are killed off by the addition of SO2.
- The 'must' is fermented in oak at 18° C–20° C by natural yeast.
- The wine is racked every 3 months and the finest will be left to mature for up to 3 years before bottling.
- Sauternes improve in the bottle. Sauternes maderises.

What has been omitted from this recipe is the condition of the grapes – and I am referring to the Semillon before picking… and this is the secret!

The picking [eight or nine times] of these grapes is done over a fairly long period, which can start in September and go on until November.

The grapes are picked individually, i.e. 'grain par grain' and must be done only in dry weather.

There are several 'risk elements' with the weather, i.e., bad weather in October, heavy rains in summer are not appreciated, possibility of hailstorms in April and May.

The Semillon is sometimes referred to as a 'flabby grape' but it is susceptible to a rot, '*botrytis cinerea* [Latin], Pourriture Noble [French] or Noble Rot.

This happens in a certain climate, which is a micro-climate, and in very special regions where the air is damp, The Sauternes is in the perfect position, situated between the Garonne and the Atlantic – creating a warm humid effect, bad for rheumatism but great for Semillon grapes! You can feel the dampness! When Autumn comes, the mornings are very misty, then the sun burns off the mist and shines on and heats the grapes. Nature is wonderful!

The grapes are left on the vine to rot, a mould forms and shrivels the skin to a wizened condition. This in no way affects the flavour, in fact it enhances it. The water from the juice escapes leaving the sugar and flavouring elements concentrated. The result is an oily-like texture.

[The sauvignon is added to give the wine a refreshing acidity – it 'lifts' the wine and the Muscadelle is also of some importance.]

This wine ages extremely well, the colour will deepen and the wine will maderise eventually. In France, it is often given as a Christening present to be drunk on marriage – or even on retirement!

The most prestigious Château is Yquem, listed in the 1855 Classification. It is a beautiful building, with gardens to match. Unfortunately, visitors are admitted by appointment only and only if related to the trade would small groups be accepted. The château belonged to the Marquis de Lur-Saluces and, on his death in 1970, was handed over to his nephew Alexandre de Lur Saluces.

Not far from Yquem is Château de Malle, which belongs to the Comte Pierre de Bournazel. The family is related to Lur Saluces. If I remember rightly, Pierre's father was a cousin.

I have visited this château for many years and it never fails to interest me. The first time was when Pierre's brother, Charles, was very young and home from school. He followed the group through the château and asked if he could come on the coach with me and the other passengers.

After you have walked through the gardens and up into the courtyard, there are a few steps that lead to the door of the château. The entrance hall is enormous with a marble-tiled floor and wood-panelled walls. On the mantlepiece above the huge stone fireplace there are several marble balls all different colours. These were given to the owners for them to choose the marble they preferred for the floor tiles.

To take you through the château, there is usually the housekeeper who carries a tape machine which is switched off and on as we progress. Normally, I would insist on a proper guide, but in this case it's different because the tape was made by Pierre's father just before he died, a very young man.

As you go from room to room, his voice haunts you, you can tell how much he loved Malle. In the sitting room there are masses of paintings and photographs of the family from way back until the present day. The sad pictures are those on the side table with Pierre, Charles, Father and Mother together.

The next room is the original office, lined with book cupboards, which hold a terrific collection of books on the history of France. On the wall beside the door there is a sword hanging with a bullet hole in the blade. This sword belonged to the grandfather of Pierre, who had used it in action.

In the bedroom there are original paintings of Mazarin and Richelieu and others at that time.

The small chapel is the last place on the visit, very peaceful with an altar, a few seats and around the walls are paintings on leather, set in panels.

Before tasting the wine, which varies a lot in quality, you have a chance to visit the Italian gardens and, in the corner of the top garden, there is a little open theatre where the family held concerts.

As I said, the sweet wines vary and I think they are too expensive because of that. The red wine they now produce is reasonably priced and value for money.

On the opposite side of the Garonne is Loupiac, where some of the wines compare favourably with the lesser wines of Sauternes. In fact, I have heard little rumours that these wines have occasionally been served as Sauternes!

My tale of this area is going to concentrate on Château Mazarin which, unfortunately, no longer produces wine. The reason is that when Monsieur Louis Courbin-Meyssan, the owner, reached the age of retirement, in order to receive his state pension, he had to give up his job as a wine producer. It was then decided to pull the vines out of the ground and this wasn't a pretty sight – or site! As we drove along the front of the château to enter it by a side lane, the château was set in vineyards and it looked very impressive. I haven't been in Loupiac for the last 10 years – perhaps things have changed – I hope so.

Château Mazarin took its name from Cardinal Richelieu's great protégée, Jules Mazarin. He was made Cardinal in 1641 and died 20 years later in 1661.

Mazarin was with the party travelling to St Jean de Luz for the marriage of the Infanta of Spain to Louis XIII's son. Mazarin hoped that the son could have married his neice, but Louis was not on good terms with Spain and something had to be done to rectify this.

Mazarin wasn't a popular man – hated by many and, when the party stopped for the night at Château Cadillac, it was thought too dangerous for Mazarin to stay with the others as there was a price on his head. He continued a little further and arrived at Loupiac, taking lodgings in one of the houses there. The next morning before he left, he told the owners that he was Mazarin and that they were permitted to call the house, Château Mazarin. The Château has been in the Courbin-Meyssan family since1534.

I took many groups there and we had such wonderful times. Anne-Marie the daughter spoke perfect English and was a character in herself. We went through the winery and, not only did Anne-Marie explain the methods of vinification, but demonstrated them to us if we happened to visit at the time of harvest. Other people had told me that the hydraulic press was no longer used, but I knew this to be untrue because it was used – when I first started to visited Mazarin.

After this visit, we went upstairs to where Anne-Marie had converted the loft into a museum. All the history of the family was displayed here: letters, invoices, tools of yesteryear, etc. At the end of that visit, Anne-Marie asked a question and the first member of the group to give the right answer was given a bottle of wine.

Lunch was then served in the dining hall, where other functions were held from time to time – such as weddings, anniversaries, etc. The lunch cooked by Marie [Portuguese] and her assistant was superb – far too much and the wine to accompany each dish was forever flowing. The family had two other vineyards, Château Barthes in Cerons and

Château Clarins in Cadillac. Wines from these vineyards were on the table together with the sweet wines of Mazarin. Such happy times!

It is often said that many who travel on wines tours do so to drink as much as possible – and some end up in a sorry state. I organized my tours where the visits were interesting and well spaced out. One of the first things I teach is that wine should not be abused – it is there to enjoy. In other words, the wine does not make you drunk – your abuse of it does that! Therefore, I can honestly say that I had no 'sorry states' on my tours. We had a few glasses in the evening with dinner and became more chatty; there was more laughter and occasionally we had a recitation from a member or two. For instance, I shall never forget the 'ode to a chip' – it was after near completion of the tour and we had the first plate of chips! Anyway, I'm digressing – back to Mazarin.

Well, Mazarin was the nearest we got to anyone having too much to drink… .

On one occasion we arrived to see panic in the face of Anne-Marie and her sister in the background. I asked what had gone wrong and they explained that Marie had sinned and gone off on a pilgrimage – she had been away for 6 weeks and, although they expected her back any day … . 'She may never come back!' The lunch had been prepared by the sisters.

I was later *intronised* as a Chevalier de Le Commanderie des Echansons du Loupiac, I received a bottle of Château Mazarin [Loupiac]1926 that had been made in the Sauternes way. I promised I would open it when my first book was published – and now I don't know … because I get so much pleasure from just looking at it and seeing how it has developed over the years. I had the pleasure of tasting a bottle of similar wine vintage 1932 about 10 years ago. It was superb and I find it difficult to find words to describe it. Old – yet not aged, well matured, honeyed with fading hints of tropical fruit, and the texture was an experience in itself as it slipped down my throat.

I shall tell you what… . To evaluate wine, you must use your 'senses', and when it comes to a special sweet wine, *tactile* is so important.

Ste Croix du Mont produces a very pleasant sweet wine, without the character of the Sauternes – or even the Loupiac, but if you want a reasonably priced, decent quality, sweet wine you can't go wrong with this one.

Vines, sea, rivers streams… . You might ask what is the connection? Many of the best vineyards are planted in areas that are near water or where the land has been covered by water at some time or other. This is a very general statement, but there is a reason for this. If you ever visit Ste Crois du Mont, there are vineyards on cliff-tops and it is possible to see the make-up of the cliff at a certain point and, guess what, there is just a complete mass of fossilised pink oyster shells. A remarkable sight!

Chapter 16
Champagne

My favourite 'tipple'

A few years ago, I had a phone call from a lady in Esher who told me that it would soon be the 50th birthday of her husband Marc and she wanted to arrange something special. She had come up with the idea of taking him to Champagne to celebrate – could I organise such an outing?

I did, and the chauffeur and I arrived at their home in Esher to take Priscilla, Marc and daughter to Reims. I had booked them into a very good hotel just on the outskirts and our arrival was welcomed by a courtyard full of Rolls Royces ancient and modern... . I couldn't have planned it better!

We had travelled from London to Reims via the Eurotunnel, and this time it gave me a chance to talk about Champagne, its history and production.

Making sure that all was correct at their hotel, the driver and I went off to our more meagre hotel, had dinner, chatted about the programme for the following day, and then I went off to bed.

The next morning we met for an early breakfast and then went to pick the family up from their hotel. It was a tight schedule as we were returning to UK that evening!

They hadn't finished breakfast, but I had allowed a little extra time so, when they came to join the car, we hadn't yet gone into panic about getting to our first Champagne House. I had already phoned Mercier and explained what was happening.

On arrival, we were taken into a special guest-room and were served two different Champagnes of very good vintage. We were well attended to by one of the Sommeliers. Gosh, I thought, this must be a thank you for all the groups I have brought here. After the tasting, we had a quick visit to the shop and then on to Charles Heidseick – another superb visit, which Marc thoroughly enjoyed.

We then rushed off to drive to the Royal Champagne restaurant for lunch. Priscilla had arranged for two very special friends from Paris to join us. We all sat down for lunch, the family, the friends, Peter, the chauffeur [who was actually my bank manager – just retired] and me. What a lunch – in true Champagne style. Marc's favourite Champagne is Bollingers and we drank a few bottles through lunch. So you see... .

Champagne is a celebration drink and, when I think about it, the mind conjures up pictures of light behind sparkling showers of froth and pale yellow liquid falling into a pyramid of long-stemmed glasses, men in beautifully tailored dinner suits and glamorous ladies studded in diamonds. When I drink it, I feel extremely special. It made its fame through the ladies in the court of King Louis XIV.

> I drink it when I'm happy and when I'm sad.
> Sometimes I drink it when I'm alone –
> and when I have company, I consider it obligatoire.
> I trifle with it when I'm not hungry and drink it when I am –
> Otherwise, I never touch it – unless I'm thirsty!
> Elizabeth Bollinger known as 'Lily' 1977, aged 78

It is the only wine a lady can drink without going 'pink' and it doesn't affect your weight!
[or words to that effect!]

Madame de Pompadour

Madame de Pompadour, Jeanne, was born plain Antoinette Poisson in 1721 and was the daughter of a municipal Clerk.

Her father was caught in some unlawful speculation and was forced to flee abroad. During his absence, her mother became mistress to Norman de Tokernheim, who educated her and her children. Then he married Jeanne to his nephew. Jeanne was instructed in all social graces; she met her first royal lover in 1745. On the occasion when she attended a Masque Ball at Versailles – both she and the King [Louis XV] were disguised as yew trees. Within a few months she became his chief mistress and introduced Champagne to the Palace.

'In victory you deserve it; in defeat you need it.'

Napoleon

Napoleon was born in 1769 and came on to the French scene in 1793. According to what I have read, he wasn't very impressive; his hair was shoulder length, ill combed and badly powdered. He had a thin face and was yellowish in complexion. His boots were unpolished and he wore a coat that was threadbare with the seams showing. But, even with this first impression, there was something arresting and memorable about his expression – an intensity and magnetism in his gaze.

On the 5th October 1795 at the age of 26 years, he moved against the rioters. It was a success and his reward was first the command of the Army of the Interior and then the Army of Italy. I think they must have thrown in a new coat as well!

Before he left to join the Army of Italy, he took 2 days' leave to get married. He had fallen madly in love with Josephine de Beauharnais – whom the guillotine had widowed. She was a Creole from Martinique, where her family owned a plantation. She wasn't young, her two children were in their teens – but she had grace and charm.

We are told that Josephine wasn't in love with Napoleon; he was referred to as a 'funny little man', but she needed a husband to pay her debts! Napoleon needed a wife, he was young, and like all his family – oversexed! Contrary to Josephine's reasons for marriage, Napoleon was very much in love with her.

The word Champagne is a variant of *campagne'*– meaning countryside.

Champagne is defined as a *sparkling wine* – its difference from other sparkling wines is that it is made in the region of Champagne and is produced from black as well as white grapes, Pinot Noir, Meunier and Chardonnay [there are other grapes in the AC but they are rarely used].

There are three methods of 'putting the bubbles into wine' and all are not natural ways but in Champagne only one method is used and that is *Méthode Champenoise* which is a natural way to create bubbles.

In ancient times, the wine made in Champagne was red and 'still'. It wasn't until an Englishman [Patrick Forbes] discovered that this wine had a tendency to effervesce in Spring that they made use of this in bottling.

In 1660, the Marquis de St Evremond, exiled by Louis XIV, arrived in England and had his favourite wine sent over. He was one of the founders of the Ordre des Coteaux, a group of influential young nobles with estates in Champagne. He arranged with his friend, the Marquis de Sillery, to send over his favourite wine, Champagne. This was at the time of the very popular Nell Gwynn and she may have invented Buck's Fizz before it was officially made at a club in London where, in 1921, they started serving fresh orange juice with Champagne. The club was called Buck's Club and the drink was named 'Buck's Fizz'.

It was actually Dom Pierre Perignon 1638–1715 who first succeeded in making clear wine from black grapes. Blind in later years, he was still able to taste grapes from different locations before breakfast and indicated how they should be blended. He was also the first to seal bottles with Spanish cork.

The breakthrough came after 1740 when Champagne created a sensation at the court of Louis XV. The ladies were responsible for its popularity.

In 1934 Champagne declared that only sparkling wine made in the region could be called 'Champagne'. *Méthode Champenoise* has been even more protected because, in 1994, it was ruled that this description of wine production could only be used on Champagne. It's all tied up!

Méthode Champenoise is a traditional method of making Champagne. The wine rests for a longer spell on its sediment, which gives a greater softness and mellowness.

An absolute record was created in 1984 when 190 million bottles were sold.

59,300 acres have been planted as vineyards on the gentle hill slopes, where they are better protected against damp and cold than on land lower down in the valley.

The zones of Champagne are:

Montagne de Reims
Vallée de la Marne
Côte des Blancs [mainly Chardonnay]
Aube [least important]

The subsoil is chalk. There are 50 different zones of chalk between Dover and Champagne. For thousands of years, this areas was part of a sea where conditions favoured the development of shellfish. The creatures lived and died here, and their shells and other parts built up into a chalk layer of exceptional quality. Nowhere is there such a wealth of belemnite [an extinct cephalopod]. There is a small concentration of it in Paris.

The chalk is 650 ft deep in places, with thin layers of top soil. It gives the Champagne certain special characteristics.

The advantages of the chalk soil are as follows:
1. It drains off surplus water in sub soil
2. It retains enough moisture to supply vines during dry period
3. It absorbs heat during the day and radiates it during the cool night
4. In storing, the chalk helps to mature the wine.

It is very important to note that the average minimum temperature in Champagne is only 10° C and this is only just above the minimum level needed for grapes to ripen. Champagne production is a very dodgy business.

What is this *Méthode Champenoise* – or 'traditional method' of making sparkling wine?

First of all, only the finest grapes from the best *terrior* are used ['terrior' means soils, climate, etc., all rolled into one]. Champagne producers are most strict about this. Most producers have to buy in grapes and the price varies according to the soil. [Piper Heidsieck haven't any vineyards – they buy in all their grapes. Some grapes cost around £5 per kilo!]

It takes 4000 kilograms to make 2666 litres and, if you press again, you will get:

410 litres from the second pressing
205 litres from the third pressing.

The pressing is called a 'taille' and the less taille used, the better the wine.

The wine is made like all white wines are, i.e., by pressing the juice – very little skin contact [especially in the Champagne region where they use black grapes!].

Pressing, then debourbage [impurities allowed to settle]. The wine is then taken to cellars for fermenting and later blending. This is done before the wine is made into Champagne. A 'good' Champagne is the result of good blending.

Once the wine is bottled, it is left on its lees to age. In this way, over a period of time, the wine is gaining more flavours and aromas from its lees, *Muscadet sur lie* is a perfect example. This is a better quality wine than Muscadet [which hasn't been left on its lees in the barrel].

After a certain time, the wine has to be *taken off* its lees. This is more difficult than just siphoning it from the barrel.

The bottle, at this time, has a metal crown cap [like a beer bottle top]. The cap has a plastic cup lining, then the bottle goes through a procedure called *Remunage*. This means that the bottles are placed into a specially designed angled hole in a wooden rack [two boards held together on hinges] called a *pupitre*. The bottles have to be shaken, turned slightly and inclined every day to ensure that the wine is absolutely clean, and all the solid yeast particles end up in the neck of the bottle. There are now *Gyropalettes* to do this automatically, which saves the work of each *rumueur*, who can turn on average 60,000 – yes, sixty thousand – bottles a day! The Gyropalettes are metal baskets that can hold 504 bottles. They turn and shake the bottles every 8 hours. The *remunage* now takes 1 week in comparison to 2 months. Another fact is that one cellar of Gyropalettes now copes with 70 cellars of manual remuage.

At the end of this 'treatment', the bottles are then upside-down and referred to as *sur pointes* – on points.

The neck of the bottle is then put into a brine solution at -15° C to freeze the wine containing the sediment. After this, the bottles are turned upright, the metal cap is removed and the frozen block pops out of the bottle. This procedure is called '*dégorgement*' [removing the throat!].

'Dosage' is next. And this is when we determine whether the wine is going to be very dry, dry, medium or sweet. For a very dry wine, just a touch of cane sugar is added to the wine, which is used to replace that lost in the *dégorgement*. For the medium and sweeter wines, more sugar is added accordingly. This sets off a *second fermentation* and gives the natural bubbles.

A vintage Champagne is made in very good harvest years. It has to contain 50% wine from white grapes and has to be at least 80% from the single vintage – all very complicated... .

A rosé Champagne is made from 50% white grapes. Later, 18–20% of still red wine is added to the base. It is best drunk at 4–5 years of age.

At this stage the traditional cork is used. A much bigger one than used for ordinary wine and, although the same shape to start, the end result gives it the shape of a mushroom! The cork has to be compressed considerably before it is inserted into the bottle.

Because of the pressure, an extra strong bottle is used, and a wire cage is fitted to secure the cork to the bottle – to avoid an explosion! Sometimes, there is a weakness in the bottle and it explodes whilst ageing! If you ever visit a Champagne cellar, you will see the empty places where this has occurred. The pressure in each bottle is equivalent to that in a coach tyre! The pressure in Cremant and other sparkling wines is not as great as in Champagne – sometimes, only half as much!

When the wine is ready, the bottle is then 'dressed'. This means an extra long foil on the neck, labelling and any other decoration the producer may wish to add. The long foil is used simply because, unlike ordinary wine when the bottle is filled automatically to the same level, the *dosage* used in making Champagne gives variation in levels and would show with a short *capsule*. Hence the luxurious neck coverage.

Opening and serving sparkling wine needs skill. Never shake the bottle before opening. Always open a bottle of sparkling wine with care – remember the pressure! This should be done by tilting the bottle away from all danger, covering the cork with a napkin and slowly releasing the cage, holding down the cork – just in case there is too much pressure. Keeping a tight grip on the cork, slowly turn the bottle and this should release the cork from the bottle. Always remember: to open the bottle with a 'bang' shows inexperience! The best performance of opening such a bottle, apart from using a 'Champagne sword', which I have seen done perfectly on several occasions, is by getting only a slight 'pop' – thus keeping the bubbles in the bottle.

When serving sparkling wine, fill the glass only half full on the first round; this allows space for the fizz. Only on the second round should you fill the glass – but, even then, not to the brim!

Have a good look at the glass. Sparkling wine should be drunk out of flute-shaped glasses and the bubbles should come straight up from the base of the glass.

It should be very fresh on the palate and you should feel the bubbles as they go down but, as this happens, you will again be able to identify the quality. Well-produced sparkling wine has small bubbles that slip delightfully down the back of the throat. If the bubbles are harsh – you will certainly feel them!

Champagne will not keep forever and unless you are a knowledgeable person, I wouldn't recommended storing it for any length of time. Stored for too long, it will lose its freshness and bubble and take on a greater depth of colour – perhaps *'maderisation'* will occur.

You have to be very careful when discussing Reims and Epernay as they are both *Capitals* of Champagne but will never agree this.... .

In Epernay, you will find the Maison du Champagne, CIVC and the Great Champagne houses, which include Moet et Chandon, Pol Roger, etc. to be found on the Avenue de Champagne.

Reims has the history. It was built of chalk from the Roman cellars on which it stands. During the 1051 days of the bombardment of World War 2, the entire population lived in these cellars!

When I think of the survival of women, the 'five widows' of Champagne come to mind, they were wives of important Champagne producers, who were widowed at an early age. Each one took over the business and built an empire! I will mention just three. For instance, there was Madame Pommery.

She was widowed at the age of 39 in 1858 and was left to run the production of red wine. She concentrated on winning the British market and introduced one of the first dry Champagnes, Champagne Nature, in 1873.

Pommery was built in 1878 and the design was largely based on two Scottish examples, Inveraray Castle and Mellerstain House. The builder was commissioned by Mme Louise Pommery and she wanted the premises built so that it would not only catch the eye but would flatter the vanity of the British – her biggest customers.

Her husband was responsible for converting the chalk pits underneath into Champagne cellars – 120 interlinked cellars. A lot of these cellars are named after the cities with which she did business. A local sculptor decorated the walls of the cellars and there is a massive relief in one of the cellars called 'Champagne au XVIII' and here you will see a group of people drinking Champagne at the table. The glasses they are using are the traditional type, shaped like an elongated V. The tail part of the 'V' was long and this was for a reason.

The latest decoration of the walls was just a few years ago and was of Madame Louise herself. It portrays her as a very beautiful woman but I have been told that she wasn't – in fact she wasn't pretty at all! But, she did a great job with the Champagne!

At the beginning, they were able to make the Champagne but they didn't know how to get rid of the sediment! By using the 'flute' type which are different glasses [I am referring to original champagne glasses], the sediment went down into the tail and left the wine clear. Of course, this takes me on to the second widow.

Madame Vve Cliquot was the widow who solved the problem of getting sediment out of the wine. She discovered that, by making slanting holes in two pieces of wood, hinged at the top so they could stand freely [which was eventually called the *'chapitre'*], then placing the bottles in the holes, turning the bottles at regular intervals and at the same time raising the angle of the bottle, would eventually take the sediment to the neck of the bottle.

There was also Mme Bollinger who followed in her husband's footsteps. She spent her days, when not working in the Chai, riding around her vineyards on a bicycle.

We also have to return to Eleanor d'Aquitaine [or Ailenor in French]. There is a town in Champagne called Vitry le Brulé and, in 1143, Royal troops [LouisVII husband of Ailenor de Aquitaine] set fire to the town and burned over 1000 refugees – mainly women and children in a church. Louis VII's troops remained in Champagne until the interdict was lifted. He later planted cypress trees brought from the Holy Land in Vitry as he was still feeling guilty.

Louis and Ailenor's daughter, Marie, married Thibault de Champagne and became Countess of Champagne.

Wine educators have to do refresher courses if they want to keep up to date. These courses aren't 'jollies' in any way and I shall tell you of one or two of them as I go along.

It was only recently that I visited Champagne on such a course. It lasted 2 days and I was asked to 'write up' on the first day – which turned out to be the most difficult. Our visit to Mme Cliquot was spoilt because of an administration problem, but I reported as follows.

Two-day refresher course in Champagne: Day 1 17 June 2004

The circular-shaped tasting laboratory with walls of illuminated glass, fitted with individual tasting booths. Before being directed to these booths we were asked to sit down around the central table which was also equipped with crachoirs. There, Delphine, one of the

oenologists for Champagne, explained that we would taste six different wines in two flights. After each flight, we would be asked for our comments and then she would expand on details of each wine.

So, off to our stations we went, sat down on the very comfortable seats and set to work tasting the first flight. I have never experienced such wonderful light for evaluating the colour. All the wines were pale but each so different under this light.

The second flight was more colourful, the first two with tints of salmon pink, but different, and the third was bright yellow. I called it 'sunshine yellow' and the thought of it being an older wine came to mind immediately. This was confirmed on tasting.

When discussing the older wine, we were asked to give some idea of the age. We all thought around 20–30 years and were truly amazed when Delphine said with pride that this Champagne had reached the ripe old age of 43 years – it was produced in 1961.

At this point, Philip Wibrotte of Public Relations, who had organised our visit, entered the room to take us to the lecture hall to continue our education on Champagne. I have always noticed the luxury of the Conseil Interprofessionel offices and this was absolute luxury. We walked through corridors, the walls lined in light oak, down the wide staircase to the lecture hall, where walls were cleverly decorated with attractive soundproof panels.

This session was to have a look at the new educational DVD and make our comments.

The DVD was in four parts which included Champagne, Terroir, De la nature au vin and Plaisir des sens. After watching the 'Champagne', which really was how they market it, comments from members heavily criticised the marketing target – young fashionable people. We felt that more effort should be made to include all ages, as Champagne is not just for the young and perhaps the 30–50 age group have more money to spend on Champagne.

The 'Plaisir des sens' was a demonstration of selecting the right Champagne for meat, fish, dessert, etc. This really took some believing … . Apart from the fact that there are very few restaurants outside the Champagne region where this would be done, there are very few people who would drink Champagne throughout a meal.

There was a very interesting point though about fish dishes that should be accompanied with Champagne from a region where the soil has a higher mineral content! In the nicest possible way, we hinted that

this section of the DVD needed a 'revamp'. Could you imagine going into a restaurant and asking if the Champagne you had selected for a fish dish came from such a region?

After viewing, we went on to discuss CIVC's present projects. Philip told us there were two projects at the moment. One was the planting of grass in the vineyards [and we had an excellent discussion about this the following day at Mailly, where barley has been planted between the vines] and the other was about expansion of the hectarage in the Champagne vineyards. Many years ago there were 60,000 hectares of vines and now only 32,000 exist.

There is no intention of reverting back to the original hectarage, but a slight expansion is envisaged, due to the future increase in Champagne consumption.

Lunch was arranged at the popular restaurant 'The Grand Cerf' on the road between Epernay and Reims. The menu gave us the chance to experiment with the different Champagnes selected. Unfortunately, the waiter was not as professional as the one on the film, some of us had a few drops of Champagne on our sleeves at every pouring!

The first visit of the afternoon was to Vve Cliquot, 'La Grande Dame de Dégorgement'. I was looking forward to this as all my previous visits had been with groups – you know the type of thing – welcome by a very pretty hostess in a uniform designed by one of the *Houses* and after introducing you to the Company and being shown examples of fraud against Vve Cliquot, you would be taken on a visit around the caves and be delivered an interesting, entertaining spiel.

Our visit was no different and it later got embarrassing. We were told in a very basic way how Champagne was produced! A few of the members kept tongue in check – in fear of showing their prowess and, later on, mumblings were heard, such comments made as 'Have we been misread?' Do you think she knows who we are? etc.

Under the circumstances, we kept our questions to other subjects, like 'How long have you worked for Vve Cliquot?' To which she promptly answered '10 months' and immediately added that she had been with Mercier for 2 years [this is where hostesses gain experience in taking entrance fees and guiding tourists down to the trains], so the poor girl had had little chance to learn anything about Champagne – apart from the spiel!

I asked her why she referred to the orange label as being a *yellow* label, to which she replied 'This shade of orange is called "Cliquot Yellow".' I didn't know that.

We were then taken upstairs to the tasting area in reception and were joined by a sommelier who had studied at WSET in London.

We were offered three Champagnes but very little discussion ensued mainly because of the noise of the tourists passing through reception. We were unable to concentrate on the tasting but later had a chance to compare the old and new style of bottle for La Grande Dame. The old style had been replaced because it looked too much like the shape of a woman!

The final insult of the visit was when the sommelier demonstrated how one opens a bottle of Champagne.

Disheartened, we returned to the coach wondering how we would be received at our next visit.

Unsure of whether or not they had been informed, we entered Mumm with trepidation. To our relief, the welcome showed a respect of our knowledge and we were led up to the laboratory. Preparation had been made for us to taste 12 different Reserve wines and evaluate each one. Taking into account the acidity, alcohol content and pH, we then considered the blending of these wines, which varied in age, the oldest being 1997. The oenologist, Didier Mariotti, explained blending techniques and discussion followed.

This was truly a most informative session and time just flew by.

We returned to the hotel with only 15 minutes to change for dinner. The bistro was a few minutes from the hotel.

After an excellent lunch, it was difficult to face the copious amounts set before us. The flavours in both dishes, entrée and main, were superb but many of us left the dessert, which was a small Bavrois with loads of red fruit, which was just too much and seemed too rich in flavours for the Champagne.

The Champagnes selected for the evening were delightful. Unfortunately, one bottle was corked. Carolyn, in her very best French, told the young waitress it was corked and those of us who had been served with the said wine held up our glasses.

The young waitress looked around us in amazement and replied... 'The WHOLE bottle?'

That a perfect way to end a confused day!

Notes on wines tasted:

Wines tasted at CIVC

De Saint	Premier Cru
Le Nombre	1995
Carte de Champagne Tattinger	1995
Grappier	1998
Pommery Pink Label	NV
Frank Bonville Avise	1961

Wines tasted at MUMM

	D°	Ph	Acidity
Assemblage 2004			
Cordon Rouge 2003	11.20	3.15	3.50
Grand Cru 2003	11.15	3.21	3.55
Millesime 2003	11.35	3.20	3.40
Reserve Assemblage			
Cordon Rouge 2002	11.10	3.11	4.00
Cordon Rouge 2001	10.70	3.10	4.10
Reserve Chardonnay			
Avise 2002	11.25	3.21	4.25
Cramant 2001	10.95	3.20	4.45
Avize/Nogent 2000	11.10	3.08	4.45
Reserve Pinot Noir			
Bouzy 2000	10.95	3.16	4.20
Verzenay 2000	11.00	3.12	4.05
Verzenay 1998	11.00	3.03	4.40

Chapter 17
Rhône

Côtes du Rhône

Reg Green had looked forward to meeting up with the Ainslies at Dover. They arranged to have lunch in the restaurant on board the ferry. The journey over the Channel is only 75 minutes so it must have been a bit of a rush for them – especially when the food was washed down with a couple of bottles of wine... .

Joyce had warned Reg not to drink too much – because of his condition [I never found out what that was…]. Anyway, we got back on the coach as the ferry sailed into Calais and Reg asked for some water. He was given the water in one of these polystyrene cups. Somehow, he broke off a piece of the polystyrene and swallowed it. This was just as we were waiting in the docks to go through customs. The next I knew was that Reg had been pulled to the floor by Celia [our Registrar] who opened his mouth and pulled out the obstructing piece of material. He was then helped back onto his seat and we continued our journey.

After the fright, I said to everyone 'We shall now continue, but bear in mind – if we have any other problems, we are well equipped. We may be only 16 passengers, but on board we have a surgeon, a registrar, two nursing sisters, and I have just completed a course in aromatherapy!

The second time we had a problem with Reg was a couple of years later. His health was failing but he loved coming on the wine tours. I arranged for us to stop for lunch on Le Loir [not to be confused with La Loire]. I had visited the bistro a few months before to make the reservation. On arrival, I was pleased to see that everything was ready and we were made most welcome. Although Reg, a retired geography teacher, was usually a very quiet man, he seemed to lose his temper during the meal; some thought it was because Joyce again had told him to be careful with wine – because of his health. He was quite angry and, by the time we joined the motorway at Tours Nord, he had passed out. Fortunately, we were at the Péage, so I asked for help; within minutes doctors and nurses were on the scene. Reg was taken off to hospital and we followed in the coach.

After X-ray, the doctor said that there was a swelling near the brain and Reg would have to stay in hospital overnight – perhaps two nights for observation – they didn't seem to think it was serious. I stayed with them as long as I could but never forgot that I had others in the coach and we had to get to Lyon that night. I explained to Joyce that, if it wasn't serious, they could travel down to Lyon by train the next day and I left them instructions for the voyage.

My passengers had been extremely patient and as they had said – it could have been any one of them. I phoned Joyce at regular intervals throughout the day and evening and Reg seemed to be making good progress. The next day, after visiting the vineyards of Condrieu, we returned to find Joyce and Reg waiting for us at the hotel. He had learned his lesson and had just one glass of wine with his meal for the rest of the week.

The Côtes du Rhône is predominantly a red wine region of great diversity. It is over 2000 years old and is one of the largest and most varied wine producing regions of France.

The wine was accepted by the Popes of Avignon, although their favourite tipple was Burgundy. It was because of this that the Burgundians managed to keep a tight rein on the wines of Côtes du Rhône, making sure they did not not reach the markets of the north.

The Rhône benefited by having the papal court at Avignon, but as the burgundy wine industry started to grow, they realised the dangers and this was mainly because the wines are heavier in the Rhône.

The powerful Dukes of Burgundy also jealously guarded their wines to make sure that wines of Côtes du Rhône didn't reach the markets of the north and it was a case of the Popes dissuading vignerons of the region from exporting their wines, thus ensuring that the papal residence was always well stocked with Burgundy!

From the 14th to the 16th century, Burgundy imposed severe restrictions on the entry of non-Burgundian wines into their territory, as the only form of transport was by boat on the river Saone. In 1446, Dijon banned wines from Lyon completely.

Until overland transport was available to take the wines to Nantes for shipment, only a few, including the papal court of Avignon, enjoyed the wines of Cote du Rhône!

The region is actually split into two sub-regions from north to south and displays a plethora of landscapes, soils and climates, which combine to produce exceptionally rich wines. Wine production varies, but *high tech* is rare. The northern vineyards are mainly on granite soil and don't produce as much as the south.

It is not difficult to understand why there isn't a lot of wine growing on the steep, wooded banks of the Upper Rhône region. Vineyards have been etched into the mountainside on narrow terraces – similar to those of the Douro Valley or the Mosel. Some are so steep that they have to use pulleys to obtain the grapes. The equipment is similar to that used in Switzerland.

The vineyards are still in the hands of the families of the region. The three biggest producers include Marcel Guigal, the planet's finest wine-maker [nicknamed 'The King of the Rhône']. His name is big and his wines are sought after all over the world, due to low yields and long maturation in oak, which makes them massively appealing in youth and exciting in old age. He has his own vineyards but buys in extensively from the hundreds of smallholders around.

I visited Guigal's winery recently and was amazed to see the progress that has been made. Everything is automatic! On my first visit the winery was just being developed, Marcel was just becoming known and, as we passed through the little reception area, I noticed that his office was full of computers, I thought to myself then that this man was truly a 'gadget man' and my visit last year has proved this!

My first visit was just after Jancis Robinson had interviewed him for *Decanter*. There was a wonderful picture of this wine producer in his blue overalls. On the visit we were taken around the original chai by a very smart gentleman in a grey silk suit who kept referring to 'his wine'. In the end I had to say 'but these are the wines of Monsieur Guigal' and the response was 'But I am Marcel Guigal!' This is when I considered digging a hole and jumping in … . He looked so different. We were with him all morning and he explained his production methods and what he thought was necessary to produce good wine. Later, we tasted his wines and he spoke of each in great detail. This was one of the greatest visits I've ever made.

The vines are trained to withstand the twin local dangers of wind damage and soil erosion. Pairs of vines are staked to meet in a point, making the roasted slopes look as though they are covered in Christmas trees.

Syrah is the principal red grape, which produces the deep-flavoured, ageing reds which fetch high prices.

The white wine of Condrieu, produced from the Viognier grape has become so fashionable that three times the production could be sold quite easily.

The wines of Hermitage, about 30 miles south 'on a bald suntrap of a hill', above the little town of Tain, are of better quality and in more demand than those produced in the nearby Crozes-Hermitage.

'Côte-Rôtie' is a series of little slopes above the town of Ampius. Only those facing south or south-east on the schist of this right bank of the river are worth the extreme discomfort of cultivating. Those to the south are known as the Côte Blonde, and the wines produced there mature earlier than those on the Côte Brune. Folklore claims these names originated from a vigneron with two daughters, one blonde and one with brown hair. I think it is more likely to do with the soil as the Côte Blonde is lighter in colour! 'Côte-Rôtie' is stereotypically distinguished from Hermitage vineyards by its perfume which is supposedly due to possible inclusion of Viognier grapes – but in most cases it's 100% Syrah. Hermitage wines are capable of ageing for 50 years plus!

While we are in the northern region with its granite soil, I must mention Château Grillet which is a single property AC, slightly down river from Condrieu, and the wines are even more dramatically priced. The wines of St Joseph are produced with the grapes of Syrah, Marsanne and Roussanne and can often produce one bottle in four of all the production of Northern Rhône.

A sparkling wine is also made in the district of Northern Rhône in the little town of St Peray.

The Southern Rhône is mostly limestone, and the principal grapes are Grenache, Syrah and Carignan. This is a warm region, producing rich red wines, which are the most alcoholic in France with 12.5° to14° being quite common. They are sought after by merchants in the North and are often sold under a Northern Rhône label. The wines made in this seductive countryside are best drunk in cooler climates. They can seem head-thumping when drunk in the region.

Perhaps it is the alcohol that makes Southern Rhône reds so easy to appreciate or perhaps it is the openly fruity character of the Grenache grape, which dominates here, concentrated by the relatively low yields forced upon it by the stony soils and low rainfall. The vines are trained on a single guyot method and if drought persists, limited irrigation is permitted.

Most wine is vinified using the Beaujolais 'carbonic maceration' fermentation to yield juicy fruity wines. However, there is greater ambition for 'Villages' wines, which are made to develop for 5 or more years in the bottle.

Châteauneuf du Pape owes its name to the new palace built by John XXII – it was his summer home and destroyed in the Second World War. This is the region's most famous and best – a model for the other wines. You'll recognise the wine bottles, as they carry the crossed keys on the seals.

There are 13 different grape varieties permitted in the AC, although only a few are used such as the principal grape, Grenache, which is usually supplemented by only Syrah, Mourvedre and, to a decreasing extent, Cinsault.

The vineyards are different from others as they are covered with large pudding stones or *galets,* which store heat and aid the ripening of the grapes.

These red wines are big and beefy with lots of alcohol and extract, which *explode* on the palate. It is one of the most reliable AC's. There are very few disappointments from the signature-embossed heavy bottles and the only faults to be found are in hot years, when it can be too alcoholic, and in dry years when it is often too tannic. Yields are kept remarkably low.

Some of the white wine can be *flabby* as there doesn't seem to be enough acidity, fruit or alcohol to make a truly interesting wine. On the other hand, I have found some very good white wine from this region!

The Côtes du Rhône region winds around the fluid centre of the river Rhône, producing mainly red wine of Appellation Contrôlée status.

The Regional appellations cover 163 communes and 6 departments, i.e. Ardèche, Drôme, Gard, Loire, Rhône and Vaucluse and there are 13 Crus.

At the head of the hierarchy are the 'Crus', the jewels of the Côtes du Rhône [95 communes]. These are followed by the Côtes du Rhône Villages, of which 16 are allowed to cite their name on the wine label. Authentic and typical of the area, they are subjected to rigorous production criteria. It's a tightly defined area and a distinct step up in quality – and often value.

It is worth mentioning one or two other areas like the Beaume de Venise, which produces Vins Doux Naturels, sweet wines which are most suitable with foie gras and Tavel famous for rosé wine. Tavel, at one time, made some of the best rosés in France, but this is not so today. On my last visit, I was disappointed; they were not of the quality I remembered and the prices were unreasonable. There are similar rosé wines produced elsewhere in the southern region, where the climate is right for sitting outside with an aperitif and the food is more conducive and rosé is a very popular wine.

Logo designed by HGP

Chapter 18
Beaujolais

'*Le Beaujolais Nouveau est arrivé*'. You will see this sign in many pubs and wine bars in November.

New Beaujolais is celebrated all over the world. As far as Britain is concerned, it is said that the Editor of the *Financial Times* once offered a bottle of Champagne to the first person to arrive in his office with a bottle of 'new Beaujolais'. This annual wine race has gone mad. Transport is by motorcycle, car, balloon, helicopter, aircraft – not to mention horses and camels!

This race to drink the first wine is not new, it has been going on for hundreds of years. In the 13th century, Claret was rushed up from Bordeaux in boats, which were often attacked by pirates, who hid around La Rochelle.

'Beaujolais Nouveau' is made specifically for early drinking and leaves the wineries one minute after midnight, on the morning of the third Thursday of November for the race to its destination. A third of the total Beaujolais production is sold in this way.

Very young Beaujolais can be delicious, but this freshness and fruitiness doesn't seem to last very long. In fact, wine-growers and merchants are not allowed to sell it after the last day of the following August. I believe that *Beaujolais Nouveau* should be drunk before the following Christmas.

You may get the impression that wines of Beaujolais are not suitable for ageing but you couldn't be further from the truth! 'Beaujolais-Villages Crus', which are about a quarter of the total production and mainly from the north are superb and will age reasonably well. There are ten 'Beaujolais-Villages', and the wines of each are quite different.

'Brouilly' and 'Côtes de Brouilly' are where you will find some of the best Beaujolais. 'Morgon' wines, with a taste of cherries need ageing and, when they have aged, the result can be quite stunning! To enjoy 'Moulin à Vent', you will have to wait at least 3 to 5 years; this wine has loads of tannin and can be quite harsh when young; as it matures, it resembles a Burgundy wine. 'Fleuri' is, as the name suggests, a wine with a *nose* of flowers as well as fruit and a hint of chocolate – quite a delightful wine. 'Julienas' can be quite a 'magic' wine, presenting itself as the best of the vintage in certain years. You'll find cherries and peaches in the taste, but watch out for the tannin – it can sometimes be a little harsh. 'St Amour' and 'Chiroubles' don't age very well, so drink these young. 'Chenas', not such a popular wine of the Crus, is good value and usually requires ageing. 'Regnié' was promoted to the 'Villages' in 1985 and isn't yet running in the 'top favourites'.

Beaujolais gets its name from the old town of Beaujeu. There is no written evidence of this wine region until the 8th century, but there is no doubt that Romans planted vines there. In fact, you have evidence of this in one or two of the names – such as Juliénas [from Julius Caesar].

Romaneche-Thorins in the north, gets its name from Roman corn, *Roman esca*, related to the time when Romans suffered a shortage of corn in their homeland and pulled up the vines in Beaujolais to plant corn. There was a corn depot here for their soldiers.

It is also interesting to note that the pruning method, 'taille à Gobelet' is a direct descendant of Roman occupation and is still used. Moreover, many of the 'patois' words of the Beaujolais vigneron are Latin.

The soils of Beaujolais vary from granite, schist and clay in the north to a more calcareous type with elements of marl in the south.

Gamay is the main grape – probably brought back from the near East. It yields a vast amount of juice but is low in quality. It thrives on granite.

The Dukes of Burgundy frequently outlawed the Gamay and, in 1395, Philip the Bold ordered the destruction of all vineyards with the grape. It was described as a 'disloyal grape' making a wine in great abundance but horrible in harshness. Some writers think Philip was fulminating against the Gamay's cousin ['Gamay a jus coloré' or 'Gamay teinturier'] and it is still held in general disrepute.

There are certain characteristics of Beaujolais wine. The barrel is called a 'piece' and holds 215 litres in comparison with those of

Bordeaux, which hold 225 litres. There is also a special wine bottle, which is called a 'pot' and holds 50 cl [an ideal size for two but usually drunk by one!]

Until Georges Duboeuf ['King of Beaujolais'] came on the scene, the wines of Beaujolais were mainly red with a little white produced near Macon. Georges Duboeuf began by introducing more whites, which were at first frowned upon by the local wine-makers. As time has passed, the producers now appreciate the publicity his floral labelled bottles have given to the wine region.

It is worth visiting the 'Dubeouf Kingdom' – the wine theme park! Be ready for the loud explosion of automatic organ music just after you sit down to sample the wines in the colourful large café-type tasting room.

Of all French vignerons, none are so dotty about their wine, so crazily devoted, as those of Beaujolais. They love their vinous, fruity wine and swallow it in beer-like quantities. In hot weather, it is not uncommon for them to drink several pints a day! Never refer to a vigneron Beaujolais as being part of Burgundy. It will be immediately denied.

You feel that every village of Beaujolais is 'Clochmerle', not only Vaux, made famous as the setting for this celebrated novel of the 1930s by Gabriel Chevalier. The Cave de Clochmerle is decorated with Pierre Dufour's drawings of scenes from the novel.

They say Beaujolais brings laughter to the table. I agree. It is the most French of French wines and is made for drinking.

One glass for pleasure
Two for happiness
Three for a song
Four for escape into dreams

Chapter 19
Languedoc and Roussillon

In January and February, when it is cold and miserable with very little sun to brighten up your day, you think of warmer places. For me this is easy, as I have to organise the itineraries for my wine tours. I was giving much thought at that moment to the wines of the Mediterranean: this is an exciting area for future wine production.

This is a beautiful part of France and you can feel the true character of the region in Montpellier, where an annual wine trade fair is held in the month of February. There are two parts to this town, ancient and modern, the old university quartier [where Jean Moulin, the head of the Resistance during the Second World War, studied] and the new part, which was until recently the 'dumps' of Montpellier. It was knocked down and completely rebuilt in Romanesque style. Just to walk through the modern centre makes you feel that you are on a film set!

Nearby is the fishing village of Sete, a beautiful spot for a holiday. Every time I tour the area, I make a point of visiting the Bassin of Thau because you can see lots and lots of pink flamingos. I was once told that the reason they are pink is because they eat shrimps!

I remember one particular trip to Languedoc with a group, when I arranged lunch near Sete in another fishing village called Meze. I always choose local restaurants – even Les Routiers because they're friendly and the food is always so good! On this particular occasion, the chef told me that he had prepared us a special Mediterranean dish. It was stuffed squid in a *herby* tomato sauce [similar to Provençal]. There were four courses and, before we started with the hors-d'œuvres, we were each asked which style of local wine we would prefer – dry, rosé or red. I asked around the table then gave our order – expecting a glass for each person. Imagine the surprise on our faces when we were each given a litre bottle. I couldn't believe it!

After finishing the crudités and the charcuterie delights of Languedoc, we then were served the 'speciality'. I was apprehensive at first – 'stuffed squid' didn't sound that great… but the squid was stuffed with sausage-meat and herbs and was superb with the sauce. This was followed by a huge selection of cheeses, then fruits to finish.

No one – but no one left anything on the plate! The chocolate served with the coffee after the meal was a struggle … .

There were a few half full bottles or more left at the end of the meal, as people who appreciate wine don't usually go mad and, knowing that we would be tasting in the afternoon, restricted our 'intake' during lunch. I very politely asked the patron if we could take the remainder to have with our picnic the next day.

As we left the restaurant, the chef was waiting to say goodbye and presented me with a gift of two baskets each containing 48 oysters. Those who enjoy oysters were delighted.

The next day, before going north to taste the wines of Faugères, north of Montpellier, we stopped to buy a couple of oyster knives, plus some local ham and cheeses for those averse to oysters.

After the tasting, we made our way to the delightful little old town of Pezanas, with Molière memories. The coach had two tables at the back and Paddy, a retired surgeon and excellent oyster opener, took his place at one table and Jack at the other. Together, they opened all the oysters. By this time the cheese and ham had been set out on our 'buffet' – not forgetting the bread from the local bakery and our many bottles of wine! What a picnic we had before having a look around this lovely little town..

Languedoc and Roussillon is an exciting wine region of the future, offering a huge selection of wines. It is a wine region of great promise after producing some very poor wines in the past and being the home of the 'wine lake'. The wine lake was actually around Beziers and is mentioned in the biography of Jean Moulin – a man in war history whom I very much admired. I was absolutely amazed when, on my first visit to the region in the 1980s I found vineyards planted on every available piece of land, right up to the sea! The only protection from the sea air was bamboo fencing, which can be reasonably protective, but much of what I saw was in very bad condition.

There have been tremendous changes in recent years because, after wine producers accepted large sums of money to take the vines out of the ground, experienced high tech wine-makers from the New World came along and, with their new techniques, have opened up the region, which now produces some very good wines.

The Carignan grape is 'king' in this region but others include Grenache, Syrah, Cinsault and Mourvèdre – the grape of the Mediterranean which must have high average temperatures. In this region you will find a plethora of styles offering aperitifs, liqueurs, eau de vie as well as table wine. So let's think of sunshine and have a look at this wonderful, warm inviting wine region of France.

The Mediterranean has a dry warm climate – the temperature can soar and it is important to choose the right time to visit. When it is hot, wine tasting during the day is not really advised; you could end up with headaches and or stomach upsets. Therefore, we have to think of before and after July and August. The wines of this region can be high in alcohol content and it is very difficult to resist the fortified wines, which are absolutely delicious but even higher in alcohol.

Travelling to the Mediterranean by coach seems an arduous task but stopping at other wine regions *en route* can make it interesting and pleasant. We drove via the Entre deux Mers autoroute – passing by the extremely well-preserved medieval city of Carcassonne and into the wine region of Corbières, where the main wine is red and full bodied, easy to drink and reasonably priced. Until the early 1980s these wines were classified as VDQS but in 1983 the region was upgraded to AC. I remember it well because I was visiting the region at the time and, by sheer coincidence, I heard on the car radio that a horse called Corbières had won a race in England!

Near Corbières is Minervois, on the higher ground, and it is here where some of the surprisingly good reds can be found. There is one in particular I should like to mention: Château Ste-Eulalie, their wines are available in the supermarkets and wine stores. These wines are produced by two oenologists, Monsieur and Madame Coustal. Monsieur Coustal is employed during the week on a premier vineyard of Bordeaux, coming home at the weekend to look after his own vineyard, which has been carefully supervised by his wife during his absence. She is absolutely charming and made our small group most welcome on a visit some years ago. We [especially the males in our company !] were convinced that it is her 'touch' that enhances the wine!

Behind every good wine man there is a good wine woman!

To the west of Corbières is Limoux, where Dom Perignon first made sparkling wine, before moving to Champagne.

Continuing south, you eventually arrive in Roussillon, which has superb reds, fruity and easy – too easy to drink. If you've had wines from here, they most likely come from Fitou. This region, in the foothills of the Pyrenees, is also the home of Rivesaltes and other popular aperitifs.

On the Mediterranean you can sample the grape with rich aromas, Muscat de Frontignan and have lunch around Sete, the wonderful fishing port with loads of history. Immediately, you start thinking of seafood and the dry white wine of the small production area of Picpoul de Pinet – or La Clape, which is predominantly red, but the dry whites have a nose of the sea!

When planning the itinerary for this wine tour, one of the 'musts' is to visit Daumas Gassac – a name that keeps turning up when one discusses this region. It is really a remarkable story of an architect, Monsieur Aimé Guibert, who decided to find somewhere quiet in the hills of Langudoc to have a 'second home'. He built his little paradise and occasionally invited friends for the weekend to enjoy the tranquillity of this rocky, barren area. I should point out that, at that time, he had no interest in vines but did enjoy a glass or two of wine.

One particular weekend he contacted a friend and invited him for the weekend. The friend, a geologist, wanted very much to accept the invitation but unfortunately had made arrangements to see an old friend. Monsieur Guibert suggested he brought the friend along.

During the weekend, they looked around the area as there was common interest. The invited friend of the party was Professor Peynaud of Bordeaux University, world renowned for his expertise in wine. He was very interested and after examining the terroir, he suggested vineyards.

Success followed. Superb wine was produced – both white and red commanding unusually high prices in the Languedoc.

From Montpellier, going north east you will find the wine region of Picpoul St Loup. Colleagues and I went down here recently to have a look at the vineyards of Domaine L'Hortus. I had been hearing a lot about this very well-produced red and naturally wanted to find out more! We were not disappointed, the wines are fantastic! The vineyards are beautifully situated, running north to south in a valley sheltered from winds and basking in the Mediterranean sun. The Mourvèdre grape enjoys, and thrives in this climate and the proprietor has reason to be very proud of his production. These wines are in the more expensive range of the region's wines – but I assure you – are a bargain!

Travelling east from Montpellier, you pass Nimes, home of the Roman amphitheatre and north into the wine region of Gard, the home of rosés of Tavel and Listrac. I must say that, on my last visit, I wasn't so impressed with these rosés which were rated very highly at one time. Gard is, of course, where you can see the famous viaduct, built by the Romans, and still standing today.

Digressing slightly, these Romans were clever chaps. Not only could they make wine, but beer for the soldiers and they were dab hands at plumbing and central heating – not forgetting their ability to build theatres – evidence of which can be seen all over southern France!

Getting back to my wine visit to the wine region of Gard … . I decided to do a little exploring and found some very acceptable wines in the cheaper range, further south. There was one vineyard in particular, where on the reds you could smell flowers and all sorts of fruit, quite delightful and surprisingly good. This producer made all styles of wine including some excellent liqueurs, then to my surprise, he produced a jar of glacé cherries labelled for sale in one of the large British supermarkets!

From this point, we could go into Côtes du Rhône and Provence – which are other regions close to my vinous heart.

Chapter 20
Provence

It is yet another wonderful region of France and I adore Aix en Provence where, apart from Sunday, there is a wonderful market every morning. Fruit and veg at its very best and the lovely patterns of the materials of Provence – it makes you feel good .

.Before I start my tale of Provence, I must recall the most frightening and disastrous tour I have ever made.

This particular tour was for my regular clients and I had more than usual on board – we numbered 20 persons. The drive down didn't seem too long because this is the time we catch up with what we all have been doing during the year... .

We arrived at the hotel, just out of Aix in time to settle in before dinner. The hotel was very comfortable, nice swimming pool and an easy walk into town. The only thing that failed it was the beef served at dinner and after tackling these sheets of leather on the first night – I asked that any other menu I had chosen with beef should be changed! I won't mention the rude remarks made by Paddy, who tried to cut into it with his surgical prowess.

Paddy and Edna travelled with me for 15 years! Edna was very good with tapestry and later on had taken up painting. On every trip with them I could look forward to smoked salmon sandwiches for lunch on the first day, as Paddy had an arrangement with his fishmonger to supply him with the very best once a month. There was also a present from Edna – usually a tapestry cushion but on two occasions I had paintings – one of mushrooms and one of a frog [for the bathroom].

When I started running my own company, I was never offered tips – I should have been insulted if I had! The driver was given money and, if we had a hostess, she also received tips. I received cushions, paintings, pieces of pottery, crystal glassware given to me over the years and are now displayed all around the house. These are my 'visual aids' to bring back lovely memories.

Edna told me that Paddy was a fine cook and we sometimes had evidence of this during the tour. I dreaded the meal not being up to standard because Paddy would utter a few choice words which could be embarrassing to those who didn't know him.... .

He was at school at Blundells in Tiverton and then went on to Edinburgh to study medicine. He became a surgeon and later became a dental surgeon in the Royal Navy. He was never afraid to say exactly what he wanted to and sometimes it was 'near the bone'. To most of us it was quite funny but I shall never forget when two ladies, Margaret and Pamela, started touring with us. Margaret, very quiet, always sat up at the back away from everyone so that she could just sit and enjoy the scenery. Pamela would usually sit in front of Paddy.

On their first trip, Pamela told Paddy that she had served as an officer in the WRNS. 'Oh!' Paddy said, 'You must have been one of Nelson's wrens'. She was unable to answer him – she was stunned, but from then on she was known as Nelson's wren.

On the next trip we had together, Pamela was ready for him and the rest of us were thoroughly entertained all week!

The funniest story from Edna was about their son, also in medicine, who moved to Edinburgh to take a post at the University. Paddy and Edna went up to visit him and his family. Whilst there, she said that two of the passengers they travelled with lived in Edinburgh and they would like to invite them to the house. John, their son, immediately said he would be delighted to have them for drinks.

Edna saw Derek and Kit get out the car and make their way up the drive to the front door. John had also been watching and, before Edna had opened the front door, John had returned the ordinary glasses set out for drinks to the cupboard and brought out the crystal! After a very pleasant meeting, the visitors left and John said to his parents that he had no idea they travelled with such charming people. Edna replied with 'Well, I have been telling you for years, these are no ordinary wine tours – they're exclusive!'

Back to Provence. That evening I went to reception and asked to pay the bill in advance – as was normal procedure – in fact, some hotels insist on full payment before arrival. The Aix hotel said that it wasn't necessary until the end of the week and I, regrettably, left it as suggested.

The next day was an easy day as we had done so much driving to get to Aix, but the following day I had planned a visit to the Lavender Museum at St Remy before tasting wine in the afternoon.

That morning, we left the hotel at about 9 am and, on reaching the autoroute, saw signs to say that care must be taken because of high winds. We obeyed and continued on our journey. As we drove on and approached St Remy, the weather got worse – in fact, unbelievably so and, on driving into St Remy, everything went black. The electricity went off, no lights, no nothing – utter darkness. Slowly we crept along, not knowing whether we were on a road – or in a field! Suddenly, we saw what looked like a car park and immediately parked. We had a cup of tea and talked about what we should do next. The rain was pouring down and the wind howling. This is when I recited the ditty my father had taught me: 'From ghosties and ghoulies and long-legged beasties and things that go bump in the night – Good Lord, deliver us.'

With some serious thought, I realised that we had to get the passengers somewhere where they could eat, and when the weather improved – enough to have a little light – I suggested we headed towards Avignon as there was bound to be a supermarket on the outskirts. When anything like this happens, they switch to generators for electric power. It was agreed.

We slowly drove in the direction of Avignon and sure enough there was a hypermarché. It was difficult to get everyone in because of the flooding, but the driver was very good and we managed to get the coach as near as possible so that all we suffered from was wet feet.

There in the complex, which was almost empty, we found a little café where the owner was busily cooking lunches on his makeshift facilities. When he saw us, his face changed colour – it was obvious he was going to have difficulty coping with so many, but I had a chat with him explaining what had happened and he did his best.

I explained to everyone that, after lunch, they were free to have a look around as we couldn't leave the building until the weather improved. I noticed that Phyllis, who was in her mid-70s, was starting to tremble.

Her son said that she was extremely afraid of thunder and, as dogs do, she would hide in some cupboard or other until it was all over. I had never experienced this before but was advised by my more knowledgeable passengers that many people suffer in this way. I kept my eye on Phyllis.

In time, the weather improved slightly, enough for us to get on the road and back to Aix. It was chancy but it had to be done. The coach drove up to the entrance and we paddled our way on – that is everyone except Phyllis – she just stood at the door trembling and refused to come out. There was nothing more for it, we lifted her out and fortunately, she was very tiny, and put her back on the coach. By this time, the trembling had become worse.

I started thinking about the Scottish remedies … . Ah yes! A hot toddie! This is what we have in Scotland when we are suffering from a cold and can't sleep. You warm some milk, add a shot of whisky and a teaspoon of sugar. Well, how can I improvise? I don't have any whisky – but, during the travelling down to Provence, we had tasted and bought some L'eau de vie to use in fruit salads.

We switched the water on to boil on the coach and I mixed a couple of spoonfuls of milk powder with some water, added the sugar and … a good shot of the L'eau de vie. 'Now Phyllis, you must trust me and drink this.' She did and slowly calmed down and went to sleep – only to wake up when we reached the hotel.

The next day we witnessed the devastation, flooding everywhere, vineyards ruined, properties collapsed and we heard that people had been killed. We were getting several phone calls from the UK asking if we were all right. A couple of days later we were receiving phone calls to say that the pound sterling had fallen! I shall never forgive Norman Lamont for this deed.

Disaster number two! The French banks refused to deal with British currency, we could not change travellers' cheques or sterling. The banks were closed to us until further notice! On top of this, the hotel bill had risen considerably due to the fall. Why, oh why, hadn't I paid the bill on arrival at the hotel…?

We had a meeting, how many French francs had we to last the holiday? Admittedly, we could use cards – but not for everything. Fortunately, I had a French Post Office account with a few hundred francs which I drew out and shared with those who had need.

Now we can get back to the wines of this region. The rosés are my favourite, I think it's the bottles that make them so… . When you're in Provence, you feel frivolous – the sun, the colours and sitting out to eat in the evening – well – the table wouldn't look right without one of those lovely bottles! But there are other wines and, in this chapter, I am going to tell you something of my latest find – organic wines from Arles.

Arles is an attractive Roman town with an amphitheatre that is still in use. It is situated in the Bouches du Rhône, Provence on the borders of Languedoc and Rhône.

There are few vineyards in Provence producing AC status wines; about 80% are in the lower category [VDQS] such as the Vin de Pays de Bouches du Rhône, which includes the districts of Petite Crau, St Remy and Carmargue. Arles is at the most northerly point of this area.

The 'Bouches' is the largest Vins de Pay-producing region of Provence and holiday-makers consume vast quantities of its wine.

The soil of this region is less rich and fresh than that of the Languedoc.The vineyards are mainly situated on granite, apart from the Camargue where you will find alluvial plains.

The wines are produced from 'southern' grapes such as Grenache, Cinsault and Syrah as well as indigenous grapes.

Arles is all about art and literature. As wine doesn't seem to have anything to do with Van Gogh or Alphonse Daudet, I was informed by the tourist office that there wasn't any wine information available. So I had to rely on the bottle of local wine I had with dinner the night before.

Actually, the wine I was looking for has a connection because it is one of the many styles produced at the Mas de Rey and the selection I tasted was 'Van Gogh'. Mas de Rey specialises in organic wines.

The owner of Mas de Rey is a lovely lady called Doloras Mazzoleni. She arranged to meet me at their 'quality products of Provence' shop, the Villa Natura, which was recently opened by her son who is the wine-maker of Mas de Rey.

I had a few minutes to look around the wines, which included prestige AC wines from Côtes du Rhône and Provence, as well as those produced at Mas de Rey.

Doloras arrived and whizzed me off to their estate. It is not far from Arles and we drove through some of the region that had once been covered in vines. A few years ago, they had been dug up because of too much plonk being produced. The owners were well compensated.

As we drove into the Mas, Doloras pointed out a patch of abandoned vines, which was due for replanting with a new indigenous variety. She said that it was very sad to see and I sympathised. I feel like this at the end of the season when all the beautiful coloured leaves blow away, leaving the branches of the vines absolutely bare.

Doloras and her father had moved to Provence from Italy when she was 18 years of age and it wasn't long before she met Mario, a man passionate about wine-making. Eventually they married.

The family house was originally built by a member of the Poncelat family around the 15th century and integrated is a small family chapel, which once stood in the main street of Arles. The main part of the house is on one side of the chapel and on the other is a conference room and barns, etc.

Patrick joined us and introduced himself, 'Son of a vine-grower who pursues his father's challenge with passion.'

Mas de Rey creates several wines, red, rosé and white. They are rich in grape skin aromas. The 150 acres of vineyards are composed of traditional Mediterranean vines.

Caladoc [Grenache Blanc crossed with Malbec] created by ampelographer, Paul Truel [ampelography – science of identification and description of vine species]. This 'crossing' has produced a vine less prone to the 'coulure' disease. It is planted to a limited extent in southern Rhône but not accepted in the AC. It may be used to add tannin and aroma in vins de pays in Provence. [The Caladoc Rosé has been most successful.]

Chasan, a crossing of Palomino [Sherry grape -known as Listan in France] and Chardonnay, also created by Paul Truel.

Aranel is a variety of Grenache crossed with St Pierre Doré, the very productive grape that is almost extinct.

Marselan is Cabernet Sauvignon crossed with Grenache Noir.

l'Alicante is an ancient black grape of the Mediterranean.

I was amazed to find 'Vendange tardive' [late vintage] included in his collection. The grapes [l'Alicante variety] were picked on 13 December 1990 and rested for 10 years in oak. The origin of this production is unique, very little is produced and is bottled in 500 ml at 160 Fr. a bottle! A bottle for Christmas to drink with chestnuts and chocolate almonds from Provence was suggested.

With such a wonderful climate, it is perhaps not surprising that you find vins doux naturel made from the Muscat grape, and it is worth treating yourself to a bottle of this fruity, luscious and robust wine! It is sweet with an excellent bouquet and strongly developed grapiness taste, keeps for a long time and gets better with age!

I was certainly impressed by the wines of this region. I never expected to find such quality VDQS wines. What's more, some of these wines have longevity – especially those bottled in the larger sizes.

As well as wines, there are some excellent liqueurs made from blackcurrants, blackberries, raspberries, citrus fruits and juniper. You may say that you don't drink a lot of liqueurs but what about using them as an additive to desserts? They are excellent when *dripped* over ice-cream, added to fruit salad and a drop or two added to the fruit tart filling! In the summer, I like making different cocktails, and adding a liqueur can truly enhance the flavour!

These local liqueurs can be purchased at Chez Irmelin, a boutique on the boulevard around the amphitheatre. Mme Irmelin sells lots of local products including artisanal produced liqueurs. She will advise you which liqueurs to drink in winter, summer or even if you are feeling 'down', and may even introduce you to the wine of the Gardien – a Camargue cowboy!

Chapter 21
Cognac

You have a choice when it comes to 'Brandy' as Brandy is the Dutch word for burnt wine [or grape juice], introduced during their involvement with France. Brandy, of course, refers to Armagnac as well as to Cognac, although the distillation varies slightly with each one. There is also a type of brandy in Burgundy and Champagne but, in these regions, it is referred to as 'Marc'.

Calvados, strictly speaking, cannot be called a brandy as it is distilled *apple juice*, but is often referred to as brandy. This is drunk mainly in Northern France, either as an aperitif, a digestif [after-dinner drink] or during the meal to help with the digestion. The latter presented in a small glass, accompanying a sorbet served after the main course, seems more fiery than brandy, although a 'fine' Calvados is really superb.

In other areas of France you are more likely to be offered Armagnac or Cognac.

In the 17th century, the Cognac trade was still largely run by Protestants, who had used their co-religionists abroad as the base of their commercial network.

The production of Cognac underwent two major revolutions. In 1860 it was marketed in the bottle – allowing the merchant to put his name on the bottle and gain publicity. It provided the buyer with a new guarantee of consistent quality as well as protection against outside fraud and against frequent temptations of wholesale purchasers of cognac in bulk to tamper with contents. In 1880 bottles sales were at one million, in 1980 this was up to ten million. Unfortunately, I fear that this figure has dropped considerably in recent years.

The second revolution was the catastrophic introduction of *Phylloxera* in 1878. 'Phylloxera' actually means devastator, but in the Charente it was nicknamed phyllo-scélérat [the second part of this word means wicked]. On chalky soil, the disaster was total.

Phylloxera first entered France in a small village called Floriac, just south of Bordeaux. It's a louse that lives on the roots of vines, and it slowly but surely ruined nearly every vineyard in France. Recovery never happened in some wine regions because so much money was spent in trying to get rid of the disease that there was nothing left to pay for replanting. A good example of this is in the Lot et Garonne where market gardening took the place of vine growing.

Phylloxera is with us forever and the only root stock immune to the disease is American.

European vines must be grafted to American roots before being planted. There are a few areas which weren't affected; not many and these are sandy regions – like Colares in south-west Portugal. The vines grow on more or less 'sand beds' and *Phylloxera* cannot survive in sand. The producers agreed that the remedy was to bring vines in from USA – wild vines called RIPARIA.

Other diseases appeared: first Mildew then Oidium; these are diseases which cause rapid rot. Digressing just a little further, when you see roses at the end of a row of vines, you may think they are planted for decoration. Not at all! Roses suffer from the same disease, but they are affected in advance of the vines, therefore the vigneron gets warning and can spray to prevent damage. The 'spray' used is copper sulphate with a little lime and is the best known cure for it. Because it was introduced by Professor Peynaud of Bordeaux University, it has been named 'Bordeaux Mixture'.

Anyway, we must get back to Cognac… .

Cognac lies in the Charente, north of Bordeaux and 'Le Cognac' was originally created because of the Charentais' eagerness to become involved with the excellent wine trade between Bordeaux and the northern countries. Henry, Count of Anjou, had succeeded King Stephen of England in the 12th century and had become one of the most powerful kings of England, taking some of the court to England. The wine trade between the two countries and others had started and Charente wanted to be part of it.

The people of Charente were envious and decided to produce their own wine. Unfortunately, it was an absolute failure because of different soil [much chalkier] and climate conditions. This produced extremely acidic wine and it was only when some Dutchmen visited the region that a solution was found to remedy the huge quantity of unwanted liquid. On tasting it, the Dutch suggested distilling the wine.

Because the Dutch made this suggestion, the new drink took the name 'Brandy' i.e., Dutch brandijwein for burnt wine. It was only when bids were made by the different towns in Charente that Cognac *pipped the post* before Jarnac, and this brandy became known as 'Cognac'.

At first, the producers of Cognac were not completely convinced that this was the answer, the result was a harsh liquid with very little colour or character. The main grape used is the Folle Blanche that contains lots of acidity.

In the 17th century, Cognac was sold only in the cask and consisted of 'brown brandies' [this is heavily sweetened with brown syrup molasses – doubtless to cover up the frequent inadequacies of distillation] and 'pale' [unadulterated]. These Cognacs were often named according to their provenance, i.e. brandies from the 'Champagne de Cognac' were already more prized that those from the 'Bois' [woodland area of Cognac]. Then you had the aged Cognacs that had taken on an amber shade in the cask, which fetched higher prices than the young, clear brandy. Today, brown brandies have completely disappeared; all Cognac is now pale.

To gauge the proof during this period, distillers relied on a device called the 'Prouvette'. This was a phial they filled with the spirit and they could approximately gauge the proof by measuring the thickness of the ring of bubbles on the surface of the liquid. The method was nicknamed the 'bubble test'.

Cognac differs with vine location, soil differences, cellar humidities and cask qualities. Only Cognacs that agree with, and complement, one another must be married and then they will need further time to blend fully into a harmonious 'whole'. Sounds like the perfect marriage! It is for this reason that Cognac remains inimitable.

I think my favourite Cognac House to visit is Remy Martin. It is so very well organised. You are met in the reception area and then taken to the awaiting mini-train, which takes you not only around the premises but into the vineyards, through the cooperage and then into the chais where you can actually smell the brandy ageing. It is a wonderful education for wine enthusiasts with little knowledge.

At the start of exportation of Cognac, there was a disillusionment which remained for a long period. The English who were drinking it were thought to be mad when they expressed true satisfaction of this firewater!

Puzzled by this, the producers made a decision to travel with the Cognac to England. In this way they could visit the négocients. It very soon became clear why the English were so pleased with Cognac and confirmed that they weren't 'firewater drinkers'.

The journey by boat took a considerable time and, as the Cognac was transported in barrels, the long journey gave the tannin in the wood time to develop the Cognac, i.e. adding flavour and colour to it. The harshness, which had displeased the producers so much, had disappeared: the wine had *softened*. Yes, ageing in wood really was necessary.

On this realisation, production in Cognac changed, chais were built and ageing was done on the property.

Cask making has remained the same through the ages. The staves are split, not sawn and are left to dry by themselves in the open air. To watch a barrel being put together is fascinating, it is all down to skill.

Oak was preferred for the barrel making and, as time passed, it was discovered that a better result came from using a 'tight grained' oak – only to be found in a couple of regions of France. Most of the good oak is to be found in France in the Limousin region and just a little further north – south of Paris in the Allier forests.

The traditional way to store casks is in pyramids two or three levels high, but often you will see in more modern chais metal rack systems holding eight or nine levels, which makes access and maintenance easy. The chais are located in relatively moist areas in order to give body and mellowness to the ageing of the brandy.

The production of Cognac became more and more involved. It was no longer just distilling, ageing and *voilà* ... Cognac! As time went on, production became more complicated. The content of each barrel was graded, and then blended – which demanded the expertise of a master blender – the most important person in Cognac production.

Unlike wine in general, where the vintage varies from year to year, Cognac styles must be the same every year and the master blender has to taste and blend many wines to get the same taste as the year before. A very responsible task! In some companies, the master blender and his envisaged successor never travel together to safeguard the expertise acquired.

Cognac is sold and appreciated all over the world and was an important income for France. Unfortunately, sales have dropped considerably and the way one drinks Cognac has also changed. The last time I visited the region, we were shown a publicity film. I was rather surprised to find it encouraged the young to have Cognac with Schweppes and other such additives. But, there is a point, if it sells in this way – why not?

There are many British names connected with Cognac: Hines from Dorset and Hennessy from Scotland, etc. Napoleon has also been here! But don't be deceived by Napoleon Brandy. It's a good brand name but it no way indicates age.

Francois I was born in Château Otard, which is now a brandy house. He is said to be one of the best Kings France ever had and, what I can't understand is, even with this association you don't find a Cognac named after him.

What you must remember is that, once brandy is bottled, it will not improve – just like whisky. You can keep it for up to 25 years or so but don't expect any improvement.

Armagnac is a similar type of brandy, but is distilled in a different way. The region is in Gascony, which lies south east of Bordeaux. The climate is a little warmer and, in contrast to the basic wine of the Charente, the grape juice of Armagnac is not as acidic, therefore producing a slightly softer and fruitier spirit.

It is the oldest spirit in France, was first distilled in the 15th century and is preferred by many brandy drinkers in the Bordeaux region.

In 1909, in order to establish the name and capture a market similar to Cognac, the region was 'marked out'.

In the Middle Ages, the people of Armagnac, led by their Count, were the leading political party in France. But their greatest heroes didn't arrive on the scene until the 17th century. They were then immortalised by Dumas as 'The Three Musketeers'.

Armagnac was the battleground during the 100 Years' War and many bastides were built in this region.

Bastides were the new towns of the 13th century, built on free land, where no feudal lord held sway and where freedom was the keynote. They were completely self-governing – no Lords and no castles – the defences lay in the construction. The towns were built so that it could be defended easily – the grid system allowed easy movement. Wide arcades were built in the main squares. These run round all four sides of the market place and were built to shelter the people from the sun and the rain.

All those living in a Bastide were free, and even serfs could gain their liberty by living in a Bastide for one year and a day.

In 1976 La Compagnie des Mousquetaires de L'Armagnac [one of the brotherhoods in France], which boasts an authentic descendant of the d'Artagnan family, celebrated its 25th anniversary and in 2001, the 50th celebration. The men arrive dressed in high boots, plumed hats and magnificent moustaches.

The brandy drinkers of Bordeaux prefer Armagnac to Cognac, and I can understand why. The aroma and flavour have much more fruit than the Cognac.

I am often asked for advice on buying brandy and really find this difficult because, as with wine, preference of taste is personal. The only comment I would make is that you usually get what you pay for… i.e., the cost reflects the quality.

Chapter 22
La Loire

Up until the 17th century, mainly black grapes were planted in the Loire. At the insistence of the Dutch, these were gradually replaced by white varieties because the Dutch were looking for suitable light white wine for distilling. The white wines would be bottled, transferred, *sulphurised* and reinforced – creating better preservation for transporting.

It would be very difficult to organise a wine tour to the Loire and take in all the vineyards.

The Loire is the longest river in France, which starts in the Auvergne and makes its way out to the Atlantic at Nantes. It is over 600 miles long, with a wealth of wine along its banks and these wines have been popular in England since the Middle Ages when they were shipped from La Rochelle.

There is an abundance of different styles in white wine from steely dry, fresh and crisp to soft honey toned sweet wines. The reds – made mainly from the Cabernet Franc grape – are generally underestimated because they are not as robust or full bodied as their 'big brothers', i.e., Bordeaux and Burgundy. The best way to describe a red from the Loire is 'distinguished and delicate' and not for keeping for many years.

To call all these wines 'Loire Wines' would not be correct as, if you study the labels, you will find very few with the word 'Loire'.

The wines of this region are best drunk young, they don't age well and they certainly don't travel well. Of course, there is one wine that doesn't come into this category and that is the 'flowery Sauternes' – or the Quarts de Chaume. This is a lighter type of sweet wine and is absolutely delicious.

The wine regions of the Loire are as follows:

Nantes
Anjou and Saumur
Tourraine
Quincy and Rouilly
Sancerre and Pouilly

The grape varieties cover Gamay, Cabernet Franc, Cabernet Sauvignon, Malbec, Pinot Gris, Pinot Meunier, Pinot Noir, Chenin Blanc Sauvignon and Chardonnay – to name just a few.

Starting in Loire Atlantique, the first wine region is Muscadet, which comes mainly from small family-run wineries south of Nantes. Only one grape is used and it is not only called Muscadet but also 'Melon de Bourgogne', which was introduced by the Dutch in the 17th century.

There are three types of Muscadet: 'Muscadet de Sèvre-et-Maine' [said to be the popular in France around the Second World War time], 'Muscadet des Coteaux de la Loire' and 'Muscadet' . These wines have been described as 'light tangy and almost salty'. More Muscadet de Sèvre-et-Maine is sold each year than any other appellation in the Loire. The maximum alcoholic strength is 12.3 per cent.

Since the mid 1980s, wine-makers have been experimenting with barrel fermentation and lees stirring. Many of the Muscadet imbibers are still not convinced that this method is better than the traditional one – even after so many years!

The best Muscadet is from Sèvre-et-Maine and described as 'sur Lie'. Lees [as in English] of wine are dead yeast cells, grape seeds, pulp and fragment of skins, which sink to the bottom of the vat during fermentation. The usual procedure is to draw the wine off the 'lees' at the end of the fermentation but this is not the case with Muscadet sur Lie. The wine, light in structure, low in acidity, makes it liable to oxidation and, because of this, is left to mature on its lees to increase the flavour of this relatively neutral grape.

This more complicated procedure of wine-making makes Muscadet sur lie more expensive than the other styles, but well worth it.

The dry light wine is not for keeping, it is best drunk young when it has maximum flavour. It's a perfect wine for quaffing as well as for the more serious job of accompanying seafood.

This wine should be served chilled but not ice cold. If you serve any white dry white wine too cold, very little of the flavour will come through and this superb bottle of dry wine with delicate aromas will be drunk without you ever finding out what you've paid for to enjoy.

The wine is pale in colour – almost transparent. The bouquet is seldom pronounced but sometimes you get a hint of wild roses.

When you sip it – it fills the mouth. There is a slight prickle of natural carbon dioxide that makes the wine tingle on the palate. Muscadet hasn't a lot of 'body' to it but the taste is dry, not too tart and immature because it is a young wine. It has a fresh clean finish, which can linger.

There are a couple of other wine areas north of Nantes and, although categorised as 'lesser' wines, deserve a mention. The Coteaux d'Ancenis, which produces rosé and red mainly from the Gamay grape, does so because of the gradually developing local interest a few years ago. The other wine, which I must mention, is the Gros Plant.

Faces drop when I utter these two words at dinner parties – or other occasions. I don't care, because if I happen to find a well-made, very young bottle of this wine, fresh and crisp, in the supermarket, I head straight for the fish counter and treat myself to a few oysters – a perfect match!

Whenever I think of Angers, I think of Roses. The Loire is known as the Garden Region of France and every year there is an abundance of roses – especially around Anger [and also Orleans where there is, nearby, a park with no less than 250,000 rose bushes.] When conferences are held during this time, the ladies are always given a buttonhole of roses. On one of my tours, we arrived a little later than anticipated, everyone was pretty tired, but as we stepped out of the coach on to the pavement we were greeted by a member of hotel staff and presented with such buttonholes. Our long journey and tiredness disappeared... . Later, we arrived in the foyer, refreshed and dressed – with the buttonholes – ready for dinner.

Well, it was bound to come out – not only rose flowers but rosé wine for which Anjou is famous. It is produced from the Cabernet Sauvignon grape and is medium dry. Cointreau also comes from here.

As we leave Anjou, travelling towards Saumur, there is for me, some of the best dry wines of the Loire – which come from Savennières. When I visit a prestige wine producer, I like to go into the vineyards – soil interests me. In this particular one, we had a long walk and a long chat. First of all, I wanted an explanation of why this wine is so good. It was explained that these vineyards lie on a bank of volcanic debris brought down the river from the Massif Central. We looked at the slate, which is very dark blue in colour. I said to Madame that this slate reminded me of the slate used on the roofs in the new part of Tours and she replied, 'You are absolutely right, the slate for roofs on the new buildings of Tours does come from this region.' The wines from here can age as well as some of the Burgundies.

We reach Tourraine. We can be sure that the Romans developed and extended the vineyards to here. The early church was instrumental in advancing viticulture and this included the Loire. The church, as St Martins at Tours, had considerable vineyard holdings –that stretched to Burgundy. St Martin was a soldier, born in Yugoslavia and elected Bishop of Tours in 371. He was said to have split his cloak in two to share with a beggar! The locals say that the art of pruning the vine was discovered by St Martin's donkey, who kept nibbling at certain vines – these vines produced more grapes!

This makes St Martin the Saint of the vineyards, whereas St Vincent is the patron Saint of French wine growers. I read an interesting account of Vincent, which states that 'his statue makes him look a little dishevelled because, being pretty thirsty – according to the legend – he asked for leave of absence from heaven. Alas, he broke his leave being found hopelessly 'plastered' in the cellars of La Mission – and was turned into stone because of such unsaintly conduct.'

Whilst talking about vines in this region, the Cabernet Franc, the red grape of the Loire, gets its nickname 'Breton' from Abbe Breton, an intendant of Richelieu. He was sent to Bordeaux for some vine cuttings for experimenting in the vineyards. He chose the Cabernet Franc because it yielded better.

The Tourraine region encompasses

Saumur – some very good sparkling wines and reds

Mont Louis – where lighter white wines are produced

Jasnières – producing light fruity wines

Bourgueil – where some very good red wines produced from the Cabernet Franc are produced

Vouvray – for its sparkling wine. What we know as Vouvray Petillant [produced as the traditional Méthode Champenoise] was created by Marc Bredif around 1920, and you can visit his chai, which is underground in the volcanic chalk rocks. The sparkling wines were introduced in 1950. The dry, acidic wine lent itself perfectly to a good sparkling wine. In the 1970s the demand for this wine fell – mainly because of competition and also the shortage of the basic wine.

Just before you reach the Sancerre, there are two small wine regions called Quincy and Reuilly. The soil may be poor but there are some lovely wines, which change character as they evolve.

Pouilly and Sancerre are in the area they call the Central vineyards of the Loire. I think that some of the best Sauvignons come from this region but they are so over-priced. It is here where the Sauvignon, grown on chalky slopes, produces white dry wines with a flinty, smokey flavour.

To write about the Loire and not mention the Châteaux – or Joan of Arc would be a sin. After all, it was the Dauphin of France [the future Charles VII] who brought the nobility to the Loire, and it was here that they built their splendid homes we now know as the Châteaux of the Loire.

Jean of Arc brought most of this about: her famous recognition of the Dauphin – masquerading as a courtier when she entered the hall at Château Chinon on 9th March 1429. After convincing him of her mission, she set off heading an Army to Orleans. It all ended very sadly when Joan of Arc was burnt at the stake in Rouen. French people keep telling me that the English were responsible but this is not the case as it was the Catholic church who were ultimately responsible.

Charles went to live in Chinon because he didn't like Paris and, of course, all the woodland in the Loire gave ample opportunity for hunting and the court soon followed him. There are about 100 châteaux in the Loire and most of them are empty.

Chenonceau was lived in by Diane de Poitiers, Catherine de Medici and Mary Stuart. It was given to Diane when she was mistress of Henry II of France [she was also mistress of Francois I]. She started the construction of the pretty bridge over the river. When Henry died, his neglected wife, Catherine, took her revenge and forced Diane to give her Chenonceau in exchange for the prison-like château of Chaumont where she was exiled.

Catherine then added a two-storey gallery over the bridge which Diane had built.

Château Ussé was also built on the Indre. The similar white château among the dark green trees inspired Perrault to write *Sleeping Beauty*.

Azay le Rideau is a beautiful château built on the Indre. It is built of white stone and has a blue-tiled roof, which is mirrored in the green waters around it. When I visited the area, I always made a point of taking the group to the Son et Lumière.

Villandry is well known for its beautiful gardens.

Chinon was where Joan of Arc told Charles VII that she had come to help him drive out the English.

Amboise must get a mention because it was here that Francois II lived with his wife, Mary Queen of Scots, and where Charles VIII died in 1498, when he accidentally knocked his head against a beam.

Blois is definitely one of the most interesting châteaux on the Loire. It has been described as a 'parade of genius, a synthesis of three distinctive periods of French Architecture, late medieval façade'. Some of it was built by Francois I and it has a Mansart roof – similar to that of the Hospices in Beaune.

The Duc de Guise was murdered in this château and there is a painting of the incident in the château. I was truly amazed when I first saw this painting – the majority of those men involved were wearing earrings and skirts!

Chapter 23
Alsace

This wine region is one of the most picturesque in France, and the German influence has helped this to be so. Many of the wine villages are set in the foothills of the Vosges. The half-timbered buildings are decorated with lots of geraniums and give magnificent colour against the wood and stone houses in the cobbled streets.

Of course, a visit to Alsace would not be complete without spending time in Strasbourg, a wonderful city of architectural delight and its canals. It is the crossroads of Europe and home of the European Commission' as well as 'La Marseillaise', the French national anthem, which Roger d l'Isle of Strasbourg wrote as a war song for the Army of the Rhine.

Colmar is the wine administration centre and is one of the prettiest and interesting towns in Alsace, very Germanic, with an excellent choice of restaurants offering the splendours of both German and French cuisine.

In most of the towns and villages it is possible to tour the surrounding vineyards in a little train. You should take the opportunity, as many of the vineyards are not accessible to motorists.

The wines are similar to German wines but that is as far as it goes... . This north-east wine region is a narrow strip, 140 km long, sandwiched between the Vosges Mountains and the Rhine. It is south of most German wine regions, slightly warmer, is protected from rain and wind by the mountain range and is, in fact, the driest wine region in France. For example, the average rainfall in Colmar is only 500 mm – which is less than Jerez in Spain!

Alsace wines are described as fine, complex, dry wines from aromatic grapes with pungent bouquets followed by penetrating mouthfuls of rich fruit and softness with predominant spiciness. The ageing potential is good and the best will continue to age for many years.

Nearly all the wines in Alsace have AC status and 150 million bottles are produced each year! Most are 'still white' and, with sparkling wines, Cremant d'Alsace, they make up 95% of wine production. A little red wine is produced from the Pinot Noir.

Alsace wine bottles differ from those from the rest of France. Only one style of bottle is permitted, the grape variety dominates the label and the wine must be made from 100% of this variety. 'Edelzwicker' [not a grape] on a label means that the wine has been made from a blend of grapes.

All Alsace wine must be bottled in the region, and this usually takes place the following spring so that the wines retain their maximum fruit.

Alsace grapes
Chasselas
A grape that was once very popular but is now a *dwindling* variety.
Gewürztraminer
This slightly pink-skinned grape was created in Germany. The 'Traminer' originated in Northern Italy and was further developed by the Germans and this added spiciness to the flavour. 'Gewürz', the German word for spice was prefixed to 'traminer' and voilà! '*Gewürztraminer*', a wine, pungent with aromatic spice and high alcohol content of around 13%. The best wines come from Alsace.
Pinot Blanc
One of the 'lesser' grapes and described by some as a 'workhorse'. It is a softer wine with a dash more spice and very acceptable.
Muscat
This is a difficult grape to grow because of its unreliable flowering, but it can produce fantastic wine. It smells sweet and 'grapey' but is fresh and dry on the palate.
Riesling
This is the 'King of Alsace', produces wine with a steely character, a detection of petrol on the nose, dry and crisp on the palate. It is the last of the varieties to ripen and because of the drier climate, which alleviates the risk of rot, the Riesling can make superb late harvest

wines. Some of these wines are capable of ageing for 50 years or more!

Sylvaner

This is the most widely used grape in Alsace.

Pinot Noir

Originally used to make rosé wine but recently, wine-makers are concentrating on using this variety to produce a more Burgundian type of wine.

Tokay d'Alsace [or Pinot Gris]

This is often mistaken as it is similar to the Tokay grape of Hungary, but it has no connection with Hungary. I have read that an Alsacienne soldier went to war in Hungary in the 16th century, won the battle and helped himself to a number of barrels of Tokay wine. On return to Alsace, he planted Tokay vines. Another of those romantic wine stories on which I thrive!

Appellations of Alsace

Alsace AC covers all the vineyards. Any of the permitted grape varieties grown in any village in any AC vineyard can qualify for this appellation.

Alsace Grand Cru AC, introduced in 1985 covers specified vineyards for specified grape varieties, i.e., Riesling, Gewürztraminer, Tokay-Pinot Gris and Muscat. If the Gewürztraminer in a particular vineyard is 'Alsace Grand Cru', the other grapes in that vineyard would not be entitled to use Alsace Grand Cru. Only the wine from the awarded grape variety can be labelled 'Alsace Grand Cru AC'.

Cremant d'Alsace AC

A 'Cremant' sparkling wine can be made in any wine region and is produced from the indigenous grapes. Cremant d'Alsace AC is rated as one of the finest in France – lots of tropical fruit and zingyness.

The method for making this wine is as for Champagne, but the coveted term 'Méthode Champagnoise' is jealously guarded for sparkling wine produced in the Champagne region only. In Alsace mainly Pinot Blanc and Pinot Auxerrois are used.

Vendange Tardive and Selection des Grains Nobles

These are two other classifications for late harvested grapes. 'Vendange Tardive' is medium sweet wine made from selected grapes. 'Selection des Grains Nobles' is for sweeter wine produced from grapes that have been affected by noble rot.

With all these super wines available, I have to recommend some favourite accompaniments, like *foie gras*, Munster cheese – strong and excellent with pungent wines, *tarte a l'oignon* and *tarte flambée*, a paper thin pastry base covered with cheese ham, onions and cream, then 'toasted' in the oven.

During a recent wine-tasting with Auchan in Paris, I was impressed to learn that their team of wine buyers includes an Englishman, Mark Cresswell, who specialises in Alsace wines.

When he heard I was writing about Alsace, he sent me one or two bottles of 'his favourites'. His existence in France is like a modern-day' fairy tale.

Mark studied at Tours University as part of his history degree. To earn his 'pocket money', he worked as a guide in one of the caves at Vouvray. He fell in love with a local girl and decided that he would follow a career in wine – living in France.

He returned to London and went to work with Oddbins where he studied for WSET Exams. Returning to France, with this experience, he took a wine marketing course in Burgundy. During this time he was offered a job with Auchan and now spends his time going around the vineyards looking for suitable wines, sometimes tasting 200 wines a day for the two-yearly 'Foire' event at Auchan. It sounds a wonderful job, but I know it is hard work.

Chapter 24
Burgundy

Where to start on Burgundy is the question and I have given it all much thought. I think the best thing to do is go back to the Dukes of Burgundy – or even further... .

Burgundy was named by the Burgondes; it was part of the Charlemagne Empire.

The Capetians reigned in Burgundy for three centuries – they were allied with the French kings and suffered terribly in 1359/60 from the ravaging of Burgundy by Edward III. Philip de Rouvres, last descendant of Robert sans Terre, died on 21 November, 1361.

I think if we centre ourselves on Beaune, records will tell us that it dates back to 52BC and was evidently one of Julius Ceasar's camps.

The name Beaune comes from the God of the Gauls – Belenus Belisana, the Goddess of Minerva or the last thought is Belna – which in Latin means a small villa.

It became a city in 1203 and was one of the favourite residences of the Dukes of Burgundy. It was a seat of the Bourgogne Parliament.

Beaune was the site of frequent battles and struggles and the people suffered from fire, famine and plague. In 1401 a fire destroyed three-quarters of the town. The walls and ramparts built during the reign of Louis XI still stand today. The town itself is built on a subterranean network of galleries and passages.

In 1362 Philip the bold [fourth son of King John the Good] was given the Duchy of Burgundy. It is said that he was given the name Philip the Bold because, after he and his father were captured by the English, they were taken to England and, at dinner one evening, the servant served the King of England before the French king. Philip slapped the face of the server and the King of England said, 'My word Philip, you are bold!' Believe this if you like... .

Philip acquired Flanders in 1384 through marriage to Margaret. You can see tapestries from Flanders in the Hospices of Beaune.

The wines of Beaune were the 'wines of France' [or the Ile de France as it was known]. The wines of Bordeaux belonged to the English.

In the 14th century the wines of Beaune kept the Popes of Avignon very happy and Erasmus attributed his good health to Burgundian wines. Louis XIV adopted Burgundian wines as 'Court' wine. Philip the Good and Charles the fearless used the wine as bait – it tipped the scales at court!

The Hospice de Beaune was formed in the middle of the 15th century by Nicolas Rolin. He built it, creating an institution that has acted as an index ever since – through annual auctions of the current price of Burgundy wines. It was the former Palace of the Dukes of Bourgogne.

The hospice is referred to as the 'Jewel of Côte d'Or'. And it has enjoyed important visitors from all over the world including Louis XIV of France and in recent times, the Queen and the Queen Mother in 1979.

Nicholas Rolin was the tax-collecting Chancellor of Burgundy, when he founded the Hospices in 1443. A hard man it seems: even King Louis XI was alleged to have said that Rolin, having made so many people poor, was wise to appease the Almightly by providing for a few of them. In fact, his words were, 'Having impoverished and disinherited so many of his subjects well might he beseech divine mercy by providing care and succour for these unhappy creatures'. Rolin was the first to give his vineyards to the Hospice and set a precedent to be followed over the centuries.

On 4th August, 1443 he ceded all of his worldly possessions acquired 'by the grace of God' in order to build a hospice. The hospice was completed on 1st January, 1451.

One of the most striking features is the elegant high Mansard roof of the hospices, covered with coloured slates in intricate patterns and, as you walk into the cobbled courtyard which is surrounded by the buildings which were once the hospital, kitchen, pharmacy and nurses' quarters, you can imagine and feel the bustle of nurses, doctors and staff rushing around doing their daily duties.

The hospice as it was, no longer exists but there is an old people's home on the top floor. The nursing sisters still wear the costumes of the design favoured by the founders.

The east window of the chapel shows Philip the Good, Charles and Nicholas Rolin. This is next to the huge ward, which holds 28 alcoves. There is a small bed in each one and I was told that sometimes the bed was used for two persons. Things have changed in the ward in the last few years. When I first visited the hospice, the layout of the ward was much more original. You could see the little bedside tables furnished with pewter water mugs next to the beds. I often thought that a few of these mugs must be taken by the 'dishonourable' to add to their collection of holiday trophies. This must have been the case, as it wasn't long after that the items were removed and put in glass cases.

The design of the tiles on the floor is also interesting: there is a single star on each one. Nicholas's design was to show to the world that his wife Guigonede was the only star in his life... but we know that wasn't the case!

As you walk through the hospice, you will come to the dining room and, in the room next to it, is the painting of the Triptych of the Last Judgement, painted by the Flemish artist Rogier van der Weyden in 1443–1445. It shows the influence of Van Eyck. You can pick out several important people of that time, such as Nicolas Rolin and son, Cardinal Rolin, Guigonede Salins, the wife of Niocolas, Philip the Good, Isabella of Portugal,etc.

At this point, I should like to digress a little because now that we're in Bourgogne the influence of the Revolution is with us... and pondering on The Last Judgement, I should like to give you my thoughts and opinion on this painting which, in a similar form, was to be found in many churches – sometimes by accident.

The Revolution took away the powers of the rich and the royal – and also the Church because the Church was rich!

One way of tackling the churches was by covering the paintings on the inside walls, *plastering* over them. These formidable paintings frightened the peasants and gave power to the church.

My example to you is a small church in the Lot et Garonne in a village Allemans du Dropt with an excellent village hotel. I often took groups there for 2 or 3 days and there was always time to have a 'wander'. On the first visit to this church I noticed that some of the plaster had been lifted and this had revealed tiny fragments of paintings. Naturally, nosey me, I had to find out why, and on chatting to one of the village people was told that these were paintings of the 15th century – no one knew they were there! One day the plaster on one of the pillars started to peel off and the locals brought in someone to repair the damage. As he worked on the destruction, more plaster came off and more paintings were exposed. It all got very exciting and the Beaux Art in Paris was informed. The representative said that this was a wonderful 'find' and the Beaux Art would take responsibility for uncovering the others and restoring the work as well as they could.

On seeing the finished work, I got more of an insight into what went on before the Revolution and understood more about why there had been a Revolution. These paintings reminded me of visual aids in school classrooms, where children sit and study each one very closely. Fortunately, nowadays the children are taught to read and write and the visual aids rest as a helping hand for learning, the difference being that, in the Middle Ages, people went to church but very few learned to read or write, and whatever was on the wall was of vital importance to the way in which they lived.

The Last Judgement shows the Saint Michel waiting for your arrival after death as you make your way through the clouds. On the right side of the picture are the *pearly gates* with an angel waiting to receive you. On the left is Hell and the burning pit and the devil waiting to push you in with his three-pronged fork!. The look of fear, anguish and terror on the faces of those who have sinned is indescribable! So, every time you went to church you were well informed what would happen to you if you sinned or didn't ask forgiveness of your sins. My view is that this was the first Reign of Terror! Now we shall return to Bourgogne and the hospice.

Since Nicholas Rolin gave his vineyards to the hospice, many other vineyard owners have *followed suit.* The hospice owns many vineyards, which have been handed over in order to maintain the hospice. Because of this, the hospice not only looks after the aged persons lodged in the hospice but gives the money earned from the wine auction to local hospitals and other well-deserved causes. It is a great charity.

To celebrate this important occasion, there is a celebration of Burgundian wines which lasts for 3 days. 'Les Trois Glorieuses' is one of the most important times on the wine calendar. The auction falls on the third Sunday in November during 'Les Trois Glorieuses'.

On the first day, the Saturday, a candlelight dinner is held in the Château de Vougeot.

Sunday afternoon is the time when they auction the wines from the harvest. Their wines are sold by auction after the vintage on the third Sunday of November each year amid a weekend of celebrations. Originally, the auction was a sale of wine made by private treaty; this sale was changed to an auction in 1851, the venue being moved to the town's covered market place in 1967 when the hospice was no longer large enough for the growing host of bidders and for others coming from foreign parts. The sale is, in fact, a wine trade occasion with almost more buyers than barrels! High prices are paid.

In the evening, a candlelight dinner is held in the bastion of the hospice. Over 600 people attend from all over the world and tickets are sold out the year before! I have a standing reservation so that I can take a small party there each year.

On Monday the Paulée de Mersault is held in the Château de Mersault. The Paulée gets its name from Poêle in which the slaughtered pig is fried This is a grand occasion for the wine-growers, when they all sit down to lunch together. Each wine-grower brings a bottle of his wine. It started in 1932 when there were 35 guests; the guest list has now risen to over 400! One of the menus I found for this occasion was as follows:

> Terrine de canard au poivre vert
> Suprêmes de lotte Jonville
> Jambon de Meursault [the pig]
> Faisons as l'anciènnes
> Cheeses
> Dessert

I don't know if it's still carried out, but a literary prize was awarded to a well-known author – the prize was 100 bottles of Meursault!

Château de Vougeot is the largest Clos, 120–125 acres, and gets its name from the river Vouge. It was mainly a forest area with one little vineyard. The history of it goes back to the 12th century, when it belonged to the Cistercian Order.

Unlike Islam, Christianity did not outlaw wine. When the Roman Empire was overrun by the Barbarians in the 5th century, early Christian missionaries saved the vine. Emperor Charlemagne gave his support to the Church and to the vine.

The Monks of Cluny were the first members of the Cistercian Order to be established in Burgundy. Peter the Venerable was the Abbot of Cluny. The Abbey was founded in 910 by the Count de Auvergne, the grandfather of Eleanor d'Aquitaine, and was completed by lay brothers. It was the largest church until St Peter's in Rome. Later, many began to feel guilty about the lavish lifestyle that was developing there. Wine-making was proving to be a very lucrative business... .

To lead the frugal life they had intended, the monks moved to Vougeot in order to observe a more rigorous discipline. It was these monks who built the walls that are still standing today and later, because of lack of space, on 13th October 1367, Philip the Bold gave permission to build the château nearby. It took 5 years to build.

Three types of wine were made at Vougeot:
- Cuvée for the Popes
- Good wine for the kings and priors
- Run of the mill for the monks

The Presses still stand today – and we're very fortunate to have them, as the Germans tried to use them for firewood in the Second World War!

Unfortunately, on 13th of February, 1790, the French Revolution put an end to the wealth. The property was confiscated and sold by auction. It was bought by Monsieur Focard, who wasn't able to maintain it so the last cellarmaster, Dom Goblet, continued cultivating.. He was so much appreciated that he was given two silver spoons and forks and enough wine to last him for the rest of his life.

Dom managed to get his own back on Napoleon in 1800 on his return from the Battle of Marengo. The Consul passed through Dijon and sent a messenger to Vougeot to obtain wine. Dom said to the messenger that he had some 40 years' old Vougeot and, if Napoleon wanted it, he had to come and get it himself!

The wines were so excellent that, during the Revolution, Colonel Bisson ordered his battalion to present arms when marching past the château, and the custom has been kept by the French Army to this day.

The château is now owned by the Confrerie des Chevaliers du Tastevines, an organisation devoted to the maintenance of quality and reputation of Burgundian wines. It was founded in 1933 and Camille Rodier is one of the co-founders.

It has been suggested that the ancient Swiss introduced wine to Bourgogne but that the Romans brought the vines.

Burgundy vineyards are completly different from those in Bordeaux and this is simply because the majority of them were owned by the Church and, during the French Revolution, they were savagely divided and sold to peasants by speculators.

The Napoleonic laws of inheritance did more damage. All land has to be shared equally among the children, so unlike Bordeaux, where one vineyard is owned by one body, a vineyard in Burgundy is fragmented and can be owned by 80 people!

Burgundy produces only half as much wine as Bordeaux in an average year, approximately four-fifths red and one-fifth white.

The choice of Burgundian wines should always be based on the name of the owner, the estate or the négociant – he alone, in fact, gives the most certain guarantee of quality.

The wines are full and robust. The Côte de Beaune produces softer wines – similar to St Emilion and St Estephe. They are slightly sweeter and softer nearer Beaune. They're said to have a little more body, bouquet and colour that those of Bordeaux, and the chief difference is 'tone'. Bordeaux is like soprano and Burgundy is contralto!

There are many great vineyards in Burgundy and I intend to mention but a few… . Let's look at the Côte de Beaune.

Corton

There is a proverb that says 'Give a dumb man a glass of old Corton and he will chatter like a magpie.'

Pierre Forgeot, the wine historian, suggests that this is the ideal wine for diplomats, barristers and politicians: the slowest developing wine in the Côte de Beaune.

Corton Charlemagne is white and this is simply because, when Charlemagne drank wine – his wife always knew by his red-stained beard – he ordered that white wine should be produced so that he could drink without telling her!

The white wine, Corton Charlemagne, is the finest after Montrachet.

Aloxe Corton

Aloxe Corton stands in 570 acres and takes its name from the Gallo Roman era, i.e. Aloxe for Alussa [land of God Alus].

It's here that the Roman Road from Marseilles divides, one road goes to Aachan and the other to Trèves.

Charlemagne, Henri II [of France] and Louis XIV owned land here. Charlemagne planted vineyards at Aloxe Corton – red and white and later, in 775, gave them to a Church of St Ardeche, the Abbey of Salieu, as compensation for their monastery being pillaged by the Saracens. The soil is of limestone and iron oxide.

Montrachet

Montrachet means bare mountain. For example, to dig up vines, in French you would say 'arracher' the vineyard. The sub-soil is mainly calcareous.

The white wine from here is reputed to be the best white wine in the world. Alexander Dumas suggests drinking it kneeling down and with head bare in respect!

It is also said that the wines of Montrachet are the best the Chardonnay grape can produce.

Montrachet is to Bourgogne what Yquem is to Sauternes.

It's a very small vineyard, shared equally between Puligny and Chassagne and just over 20 acres.

Puligny-Monrachet has a total production which consists exclusively of white wine. The taste is described as 'Incomparable fruitiness, subtle flavours of almonds and honey'.

Chassagne Montrachet vineyards produce more red than white. The red wines have a slight peppery flavour, deep in colour and a magnificent bouquet of wild flowers and ripe fruit.

Le Chambertin

This comes from slopes of 60 acres just to the south of the village of Gevry 'Le Roi des vins de Borgogne'.

This was Napoleon's favourite wine. He preferred it at 5 to 6 years of age and never drank more than half a bottle at a meal. [He had to drink Claret in St Helena!]

The wine has been compared to 'The good Lord gliding down your gullet in a pair of velvet trousers' or the 5th 7th or 9th symphonies of Beethoven.

Meursault

This is the great white wine of Burgundy and my favourite! These are fresh and fruity in youth with a long finish, which stands for quality. With bottle age, they tend to oxidise, taking on a deeper golden colour and richer bouquet. Rich in glycerine, a soft, round taste with a high degree of freshness. A faint odour of nuts and spicy flavours – in a very fruity bouquet. It ages well.

Meursault gets its name from 'Murasalt', which means a high fortified camp – perhaps another one of Ceasar's!

The village church with its 15th century tower has a spire of 187 ft, which is the highest in Burgundy. The local legend tells of it being built by the fairies!

The château is owned by Patriache [with a Japanese interest], who have a superb wine cellar in the centre of Beaune. I have always been made most welcome here and the tastings have been appreciated by members of the groups that I have accompanied. But, things are changing at Patriarche. At one time, for your entrance fee you were given a silver[?] tastevin for tasting the wines. This was a lesson in itself as these were used in the cellars to evaluate the wines by the cellar staff. You can tell quite a lot about the wine by just studying it in this shallow cup. As you left the cellars you were given a small bottle of the famous Kriter, a popular sparkling wine made by Patriarche. The quality of the wine is good enough for the French to serve it at celebrations where they know Champagne will not be appreciated.

Pommard

The Gauls built a temple here and dedicated it to Pomona – the protecting Goddess of Fruit. In 1005, the village was known as Polmarium.

This was once an important posting stage and the inn was used by travellers who had to 'ford' the Vandaine river between Beaune and Chagny. Before the bridge was built in 1670, this was the only way to cross.

Pommard vineyards cover 850 square acres, the production is entirely red and the full-bodied wine will age well.

The colour is a fine deep red but with fairly unsubtle bouquet which may suggest leather, ripe plums or blackcurrants – even chocolate has been suggested. Because of its strength and robustness, this wine needs to age for a long time.

Volnay

Volnay is situated much higher up than Pommard or Mersault. The Dukes of Burgundy built the château and it was destroyed in 1749.

In 1328, these wines were served at the coronation of Philip de Valois in Reims. The King was so impressed that he visited Volnay with Duke Eddes IV and gave him a present of 4000 gallons!

Louis XI loved Volnay and, after the conquest of Burgundy, he confiscated all the 1477 vintage and had it transported to his château.

This was the wine of kings because Louis XIV and Louis XV were also fond of it and had it served with Beaune and Pommard at the Coronation.

Before the French Revolution, the colour was much lighter – more of a tawny gold colour, which was popular with fine wines. Short periods of fermentation must have given the wine very brief contact with skins. They were drunk early – because they didn't age.

After the Revolution the wines were produced to taste and colour to suit the Dutch and German and because of this Volnay stopped making white wine.

Volnay wines are described as of smooth taste, perfect balance, delicate bouquet – with a scent of violets or budding wild flowers.

There was a company of crossbowmen here and, at the times of the 'Dukes', they were the élite corps first of the Burgundian army and later to the King of France. In order to test and improve their skills, there was an annual competition which started in 1393. The competition was to shoot a parrot, and the winner was crowned king and excused work in the vineyards and military fatigues, etc.

If we travel a little north of Beaune to the Côte de Nuits, the wines are red and are produced from the Pinot Noir grape.

The Pinot Noir grape has been described as the sulkiest, trickiest and most tempestuous fine wine grape in the world! It is the exclusive grape in all but a tiny proportion of red burgundies.

It needs a more delicate balance of spring, summer and autumn climate than any other wine in order to achieve greatness. When tasting a good Burgundy, you should look for a light, fragrant wine, perfumed with cherry and strawberry fruit. It is sometimes, meatier, intensely spicy – but as a rule, light.

The best wines of the Côte de Nuits are highly individual and their detailed origins can be identified to within a few hundred yards by people who are familiar with them.

No other wine-producing area in the world has yet succeeded in planting Pinot Noir vines and producing wines of the complexity and fascination of the best Côte d'Or bottles. To do this, the region needs long hot summers for the pigments in the pinot noir grape skins to develop satisfactorily. You get summers like this about once every 3 years, and the wines from these vintages have made the reputation of the Côte de Nuits.

These are dry invigorating wines, such as Gevrey Chambertin, Nuit St Georges, Clos Vougeot, Romanée Conti. They need longer to mature than Côte de Beaune.

White grapes are occasionally used in the vintage – the law permits up to 15% Chardonnay with the Pinot Noir.

The soil of this region is on 'pink stone', which is marble, and this is quarried at Comblanchien. The marble was used to build the Palace for the Dukes of Burgundy in Dijon and later for the Opera House in Paris and Orly airport.

Every time I see the word 'Comblanchien', it brings back happy memories because in the village there is a little Les Routiers restaurant where we had very reasonably priced lunches – and were made most welcome. We didn't eat with the lorry drivers; instead, a little room was prepared for us away from the bar and the smoke!

We had at least six courses, which included soup, about six different hors d'ouvres. It was typical 'transport' eating, with half a chicken each and huge plates of chips, a selection of cheeses, ice-cream, coffee and Marc de Bourgogne. We started off with a Kir – and the way it should be made, with Cassis Double… . The wine bottles on the tables were replaced throughout the meal as we finished them. It was such fun and, as we left, we were all given a present of a key ring or something similar.

Gevrey Chambertin, which has been named 'The Real Burgundy', produces excellent wine and has Grand Cru. The village of Gevrey was built in 630 and called Gibriacus, derived from Grabos [meaning goat or beard].

In 1257, after much suffering, the Abbot of Cluny gave protection to the château but, in 1336, it was pillaged, destroyed and rebuilt. What was left of the château still exists, although it was badly damaged by fire in 1976.

The village name, Chambertin, originated from Bertin's field of 30 acres, next to Clos de Bèze cultivated by monks. When Bertin died, the monks took over the vineyard and called it 'Champ de Bertin' – later changed to Chambertin.

This was another favourite wine of Napoleon; he took it to Egypt. He liked it to be 5–6 years of age. He also took the wine to Russia.

I read lots of different stories about Napoleon and his wines and how he left his hat at his favourite producers but, on travelling around many vineyards, it seemed to me that he made a habit of this! I don't entirely agree with his knowledge of wine, i.e. he favoured wines of 5 to 6 years of age. One account I read about him was that his table manners were appalling and his food was shovelled in and *washed* down with the wine! The mind boggles... . Can you imagine any person with wine knowledge using good Burgundy to wash down his food?

Nuits St Georges

It was also named the kidney of Burgundy, The area was covered with walnut trees hence the name, as Nuys is the Latin word for walnuts. In the 19th century it was under German influence.

As well as the well-known wines of Nuit St Georges, which were very popular in Britain a few years ago, there are some very good producers of liqueurs here.

It was here that the Pinot Noir Blanc grape was discovered. Henry Gouges, owner of Clos Porrets, in 1934 found some rows of Pinot noir producing bunches of white grapes, He took several grafts and planted them out in one acre parcels of La Perriere.

Chablis

Charles the Bold gave this land to the church in 867 AD.

The town itself is a friendly place and I enjoy visiting these most northern vineyards. There is tranquillity about the area and, as you drive into it, you can see patches where the ground is 'resting' before the replantation of vines.

The area is on Kimmeridgian soil [clay and limestone] – about 1350 ft above sea level. The hillsides are stonier and deeper than the Côte d'Or There is a rare belt of bituminous clay in Chablis, which must be the secret in the production of this very special wine..

It is an isolated pocket in the Yonne Department and the grape used is, of course, the Burgundy Chardonnay.

If you like dry wine – you can't get it much drier than this. The best wines can age for up to 15 years.

This region – like Champagne – is susceptible to frosts and doesn't get as much warm sun as the others. Therefore, to give you some idea of the alcohol degree achieved, have a look at the following:

Grand Cru has a minimum alcohol content of 11%

Premier Cru has a minimum alcohol content of 10.5%

Chablis has a minimum degree of 10%

Petit Chablis is a little different from the others and has a minimum degree of 9.5° C

The 'Grand Cru' is the best and should be left in the bottle for the longest time to develop. I wouldn't drink it under 3 years old and would probably leave it until it reached about 8 years of age.

The colour is very pale gold with a greeny tinge. The taste is utterly dry, yet never tart and, in good years, it has a majestic depth of flavour. Some dry wines have a metallic taste – you will never get this with a Chablis Grand Cru.

The others vary in dryness, apart from the Petit Chablis, which is crisp and fresh but sometimes needs chaptalisation.

Chaptalisation was introduced by Mr Chaptal, one of Napoleon's greatest Agricultural ministers. The most northern vineyards have the greatest problem in getting enough sun on the grapes to bring the sugar content up to a reasonable level – bearing in mind that all wines under AOC have a recognised minimum level of alcohol. In particularly bad years, wine producers are allowed to add sugar to the must to get this minimum level. This procedure is strictly controlled and is never used for good white Burgundies. To increase the alcohol content by 1% it is necessary to add 3¾ lbs of sugar to 22 gallons of wine, that is to say 4/10 of an ounce per bottle.

Not only is chaptalisation used in the northern vineyard regions, but further south it is occasionally necessary in particularly bad years.

I'm not sure whether Chaptal's reason for this was strictly to look after the wine because I read somewhere that he was very much involved with agriculture and there was so much sugar beet production in the area – he had to get rid of the sugar!

There are some very good vineyards to be found and you may be interested to know that Brigitte Bardot owns some of them!

In recent years when visiting with groups, I have concentrated on the Co-operative of Chablis, Le Chablissienne. They produce some good wines in favourable years and their prices don't break your bank account.

Aligote

This is a white grape included in the AOC of Burgundy.

It is not planted on the best sites of Burgundy and the wine itself is used mainly as a spritzy aperitif café wine – a great favourite of the bistros in Paris.. If the wine is produced from older vines, it can be refreshingly scented but it still remains sharp to the palate.

The most important fact is that this is the wine to use in the well-known 'Kir'. The traditional Kir was introduced by Canon Kir, a Resistance hero and, at one time, the Mayor of Dijon, whose evening tipple was originally a glass of Aligoté – until it got too sharp for his taste. He remedied the problem by adding Casis Liqueur. His recipe was 1 pint of Cassis to ¾ pint of Aligoté. This solved the problem.

Nowadays, you add a little Cassis to the glass before pouring in the Aligoté. And the aperitif has now become very popular although somewhat enhanced – you can now have a *Kir Royale* which should be Cassis and Champagne – but very rarely is … . Sparkling wine is more likely to be used.

A little mention before leaving Burgundy. A few years ago, I gave a couple of lectures at Exeter University and the French tutor came to discuss the programme with me at my office. He said he was in a rush as it was his wife's birthday and he was cooking a special chicken dish for her. I asked about the wine he had selected for the dish. His reply was, 'Ah! On these special occasions there is only one wine and that is a Chardonnay from St Bris. I honestly think that he thought that I wouldn't have a clue about this wine – but, thanks to my education, I was able to say that he would probably find that it wasn't a Chardonnay but a Sauvignon! This didn't please him – a Scotswoman – telling him about wine! Anyway, a few days later he popped in the office and confessed that he had always thought that all white wine from Burgundy – apart from Aligoté – was Chardonnay.

St Bris, in the northern part of the main Burgundy region is an area where the Sauvignon is produced, but it is a lesser wine.

And just to add a footnote to all of this… . When, later, during a talk with the same group on Champagne, I truly upset the same French tutor when I 'announced' that it was an Englishman who had introduced Champagne to France!

Chapter 25
Rioja

When I open a bottle of 'Rioja' – one of my favourite reds, I take a sip and memories of my visits, and the history associated with the region, immediately come to mind.

The word 'Rioja' comes from the river Oja [rio Oja], a tributary of the river Ebro.

Wine has been produced in this area since Roman times; this was one of their main centres of production. The town of Cenicero meaning 'ashtray' in Spanish was so named because it was here where the Romans cremated their dead.

In the region, you can find the remains of a large Roman winery dating back to the first century, which to judge from the size of its fermentation chambers and storage vessels, produced 75,000 litres annually. The Romans made wine to ship to Italy as well as supplying the legions in Spain.

The area is split into three regions, Alta, Alavesa and Baja. Alta and Alavesa produce the best wines.

There are 14 varieties of grapes in La Rioja, but only six are used to make wine. The main grapes for red wine are Tempranillo and Garnacha, for white, Viura and Malvesia.

Oak fermentation barrels were introduced in 1868 and, because of the French influence, they are similar in size [225 litres] to the Bordeaux barrel.

Owing to the American influence, labels are like those of California, named after the bodegas, names of the shippers and not by the vineyard.

To mention something of each of the principal Bodegas is not possible, they are too numerous but some with special interest are as follows.

Marquis de Riscal was the first bodega to be purpose built for making wines in Bordeaux fashion in 1860.

CVNE – [known as Cune] Compañía Vinícola del Norte de España, was one of the first six Bodegas, founded by the Asau Brothers and Frenchman Louis Perre in 1879. Their *Monopole* dry white wine was first launched in 1915. It is aged in oak for 16–20 months. For those who enjoy a dry wine with just a touch of oak – this could be your wine!

Marqués de Murrieta was the first wine-maker to introduce up-to-date Bordeaux methods to the Rioja wine. [Don Luciano de Murrietta later created Marqués de Murrieta in recognition of his services.]

Bodegas Muga is a good example of a more modern winery, founded in 1932. Very traditional in style and located in the old station district of Haro, they have their own cooperage and there is a very personal approach to their production.

Bodega Bilbaines has underground cellars, which are the largest in Haro. It was the first firm in Rioja to produce a sparkling wine by the Méthode Champenoise.

Bodegas Olarra is in Logroño and one of the 'high tech' wineries in the region I have visited.

The Moors invaded the region in 711 and, of course, wine production ceased. It was not until the Christians recaptured the country that wine again went on the table.

Logroño, the capital and administration centre for the region's wines owes its existence to the pilgrims to Santiago La Compostela because their route from the south followed through Rioja, and Logroño was the resting area. Some of the French merchants who mingled with the pilgrims settled in the region; a few of the old houses in the Barrio de Francos [French Quarter] still survive.

In San Domingo, further north-west in the region, one of the now luxurious paradores was originally a hospital for pilgrims.

Haro – in between the two cities – became the 'capital city of wine'. They had actually started exporting wine in 1805 – mainly to South America and France, but when the railway system was introduced in 1880, the export business exploded! The French were big buyers.

It was around this time when the disease *Phylloxera* struck Bordeaux – one of the first vineyard regions to be affected in Europe, and absolute panic broke out. Wine producers were desperate to find a solution – and many producers decided to cut their losses and headed south – thinking that the Pyrenees would prevent *Phylloxera* from spreading into Spain. They joined their predecessors, who had moved to Spain when powdery mildew had ruined the wine production and took their expertise into La Rioja and other northern vineyards of Spain. The grape varieties of Bordeaux were also imported and, before long, the vineyards of this region were producing wines similar to those of Bordeaux. The wines became known as 'cepa Sauternes', 'cepa Graves', etc.

[*Phylloxera* known as '*the devastator*' is a small yellow beetle – scarcely visible to the naked eye. It attacks and lives on, and spreads through, roots. It can also be carried by air from vine to vine and you can't control it by spraying, etc. You just have to watch your vines die – one by one – or take drastic steps such as pulling up all the vines. It was responsible for the devastation to almost every French vineyard at the end of the last century and it took nearly 20 years to get rid of the infected vines and replant – but replanting wasn't straightforward.

This little bug lives on American rootstock, a different species of vine to the one grown in Europe, which is immune to the bug. It was not known of when the decision was made to introduce these vines into France.

For this reason, when it came to replanting, great care was taken to make sure that this bug could never cause such havoc again. This was done by grafting European vines to the American stock, so that only the immune roots are in contact with the soil.]

All went very well until about 20 years later, at the beginning of the last century, when the dreaded disease caught up with the region and a similar sight of that witnessed in Bordeaux only a few years previous, re-occurred.

After this, wine production declined and it wasn't until the end of the First World War that it was started again. Unfortunately, in 1936 there was the Spanish Civil war and in 1939 World War II broke out. Only after the war ended, did wine production restart.

In the early 1980s, the wines from this region seemed to go right out of favour. The high quality and character of the wine, which those who appreciated and looked for each time we pulled the cork, seemed to have disappeared. This was mainly because of over-production.

It was soon realised by many of the producers that, if nothing were done to resolve this, Rioja wines would *nosedive* out of existence and be replaced by New World wines.

Extremely sad... . La Rioja has a character of its own and, once you taste this wine, you will remember it forever. The main reason is because of a longer ageing period in oak, some of which comes from the USA because of the historical connection between the two countries. This gives the wine a slightly softer flavour and with huge fruitiness and distinctive flavour the indigenous Tempranillo grape, creates the character of Riojan wine.

Fortunately, wise producers, such as Marqués de Riscal, Bodega Breton, Palacio, etc., put on their thinking hats and went into action. They looked to the vineyard, planning not only a revival of quality but also adopting new techniques to improve production.

It has worked and been proved with the wines of the 1990s. I am extremely happy about this because wine from this region gives me so much pleasure.

When you first decide to tour a wine region, it is necessary to do a 'recce' – reconnoitre. This can be most interesting but it takes time. I remember vividly my 'recci' of Rioja in the late 1980s.

As I wandered around the area, I came across a little wine stand at the side of the road. They were selling sweet wine and I was informed that this was produced at the nearby monastery.

'Curiosity killed the cat', I made my way to the monastery to find the winery. I banged on the huge door and when I didn't get a reply, opened it and diplomatically shouted 'Hello'. To my utter surprise, someone answered me in English!

Father Thomas greeted me saying there wasn't a winery in the monastery [although everyone was told that – probably good for sales ...] but there was a school, an international one, and when I mentioned the similar school in England where my friend's son went, we discovered that the two schools were connected.

Then we started talking of wine – my favourite subject! I explained that I was looking for suitable small, individual vineyards to take groups and Father Thomas offered to help. We started writing to each other and, when I informed him of the impending visit, he sent me instructions to bring the group to the monastery on a certain day and time.

We arrived, and there waiting for us was Father Thomas and a vigneron. I was told to get into the little car – with the vigneron, and the coach would follow.

We were taken to a vineyard and there to greet us were about 12 grape-pickers who had obviously finished work. We were warmly welcomed and shown around the vineyard. After this, it was back into the vehicles and on to the winery. We were absolutely stunned to find that this 'small winery' was Paternina, one of the most important Bodegas in Rioja and the Spaniard with whom I had been driving around was none other than the owner!

Someone was waiting to guide us through production and by the time we had finished, it was lunchtime – which is later in Spain.

Surprise number two then happened. We were taken to one of the oldest villages in the area and there, in the centre, an impressive oak door was opened, we all went in – and upstairs. It was a most beautifully decorated, traditionally styled, spacious sitting room. This is what they call their 'social house' for entertaining clients. Father Thomas asked me to help collect the lunch baskets from the back of the car, which the monks had prepared for us. We took these into the kitchen situated off the sitting room and prepared the plates. Ham, cheese, nuts and apples, etc. – with bread – of course.

The wines were opened, Reservas and Gran Reservas of at least 10 years old. What a feast and what a treat!

Time to go – and on to the cellar. There are **old** and **old** cellars – but this was very old and massive … seemed to go back to ancient times! We went along the tracks feeling the chill and dampness. There were bottles stacked on both sides, covered in mould, some so old that the only indication of age was the chalk mark on the stone shelf.

From here we were taken into a small private cellar – actually two but the first one was an exhibition of photographs … . Of whom? When we took a closer look, they were all of Ernest Hemingway and his family, and in the next cellar was a huge barrel and this was the family's wine supply!

It was a wonderful experience and I shall be eternally grateful to Father Thomas and the owners of Paternina for introducing me to La Rioja in this way.

Chapter 26
Portugal

Colin and Nancy Brokenshire made friends with Mary Morgan, who later shared a room with their friend Barbara. The ladies later became known as Colin's harem. On my first wine tour to France, by coach, everything went well until our arrival at Portsmouth to board the ferry.. I looked at the list of passengers to meet and there they were – all waiting patiently. After the driver had taken their baggage, and they had found a suitable seat on board they then joined the others who had gone for a walk or to have a cup of tea.

It was then that a young girl came up to me and said 'Is this a coach from Wessex Coach Travel?' I replied that it was. She then went on to tell me that her mother, a nursing sister from the Queen Mary Hospital, had booked a holiday with Wessex to go to Spain but had missed the coach! She then asked if her mother could join my tour. I explained it wasn't that type of holiday, my passengers were wine enthusiasts and her mother might not be interested in wine.

The daughter then returned to me and said that her mother would very much like to join the group. I had to explain that we might have a problem with accommodation at some of the destinations and, if this arose, all I could offer her would be the driver's cabin for the night! Mary Morgan was quite willing to take a chance, she was desperate for a holiday – so I agreed to take her. She enjoyed the holiday very much and travelled with me for the next 10 years – probably more… . She had been a widow for some time and decided that, as she now had an interest in wine, she was out to find a rich wine producer!

Every year, I offered certain wine regions and asked my regulars which area they most favoured. Colin would hold a Committee Meeting weekend in Devon and he and his harem made a decision on where they would prefer to go. It was usually the same area as everyone else had chosen.

When I suggested the Douro Valley one year, there was a little hesitation from the passengers – it was a long journey, they didn't know much about it, etc., etc., but in the end it was agreed.

I had visited Portugal many times. I found the people warm and friendly, the scenery outstanding – especially in May when you drove through the Douro and the hillside was covered in an abundance of wild flowers. Nature had been allowed to survive uninterrupted.

This was the first time I had taken a group to study Port, and it was quite an experience. Tourism hadn't really taken off in the region, and arranging a programme was difficult. It was even more difficult because, when I first announced that I was considering a tour here – there was very little interest shown, so I put it aside. Then, all of a sudden, I received several bookings.

Normally, I do a *recce* before the tour, checking the hotel and menus but on this occasion I didn't have the time. I had to find a hotel and, after studying one or two and getting all the necessary information through faxing, etc., I chose one in Regua. It was described as having bedrooms of certain dimensions – all of a fair size. The menus were interesting and it had a swimming pool. The latter wasn't that important because it was for the month of May.

On arrival, we noticed from the parking area that the swimming pool was empty and obviously had been from the year before! We went into the hotel and had a friendly reception – then we were shown to our rooms. Every room was smaller than any of those of which I had details – I was furious. No way could my passengers stay in such small rooms for four nights. I went to see the manager and told him that, if this had happened in England, I would have started proceedings to sue him under the Trades Descriptions Act. He explained that a German group had arrived before us and had taken our rooms – but not to worry – they were only staying two nights and we could take over after that! My blood boiled.

There was very little time to settle in before dinner because of our late arrival. I didn't go for dinner. Instead, I went out and had a look around. There was a little café nearby, so I popped in to ask if he knew of any other hotels in the town. Fortunately, the manager spoke French and, after explaining to me that he had spent his working life in France – which he enjoyed very much – he had returned to buy the café. I told him of my plight; he went off and made a phone call. The next thing that happened was that I was whizzed off in the back of a van. The Frenchman explained that he might be able to help and it was a pleasure as France had done so much for him!

We arrived at a large austere-looking hotel, which was closed – but not for long because a lady arrived – gave the café owner a kiss and opened up the doors. The hotel was huge, with a small reception but, once you were past that, it was just space, space, space. If I remember well, there were three floors and the bedrooms were on the balconies on each floor. The rooms were huge. It must have been built years and years ago for the rich who visited the region to look after their interests in the Port trade.

Well, what could I say… ? Although we would have to eat out because the only staff would be the lady or her assistant looking after reception, there was no question about it. Yes, can I bring my party of 16 here tomorrow?

I went back to the hotel. My group were in the restaurant and I told them not to unpack as we would be moving out tomorrow. They were delighted. I informed the manager and rushed up to the room to prepare the programme for the holiday, which included eating out every evening at the different eating establishments around.

The next morning, after breakfast, we made our way to the coach. I didn't know what to expect from the hotel manager. He was losing a lot of money and I had no intention of paying him. To my amazement, he came carrying a couple of bottles of Port, apologised profusely and said he hoped that we would come back another time! I told him that his hotel wasn't suitable for a 4-day stay, and that the only terms I would consider would be an overnight stop in the decent bedrooms!

Touring the vineyards was difficult. It was obvious that very few groups had ventured here. We were about an hour late for the first place we visited because the directions given were just useless.

I had made an appointment for a Sunday afternoon visit and, surprisingly, we found it quite easily. On arrival, we found that the gate was closed. We made the usual noises and it wasn't long before a gentleman arrived and said he regretted that there wasn't anyone who spoke English to take us around the Estate [known as a Quinta in Portugal]. I explained that we were a group of wine enthusiasts and had come a long way to find out more about the production of Port. I then said that, as he could speak English, why couldn't he show us the

Estate? His reply was 'Oh!... but I am the owner.' He softened, and said something about a brief visit.... The gates were opened and in we went. As we walked down to his mansion, I asked him serious questions about production and sales and what did he think about wine-makers in the Douro Valley producing their own wine in bottles – rather than sending it to Oporto for Port production. I could tell he was impressed with my line of questioning and especially that he was talking to a woman with wine knowledge – there weren't too many of us around in those days.

After a brief discussion with the group, he called one of his staff, chatted to her and then suggested to us that we get back in the coach and he would show us his Social House [It's where they entertain visiting people of the trade]. One or two of the group went in his Mercedes and we followed. We started to climb a hill, which was more like a mountain! Fortunately, I had my best driver, Colin Holt, for this tour, so we knew we were in capable hands. Up and up we went and round and round – the road was getting quite narrow – and we were getting a little anxious. We noticed that the peasants we met *en route* were bowing to the Mercedes as it went past. A little further on, we arrived at a gate, which was the width of the road and there were two armed guards – one on each side. The gate was opened and we continued driving. The dust from the road was orange and the coach was being sprayed continually with this dust from the Mercedes. At last we arrived at the top – on to an esplanade.

On the esplanade there were several relics from what I supposed were the Napoleonic wars! Having no knowledge of these events, I couldn't draw any other conclusion. There were several cannons and something like part of a ship's mast between two of the cannons.

He told us that this was the highest point of the Douro valley and, as we walked around, I asked him about the 'ship's mast'. That's a television mast for all my workers who live below and – wait for this – 'if the work in the vineyards isn't done to satisfaction, I turn off the television'. Now, *hold on* I thought, either we have a man who likes joking – or one who is extremely powerful.

As we continued to walk around the esplanade, we came to a helicopter pad and were informed that this was used regularly as he travelled a lot and it made it so much easier to get to the airport. By this time, I could see the entrance to the house, which was called the 'round house' – as it was. A huge hole had been dug down into the rock, big enough to hold a spiral staircase which led off to different rooms on different levels. We made our way down to the bottom where his wine cellar was. It was just an array of pigeon holes round the walls – he said there were 800 bottles stored here and he knew where to locate every bottle.

Jack challenged the gentleman by suggesting that he would point to a certain bottle and ask the owner to identify it. He did – and was correct each time! Jack was a member of 'The Last of the Summer Wine'.

Not long after I had started organising tours myself, Harold, Derek and Jack came on tour with me to France. They said they had spent many years going on holiday together around the vineyards of France, but had now decided that they didn't want the responsibility of driving, which deterred one of them each time from sampling the wines. They travelled with me for many years.

I nicknamed them 'The Last of the Summer Wine' simply because they behaved very much like the characters in the series. Harold was the wise one – always giving advice. Derek went along with everything but did not want to get too involved, and Jack came every year dressed in the same light tan leather jacket, which he wore all the time – hot or cold! They were super chaps and, my word, did they know about wine and beer, that is, real ale? They were members of CAMRA.

When we stopped for lunch in one of the towns, most of us went off to restaurants, cafes, etc. – but not the Summer Wine. They would find a local grocery store, buy the local cheese and wine and have a picnic – just as they did when they travelled alone.

We then starting making our way back up and on the way stopped off to look at some of the accommodation. The sad room was the host's bedroom, a bed with a television at the end of the bed. He admitted watching TV regularly and then we saw a photograph of his wife who had left him. Yes, he was a lonely man and he was enjoying our company. By this time, we were becoming quite 'attached' to our host and were certainly enjoying the visit.

The hours were passing, and I suggested we made our way back and perhaps taste his Port. Before leaving the 'round house' we did spend a few minutes in his 'observation tower' and the views over the Douro were magnificent.

We could hardly see the name of the coach company on the coach – it had been obliterated by the dust and we collected more dust on the way down. I advised everyone that we would be tasting a white Port and the traditional red. I said that, if we had a chance to buy, I would prefer to have the orders before the tasting to save time – it was getting late!

We were expecting to be taken to a chai or similar type of tasting room – but no – we were led into the mansion, then the beautiful dining room. Underneath two wonderful chandeliers, the table had been set with plates of local ham, cheeses and several types of nuts. What a spread – we could hardly believe our eyes! The staff came in with the Ports and served us. By this time, we were well into discussion and had lots of questions, which our host was only too willing to answer. I had to call a halt and thanked our host for a wonderful visit. He said he had enjoyed having us and when I asked if we could by a few bottles of Port, he said we could have as much as we wanted at approximately 25p a bottle! Of course, everyone wanted to increase their orders – but I refused. We had had such a wonderful visit.

A few years later, I visited the region in my capacity as a wine educator and wine writer and, during my visit, asked about the gentleman. Oh! my host said, 'he is in prison for bottling wine from other vineyards under his own name!'

We had several problems with restaurants in the town, They weren't very keen on taking groups – and let's be honest, very few were big enough! There was one we went to twice, the menus were reasonable but – there was cabbage with everything. On both evenings we had cabbage soup and this was followed by a very nice meat dish – served with potatoes and cabbage!

One night, we went to a small restaurant where the lady specialised in fish – the fish dish of Portugal, Bacalhau – salted cod! We all found a seat around the small tables and watched her take the fish out of a pail of water and proceed to cook it. It wasn't long before she served us and the fish was horrible. Not only was it as salty as could be, there was little fish on the bones! Colin Brokenshire blew his top and made some exceedingly derogatory remarks. I felt like crawling under the table, but I remembered I was in charge and had to think fast. A quick analysis was required…. . Who was to blame? – the Chef, so I went for her… I told her that we couldn't possibly eat this fish and would she please prepare veal for us. She did and, with a few glasses of local plonk, we soon forgot about the fish and started to discuss the programme for the following day.

It was strange, because, a few months later I was watching a travel programme and the expert started talking about the Douro Valley. He said it wasn't yet ready for tourism but soon would be as so many people were visiting the region. How true!

A few years later, Colin and I were having chat during another tour and he said to me, Do you know, Helen? The tour to the Douro is probably the best you've ever done – it was so different and so interesting. I wanted to add 'and the most difficult' but rested with the fact that the hard work had been worth it.

The French are great Port wine drinkers – but in a different way. They drink it as an aperitif and you will often find a choice of either ruby or white offered.

In Britain, *Port imbibing* can be quite serious. The British have become connoisseurs, and the selection of Ports available in UK far exceeds those available in France and other European countries. The reason is that we have educated our palates and know what we are looking for. If it is not available, we ask the retailer to order it for us. This is how the selection available in the store improves.

What has made the British like this? Well, believe it or not, it is all because of Claret!

The British were always Claret drinkers – in fact, Claret was the drink in Scotland before whisky came on the scene.

The English went to war with France, resulting in one-third more customs duty being charged on French wine than on Portuguese or Spanish wine. Because of this, the importation of red wine from Aquitaine ceased and traders had to look to Iberia for an alternative source.

Northern Portugal was one of the main areas simply because of our trading relationship. Alas, the red wine of Portugal was very astringent and harsh and wine buyers were becoming rather concerned. This wine was never going to replace Claret! That was until some exploration was made inland along the Douro Valley.

Two traders, in particular, arrived at a monastery and, cautiously, accepted a glass of red wine before dinner. They were elated as it was quite different from previous wines of the Douro Valley they had tasted! Their search had been worthwhile – surely being inland couldn't make such a difference! On questioning the monk, they were informed that the red wine from this region was extremely harsh, so much so that, to make it drinkable, he had found that adding a little brandy to the *must* [grape juice] before fermentation is finished considerably softened the wine... .

Well, this makes sense because what he had actually done was 'stopped fermentation' – leaving residual sugar in the wine, which results in a sweeter, fruitier wine. The drink which we call Port had been created in the Douro Valley.

It wasn't long before Port was being commercialised in Oporto. The wine from the Valley would be taken by boat [rabelo] to Oporto, blended and aged for several years according to taste, before being shipped to England.

The Methuen Treaty was signed in 1703 and this established trade between England [and in later years, the United Kingdom] and Portugal. In exchange for wine, they imported wool from us. Very fair, I would say!

Port was now being viewed in a new light, and the Scots, as well as others, were not averse to cashing in on the wine's commercial potential. Because of the troubles in France, this growing interest in Iberian wines further reinforced them on the British market. The plethora of Scots names included on the list of Port wine shippers gives some indication of the Scottish interest.

In May 1790 George Sandeman was one of the first, who like so many Scots went to London to widen his 'commercial and social' talents and soon involved himself in the trade by borrowing £300 from his father to buy a wine vault in London.

The present George Sandeman is very much involved and active in his company. I've seen him on many occasions at the trade fairs in London, and had the pleasure of dining with him in Oporto when he hosted a group wine educators from London and merchants from Chicago. I was quite taken with the Scottish 'lilt' in his accent and taken aback when he told me that he had very rarely been to Scotland!

When I say 'I'm off on a refresher course' people keep telling me it's a glorified holiday. I can assure you that it is not. It is intensive and a *hard slog*, and to prove it this part of the chapter will tell all about the last trade visit I made to Portugal.

We arrived in Oporto on the Sunday evening and were taken to our hotel, where we had an hour to settle in before dinner, which was at one of the very good fish restaurants at the docks. Our hosts were members of ICEP London, who had organised the visit and our programme was discussed.

After dinner, a weary group made their return to the hotel. I was really tired as I had been up since 5 am – having to travel from Devon.

The next morning, we were *en route* by 8.30 am. We had three visits in Vinho Verde and the Douro region, where the wine is produced, and then taken to Oporto to make Port.

Vinho Verde is a region where you find crisp white wines with a refreshing acidity. It is called 'green wine' because the grapes are harvested early. We visited Casa de Vila Verde where two other producers joined us. Later in the morning, we went to one of my favourite Quintas – Aveleda. The fantasy gardens never cease to amaze me. I'm quite familiar with their wines and when we reached the 'Grinaldi', I thought of wine enthusiasts I had brought here, not so long ago; this was their favourite. Since that time, Aveleda have introduced other styles and the quality is quite remarkable.

The sparkling wine is dry and crisp made by the traditional method. We finished lunch with the brandy aged on the estate – a sip was sufficient, enough to tell me that the quality of this had not changed. Brandy in Portugal is called Aguardente.

After lunch, we moved on to the Douro Valley. I love this wine region! Our final visit of the day was to Quinto Valado on the banks of the Douro. The production method mixes new with traditional and this Quinta is obviously preparing for future competition on the British market.

Until about 10 years ago, nearly all red wine produced in the Douro was for Port. The producers were paid very little and there was tremendous poverty in the region. In recent years, since joining the EC, a mini-*rebellion* has been quietly taking place and some producers are now making their own wine and bottling it on the estate. I witnessed the start of this on a visit a few years ago. Some estates were producing reds, which were acceptable, but many producers were experimenting with other grapes – especially white varieties. It was best described as a 'shambles' as these wine growers were really tampering with the unknown and using varieties from cooler climate regions which were not really suitable in the climate of Douro where, although they have a lot of rain, the summers are very, very hot. I am glad to say that this has changed and they are now producing good reds and a very acceptable white, 'Douro Branco'.

They are also reverting back to the traditional way of crushing grapes – using their feet! The grapes are fed into granite lagars [treading tanks] and the 'stompers' start by slow marching on the spot – this is to break the skins. When this is done, 'line dancing' and singing can commence! It is done like this as there could be a few nasty accidents by sliding about on grapes full of juice with unbroken skins. Don't worry about dirty feet …. Alcohol *kills all known germs*!

Our day didn't finish until 8.45 pm and, by the time we reached the hotel, the only thing I wanted to do was go to bed, knowing that we had an early morning start and it would be necessary to pack as we would be changing hotels yet again.

The hotel was excellent, in fact, best of the whole week! Regua has changed considerably since my last visit when a tourist stood out like a sore thumb! New hotels are popping up everywhere.

We stayed in the Douro for the first visit to Quinta Noval, where grapes are grown for Port production. We had an interesting tour of the vineyard, which included a look at a couple of rows of vines which had survived the dreadful disease, Phylloxera, at the end of the 19th century and now produces grapes which are used to make Noval's finest Port.

After a 20-min sandwich stop in Pinhao, we travelled south to the Dao [Don – with a nasal 'n'] region. Until recently, these were some of the only red wines worth buying in Portugal – how things have changed! The tasting at Quinta Carvalhais, arranged by Sogrape, was superbly correct. We sat down in separate open cubicles and the different styles of wines were poured into each of six glasses on a white table top underneath which was fitted a spittoon with its own cold water tap. The wines we tasted were as expected. One or two were exceptionally good. An educator was chosen at each venue to give a vote of thanks and it was here where I said 'thank you' on behalf of the members. I explained that my tours to Portugal had been to the Douro Valley only – with a quick supermarket stop in Dao on the return journey. During the visit I had decided that a visit to Quinta Carvalhais would be included in all future tours.

The last visit of the day to Quinta des Roques was a wonderful experience. The Roques family have been making wine for nearly a century, at first for home use and later on for the Co-operatives. All changed at the beginning of 1980 – they decided to produce their own wines.

We were taken into the winery where a table had been arranged for the tasting. The whole family was there – from grandfather down! The ladies of the family had prepared an array of local dishes, cheeses, sausages and other delicacies. Grandfather looked proudly at his son who proceeded to describe the wines.

They were superb, aromatic and fruity. The white wine gave hints of tropical fruit and the reds were rich in colour and body with the concentrated aroma of blackberries and raspberries – complex wines, velvety on the palate.

The only problem the family now has is producing enough wine for the demand!

We stayed in Viseu for the night, but the arrival at the hotel was so late that no one had the strength to visit the town.

Day three was in the Bairrada region, known for its ever improving red wines. The principal grape is the 'Baga' – a difficult grape that can give an acidity and dryness that makes the wine harsh. Many wine producers think twice about using this grape, but not Luis Pato, the King of Bairrada! His wines were amazingly good, *fruit driven*, good tannin and full bodied – and this was our opinion from new wines drawn straight from the barrel. Luis Pato is a genius! Rebelling against tradition, this man is taking the best methods of the *new world* 'high tech' and using this in a traditional way. He is creating WOW Wines!

He had arranged lunch at the local restaurant, and his wine went perfectly with the celebrated 'suckling pig'.

Our second visit was to a large wine exporter of all Portuguese wines, Cava Alianca. The visit was hosted by Mario, chief of marketing, and his enthusiasm was infectious as his commentary on the wines from different regions was most interesting.

Our stay that evening was in Coimbra, the old University city. We didn't get to the hotel until after 9.30 pm and some of the group, desperate to have a look around Coimbra, took a taxi late at night – but unfortunately didn't see very much.

The hotel was a Relais Château built in the 18th century and Arthur Wellesley – better known as the Duke of Wellington – stayed here and fell in love with the gardens, so much so that two trees were named after him.

On the fourth day we had an early start to study the wines of the Ribatejo region where the predominant grape is the 'Periquita'. As well as grapes, there is an abundance of oranges, lemons, melons, etc. It was heartbreaking to see all the fallen oranges on the ground.

The first visit was to Fonta Bela. A busy morning, tasting 21 wines [a lot at that time of the day!]. We were fortunate to have José Neiva, described as Portugal's most ubiquitous wine-maker, to tell us about his methods of wine-making. I absorbed every word and was pleased that he joined us for lunch when we were able to ask more questions.

Our afternoon visit was to Quinta Abrigada, a family-run estate. The weather had been terrible all week and it was pouring with rain as we drove into the estate. The coach was taken right to the front door to help keep us dry. Once inside, we were shown around, then taken into the main reception room where a large wood fire was burning in a huge fireplace. We sat around a large table where we tasted and evaluated the wines. These wines are exported to Germany and Sweden.

We arrived in Lisbon at about 7.30 pm and were off to dinner at 8 pm. That evening we ate with the representatives of ICEP Lisbon.

The fish was excellent – but the event of the evening was the *vinious fracas* which started with the first glass. It was 'Doura Branca', deep yellow in colour – quite different from the pale excellent example on the first night. It was oxidised, so we complained. The next one was slightly paler but not right. We asked to see the bottle to check the age: **1992**! Out of date and should never have been in the cellar! We revealed exactly who we were and a different wine was served. Shock upon shock: it was well and truly corked! This brought the manager to the table, who changed it immediately – but the second wine was also corked! It was now embarrassing for all, and the manager again appeared, most apologetic – it wasn't his fault. A different wine was served immediately, which was most acceptable but unfortunately, by this time, we had finished dinner!

On return to the hotel, I treasured the thought that we would be staying in the same hotel for more than one night.

The next morning was an early start for the long journey to the Alentejo region, where some of the elegant complex rich red wines are still made in clay amphoras – taking you back to Roman times … .

We arrived at Herdade do Esporao at about 11 am and were warmly welcomed by David Baverstock, who was responsible for the construction of the winery for Cliff Richard. Here, we saw how this modern winery had been built on the side of a hill, cleverly planned on different levels for receiving the grapes, pressing machines, vats and ageing barrels. Gravity with a capital 'G' is the word for this Quinta! David gave us a detailed explanation of the whole production. The tasting was most interesting – rustic Portuguese wines with traces of Australian 'high tech' production. These wines were quite different.

The Quinta has been specifically built for tourism in the wine country. There is a lovely restaurant, sitting rooms and terraces. Perfect for the day out!

The day was not yet finished. From here we went on to meet one of the most outstanding Portuguese wine producers, Joao Portugal Ramos. Female educators were warned: he was handsome! I noticed he had the same blue eyes as some of the other men we had met *en route* and adding the dark hair and tanned skin to these eyes made him very attractive … and so were his wines! I especially liked the wine produced from the 'Bastardo' grape. Later, a buffet was served and his wife joined us. We didn't get back to Lisbon until very late.

Saturday morning was a special day; we didn't leave the hotel until 8.30 am! As well as this, we were told it was going to be a shorter day – allowing time to shop.

Setubal is well known outside Portugal for Molscatel and Periquite wines. The first visit was to JM Fonseca in Setubal. This was an interesting visit as the building with a beautiful façade was a museum in itself. We tasted seven different styles – ending with the famous Moscatel. Oranges and honey impregnated the palate.

The next visit was nearby – a large modern winery, with yet another gorgeous wine-maker! He spoke very good English and delighted in showing his winery to us and explaining the methods of production. We were then taken to lunch – which I didn't expect, and the main course was the renowned Bacalhau, [cod] – well, one of the 700 recipes! The pudding was a Swiss roll type of dessert, but it had been made solely of eggs. We had been served something similar the day before when the eggs had been cooked and beaten, with sugar added and sprinkled with cinnamon.

We didn't get back to Lisbon until around 5.30 pm! No shopping but a little time to relax before dinner in a 'Fado' restaurant. This was quite an experience as the coach had to drop us just outside the old quarter and we saw something of the oldest part of Lisbon as well as enjoying some of the traditional music of Portugal. It was very late when we left the restaurant because each time we 'made the effort', another singer would come on stage and you are not allowed to move until she/he has finished! A synchronised attempt had to be made… .

The next morning there was a 'wake-up' call at 5.45 am. The return flight was at 8 am.

I was absolutely exhausted but what a wonderful experience! I had learned such a lot. I feel such progress has been made in Portugal and very soon you are going to see quality Portuguese wines on the market. In a couple of years' time there is going to be a 'vincanic' eruption in this country and I have just spent a week in the 'rumblings'!

Chapter 27
Italy

When I am asked to talk generally about an individual wine country, I have given up trying to go into any great depth about the regions as each one is so interesting and I never seem to have enough time! This is particularly so with Italy, the largest producer of wines, with 20 wine regions and, at the last count, 240 DOCs [wines of particular reputation and worth] and 12 zones of DOCGs [wines of particular reputation and worth – guaranteed authenticity]. According to the WSET publication, there are in excess of 1000 different varieties of vines in Italy! This should explain my reluctance to say more than a few words about each of the country's wine regions in one session.

I always seem to have problems when organising an Italian wine tour. I start to arrange my programme, contact the vineyards and the next thing is I receive communications suggesting that I have an agent to organise the wine holiday. It is difficult to explain to these people that I don't want an agent and once I got really angry. They wrote to me to say that it would be better if I had a wine tour guide from this particular agent. I answered by challenging them about their knowledge of wine compared with mine. They never answered.

When touring Italy, we drive through France and make an overnight stay in Annecy. The next day is a drive taking in some fantastic scenery through Mont Blanc, to the Val d'Aosta, where the hills are covered in vineyards and wines are produced from Swiss, French and German grapes. Because of the history of the area – on the border of France and Italy and once belonging to France – the French language is spoken and labelling on the wine bottles is usually in both French and Italian.

As you drive out of Aosta, you arrive in Piedmont, where some of the very best and most expensive wines are to be found. This region, with Tuscany, is my favourite Italian wine region and Piedmont has all the big 'BARS' Barola, Barbaresco [DOCG], and Barbera d'Asti. The wines are very, very good, but unfortunately, they are difficult to find because of their exclusivity. The last time we were in this region we were unable to buy wines at some of the wineries because they were sold out and in a couple of *cases* – [not *viniously]*, most of the wines of the following year's harvest had been ordered!... This is also the region where the extremely popular sparkling wine [*Spumante]* is produced in Asti.

Finding a hotel in a spot convenient for touring from can be difficult. We were very fortunate on this occasion. The very modern hotel was near Asti and the rooms were large. They were obviously very pleased to have my small group because we were very spoilt in the restaurant. Every evening there were delightful local dishes prepared for us and the waiter enjoyed telling the group about each dish. The only problem was that Piedmont is a rice region and to put it mildly, we had a lot of it... .

Going around the vineyards was interesting but the visits lacked the ambiance of the French 'degustation'. They told you about the production, you tasted the wine and that was it at most places. There is nothing more delightful when touring vineyards than finding out the little differences in each wine producer's method of production – and we didn't seem to have enough discussion to find out much. There is one thing I can say for certain: the reds from here are wonderful and when you are told that some wines smell of violets – these are the wines. It wasn't just a hint of violets – in some cases , it was like holding a whole bunch to your nose!

The most enjoyable Italian tours were to Tuscany, I did two – one after the other.

Tuscany – together with Piedmont – gives us the prestigious wines of Italy but Tuscany has something else to offer and that is tremendous scenery and history. This was a very popular tour and I enjoyed every minute of it! As well as the wine, there are so many places of interest such as Florence, Siena and San Gimignano – a name which is always a devil to get your mouth around! [Pronounced 'san jim in yano'.] A superb Tuscan white wine is produced here and is called Vernaccia di San Gimignano. Tuscan whites rarely enjoyed much prestige in the past but this little wine has made a revival and is quite delightful.

This is the home of the Sangiovese grape which gives us the the very popular wine, Chianti, found in all Italian restaurants, but the best Chianti comes from the heart of the region and is called Chianti Classico [DOCG], which is sometimes referred to as the 'Italian Bordeaux'. The black cockerel is on the label of the bottles of this wine so you can always recognise the wine.

Brunello di Montalcino DOCG is the greatest wine from this region. It ages really well and the town of Montalcino is situated just south of Siena.

We stayed in a lovely hotel, high in the hills of Tuscany, the proprietor had never accommodated groups before and the reason was obvious, the hotel was small and difficult to find. We enjoyed every moment of our stay, the food was traditional and, each evening, the manager would talk to us about the different wines of the region.

One night, we discussed Brunello di Montalcino DOCG and it was interesting to hear that the Italians prefer this wine when it has really aged. Some in the group thought the wine he suggested as perfect for drinking was really on its way out! But then my memory went back to the Dordogne where a lot of the older men preferred their wine at this stage.

Vino Nobile di Montepulciano was the first wine to have the DOCG. It has been produced as a religious wine since the 13th century. It is produced from the Prugnola Gentile grape, which is a species of the Sangiovese. This wine can age 20 to 30 years! Its home is in the southern part of Tuscany.

A speciality of the region is the oxidised dessert wine, Vin Santo – well worth trying … .

There is a great diversity of climate – a difference of 10 degrees from north to south and, because of this, there are several methods of growing vines. In the north you will see lots of vineyards where the high trellising method is used, whereas further south you will see the more usual Guyot or Cordon method.

In the Veneto region there are more important wines, such as Soave, Valpolicella Amarone and Bardolino. The latter, I have been told, is a great favourite of Prince Charles. It is here where you find the Recioto della Vallpolocella made from semi dried grapes. The grapes are laid out on trays until they are almost dry. This results in a sweet red wine. When we visited Masi, Italian wine producers – owned by Americans

– we were able to see the trays and taste the wine. Surprisingly, some of the traditional red wine drinkers found it quite delightful. To me, it was interesting, but too sweet for my palate… .

Winston Churchill must have imbibed some of these wines because he spent a lot of time painting on Lake Garda, which is near this wine region.

I visited Lake Garda not long after the wine scandal when two men died because of 'doctored wine'. I remember seeing notices, similar to a certificate on shop windows stating that the premises didn't sell any of the wine in question.

What was it all about? Some cheap wine producers had decided to up the alcohol content of their wine by adding methanol.

The two men who died were alcoholics and had obviously drunk a huge quantity of this adulterated wine.

On a visit just north of the lake to a sparkling wine producer, who supplied fizz to the night clubs of Paris, the owner told me that this had happened at a very bad time because the Italian wines were doing well on the market before this scandal, which had set them back at least 5 years! All very sad… .

The Apulia region lies on the 'heel' of Italy and has a rather warmer climate. Some very good average wines are now being produced there, and one that opened up the region was Salice Salentino.

Chapter 28
Australia

Australians celebrate their special day on 26th January – not only in Australia, but all over the world.

The annual Australian Wine Trade Fair is held in London on this day, and anyone who has connection with Australian wines will be there.

These wines are known as New World wines and when we talk of 'New World' wine-making, we're referring to new methods of production, which have been created by using high technology –introducing new methods of vinification [wine-making] and styles of vineyard care procedures.

Before the Australians had 'high tech', the red wines tasted 'burnt' – simply because the grapes had too much sun in the vineyards and much of the white wine produced was flabby, very little aroma on the nose, or fruit on the palate. This type of wine has gone forever.

'New World' uses very modern machinery and 'high tech' to create wines, which are ready for drinking when they reach the wine market. Some are capable of maturing with age but not in the same way as the traditional wines.

Cleanliness is high in priorities – everything must be sterile!

White wine has benefited most from this revolution. 'Cool fermentation' gives a much fruitier, fresher wine than before and machine picking plays a very important part. It enables harvesting to be done early in the morning – before the sun comes up – so the grapes can be brought in at a cool temperature, which is vital in this new method of production.

The Australians put Chardonnay on the market! With 'high tech' the wines have beautiful aromas. They are fresh and full of flavour and are a great favourite with white wine drinkers. However, a few years ago, it went out of favour and oak ageing was the problem.

Chardonnay is most versatile and can take oak ageing of a few months – or longer. The trouble was how much oak and whether the barrel should be lightly, medium or heavy toasted. Oak 'chippings' were even introduced! It had got out of hand. In some cases you couldn't taste the fruit for the oak and there was so much being produced! This was when I heard the phrase 'YAC' wines [yet another Chardonnay!].

Sales plummeted and it was soon noticed. The overuse of oak was rectified and suddenly, 'unoaked' Chardonnay was available and the new oaked Chardonnays were certainly much improved. The wine-makers have now got it right!

Australia has created full-bodied, fruit-driven red wines. They are drinkable at a very early age because they haven't got the amount of tannin found in the more traditional wines, which gives the wine longevity. New World 'reds' are for drinking young; although some produced now are ageing beautifully. This style has revolutionised and changed the mode of red wine drinking in recent years.

The history of Australian wines is also of great interest.

When Napoleon's emissary visited the country in 1801 – to check England's new colony – the report stated that 'Australia should become the vineyard of Britain'. If only Napoleon could see what has happened since then … . He accused us of being 'a nation of shopkeepers and tea drinkers'. Little did he know that, during the following century, we would become a nation of Australian wine drinkers and that the French wine market would suffer greatly because of this development!

It was in 1805 that James McArthur planted the first vines in Australia and in 1815 he visited Europe and returned with a various grape varieties. In 1822, 32 gallons of red wine were exported to UK.

In 1824, James Busby [born in Edinburgh] went to Australia – intent on developing the wine industry. He had already studied wine-making in France. In 1831, a year after his first book on wine was published, he returned to Europe – amassing 665 different named grape varieties from Spain and France – many were duplicated. Out of the 570 varieties, which actually arrived in Sydney and were planted in the Botanical Gardens, 362 were successful. This collection, along with the others brought in previously, formed the backbone of the Australian wine industry.

Busby planted his vineyard in Hunter Valley, New South Wales; in 1834 vines were planted in Victoria and 3 years later in South Australia.

It was during this decade that famous names were established including Christopher Penfold, Henry Lindeman and John Francis Brown, a grandfather, who had dreams of owning a vineyard and in 1885 planted his first vines. Four years later, he tasted his 'own' wine. Today, three generations are involved in making some of the premier wines to come out of Australia.

At the recent Wine Trade Fair in London, I had the pleasure of meeting Tim Adams, another terrific wine-maker from 'down under'. I can't remember whether he won seven or nine awards. I was asked to taste a few of the winning wines because he didn't agree with the decision made on the wine that achieved the gold medal. To my surprise, I selected the same one he thought should have gained the great *Medaille D'Or*, but they were all exceptionally good.

These families, with many others, are among the well-known producers of today in a country that is the 11th largest producer in the world.

Although Australian wines now have to share their glory with those of other New World wine regions such as Chile, which is producing some stunning reds, California, South Africa, Argentina and New Zealand with wonderful white wines, Australia still has the 'lion's share' of the British market.

This country is the origin of New World Wines and Australia's wine industry should also be celebrated on that 26th of January.

Chapter 29
The Whisky File

Introduction

As a Scot, I have always had an interest in Whisky, but my knowledge has been limited as I haven't ever had the pleasure of tasting many of the large variety available on the market.

I studied the subject for exam purposes but this textbook knowledge slowly faded into the past as I continued in wine and spirits, concentrating on wine.

A 'blended' was my usual tipple – with an occasional Malt. This has all changed since my recent visit to Islay to study the production of Malt in much more depth.

I have been fortunate enough to participate in a 4-day study course of Malt Whisky on Islay. The Master of Malt, John Lamond who is also a member of the Association of Wine Educators, led the course.

As the barley is steeped in water, my textbook knowledge was immersed in *developer*, which resulted in the most wonderful film of the production of Malt Whisky, thus replacing the limited knowledge of the subject that I had held in the past.

What is Malt Whisky?

It is a whisky made from barley that has been screened for any foreign matter such as stones or metal. It is then soaked for 2 or 3 days in tanks of water known as steeps.

The wet barley is then spread out on a solid floor [malting floor] and allowed to germinate. This can take up to 12 days – depending on the season of the year. Temperature and rate of germination must be kept under strict control.

At the appropriate time, germination must be stopped and this is done by drying the barley in a kiln. The floor of the kiln is perforated – it looks just like wire mesh, and this allows the hot air and smoke from the peat furnace to percolate upwards through the grain.

Peat is a form of fuel used in Scotland. There are two types of peat, marsh peat – of decomposed mosses, and forest peat – of decomposed leaves. It is the marsh peat that is used for whisky. In Islay it is cut from the ground under the heather, about two shovels deep, either mechanically or by hand. It is then left to semi-dry and is then chopped up into 'easy to handle' bricks. No one could fail to notice its smoky, pungent sweet smell as it burns. I should point out here that, during my 4-day educational visit, my clothes and hair were delicately perfumed with this 'aroma of Scotland'.

When the barley is dry, it is then ground in a mill. The end product is called grist, which resembles flour with bits in it! The bits can be large or small, in other words, it can be fine or coarse according to the demand of the distiller.

The grist is then put into a large circular container called a mash tun. Hot water is poured on to it and the grist is mixed by an arm with turning forks attached to a circulating central cylinder. This is when the starch is converted into sugar liquid known as wort. The liquid is then drawn from the remaining solids which are later used for cattle feed.

The wort is very hot and has to be cooled down before passing into larger vessels called washbacks. It is in the washback that the wort is fermented by yeast. It doesn't take long to start and there's froth everywhere – especially if the washback hasn't been sealed properly!

After about 48 hours the result is a weak form of alcohol liquid, known as 'wash' and it is from this liquid that the distiller ultimately produces Malt Whisky.

The liquid is distilled in huge copper kettles, usually twice, sometimes three times. In the case of Springbank in Campbeltown two and a half times. The first 'run-off' is called foreshots and the last called feints. The procedure sounds quite complicated but is really quite straightforward. Great skill is required and this results in pure alcohol being given off and what is known as low wines. The latter is then distilled again.

Whisky is usually about 70% alcohol by volume when distilled – slightly higher in the case of triple distilled whisky. The remainder of volume is water from steam condensed with the distillation. It is a clear colourless spirit.

After distillation, it is then put into casks to mature. The longer a whisky remains in cask, the more flavour it will acquire and the less spirit will remain. A 21-year-old whisky will therefore usually have more complex flavours than a 12-year-old whisky – but it will be more expensive.

All the malts we tasted were superb – and varied from very peaty to slightly peaty. Ardbeg was definitely at the top of the scale, with loads of peatiness on the palate, whereas Isle of Jura was quite different, subtle peaty traces on the nose, a sweetish palate and light, soft body, with a long finish and slightly salty tang.

Chapter 30
Buying A Vineyard

More than once, I have witnessed on the programme 'Who wants to be a millionaire', when a contestant has been asked 'What would you do if you won the jackpot?' the answer has been 'I'd like to buy a vineyard in France', and so many people seem to have this dream!

One of my regular travellers from Portsmouth, a nursing sister, has often said to me that her dream was to marry a vineyard owner. Owning a vineyard isn't all it is cracked up to be... it's hard work and, because of the demands made on you, you sometimes feel like a prisoner! You have to be around all the time during the growing season – there is always something to see to – such as machines going wrong, supplies coming in and the infernal bureaucracy which can drive you crazy. Each month you have to send in a record of all the wine that has been sold and, in the case of bulk sales, this has to be accompanied by the papers of transport, giving details of when it left the château, matriculation of the vehicle, etc. If the wine has been given its AOC, this also must be noted. This 'register' must be taken to the local office before the fifth of the following month. Too bad if you are on holiday! On top of this, an annual stock-taking is done once a year and this form has to be handed in with the register.

I have often been asked for advice on buying a vineyard. This needs a lot of thought. I've seen people rush into it, ignoring the responsibility they are taking on and my advice to anyone contemplating this would be as follows:

a.   If you want to make a small profit, you must be able to put in a huge investment. A vineyard requires money to be continually poured into it!

b. You must have a knowledge of the French language.

c. The bureaucracy is top heavy in France, to which the rules must be strictly adhered. It is no good moaning about it – it has to be accepted along with the better climate, the gastronomic delights accompanied by wine at reasonable prices and all the other joys that have attracted thousands of British to uproot and move to the south-west region of France.

d. It is futile buying a vineyard unless you have money to invest in it. No matter how good the machinery, etc., included in the sale, it will have to be maintained and replaced. Just imagine a tractor or grape-picking machine going wrong during a vendange [harvest] – it's got to be repaired immediately and can be a costly business. It is most unlikely that you will be able to hire one as they are in great demand.

e. It is wise to be able to invest yourself rather than have investors; the latter take a good chunk of your profit on wine, which won't be great in such a competitive region where wines prices have a 'ceiling' in the lower range. In some cases, the shareholders may own part of your property and, in this case, if you ever want to sell, a lot of the profit will go to them – assuming they are willing to sell!

f. A British wine grower will have more difficulty getting on to the French market and a French wine producer will have equal difficulty getting on to the British, Belgian and Netherlands' markets. These markets are mainly interested in bulk buying at low prices, and small vineyards such as those being bought by the British don't stand a chance in this field of competition.

g. It is easy to grow grapes, I agree, but growing successfully for wine production has its problems. You have to be constantly alert to disease and bad weather conditions, such as hailstorms, frost, etc.

h. The regional federation is there to support wine producers of small vineyards. Their teams of oenologists and analysts will advise you throughout the vinification, but you have a responsibility, which can absorb a fair amount of your time. Samples have to be taken in every few days, and on receiving the results, the wine-maker has to adjust the wine accordingly.

i.   The federation is also the body which will approve your wine for 'AC'. Without this, your wine has to be downgraded and this will affect the selling price. It is not necessary for your wine to 'pass' the first time – you have more than one 'try' – but each time your wine goes for approval, it costs.

j.   Another big factor is the cost of employing people. There is a minimum wage, but this is nearly doubled with the tax for Social Security.

My advice would be: buy a vineyard of a size that is easy to manage, make sure that there are one or two properties on the land, such as a house that doesn't need too much restoration for you and one or two barns which could be made into gîtes to give you a 'bread and butter' income.

Chapter 31
The Americans

I enjoy taking small groups around the vineyards of Bordeaux and aimed towards private tours.

In 1994 I had a phone call from an American who had found my name in the *Decanter*. He explained that he knew nothing about wine and wanted to learn so that he could talk wine socially. He was interested in going to Burgundy. I explained that I would not be going to Burgundy until November and if he wanted to study wine in April/May, I would be quite willing to do a 5-day course for him in Bordeaux. He wasn't interested so I thought that was the last I would hear from him.

Two months later he phoned again saying that he had decided to study Bordeaux. I agreed and the programme was organised. Bordeaux Airport was in its primitive state, one departure hall and a tiny arrival area.

As I prepared for his visit, I became a little apprehensive – realising it was going to be 5 days with someone I hadn't met – and alone! The panic got worse and, as the day approached, I made the decision to 'vet' him on his arrival and, if I were in any doubt, he would take the next plane back to London.

The day arrived and I went to the airport. The arrival lounge had one or two pillars supporting the ceiling and it was behind one of these I hid and watched for an American to arrive. Henry was instantly recognisable, tall, slim, wearing jeans – his American-type hat confirmed I had the right person. 'Well', I said to myself, 'he looks quite safe!'

We went to collect the hire car and started work immediately.

During the next 4 days, we visited Medoc, St Emilion, Sauternes, Graves, Loupiac and, of course, Pomerol. I have Henry to thank for my name 'winewoman'. He called the office one day and asked for 'his winewoman' and the name stuck. I then added it to my email address and website addresses. Henry's emails to me are Dear WW and I end with WW.

Every morning we would meet for breakfast at 7.30 am, leave the hotel just after 8 am and head for our chosen region. Henry would sit there with his notebook and pen, writing furiously, and I would be driving and explaining vinification and viticulture of each area. We stopped at several vineyards where Henry tasted and I spoke about the cepage, age, etc.

We did stop for lunch – or should I say snacks – Henry would still be asking questions and writing. We never got back to the hotel before 8 pm [Americans want their money's worth...]. By that time it was too late to have a decent dinner so, again, it was self-service or a bar snack.

By the second day I was peeved off! This is not the way I'm used to eating. French dinner was very special, sitting down about 8 pm and just letting the evening roll on, enjoying good freshly cooked food, accompanied by wine. Did this American know anything about the French way of life?

On the third day, I lost my voice! It went slowly – but surely. So many questions to answer – so much explaining to do – and there was no let-up from sun-up to sun-down!

After a very unsettled night, I phoned my friend Christianne to ask if her husband could come out for the day to help me with this very demanding character. Jean Pierre Canot, retired bank executive of Credit Agricole has a terrific knowledge of the wines of Bordeaux. Before joining the bank, he had studied oenology.

It took ages for Christianne to understand what I was talking about, as my voice kept breaking during the conversation. At last, she realised my problem and apologised profusely, saying that J-Pierre had gone off to eastern Europe to advise on financial matters in an under-developed region. My heart sank.

I plodded on, hoping that the questions would become less – but no way – he was out for his pound of flesh!

I was very pleased to say goodbye to him at the airport.

I later learned that his wife, one of the vice-presidents of Shell Chemicals, had told most of the staff about Henry's arrival at Bordeaux Airport and my concerns.

It took me several days and copious amounts of throat linctus to recover.

Henry's life had changed – he was now a 'Wine Expert'! Mind you, I felt I had managed to condense 20 years of learning into 5 days.... . But this is typical of Americans, a little knowledge.... .

It wasn't long before he contacted me again, this time for 'wine buying'.

I met him at Bordeaux and we went buying. Supermarkets, wine stores, vineyards wherever.... . Henry was starting a Collection. At that time, Fran, his wife was returning to the States to work, so this wine could be included in the shipment. J-Pierre came with us to assist. Henry spent nearly £7000 on wine and it had all to be taken back to my home in Bergerac to be stored.

Several months later, a neighbour kindly packed the wine on a pallet and it was collected for transporting to London, for onward shipment to Texas.

This was the start of an established relationship. Henry visits us in France, and he and my husband are very good friends.

Since this time, I have accompanied other Americans and one small group in particular I shall never forget.

It was a party of eight – all from Texas and all in oil – in fact, they were friends of Henry's who had asked me to arrange a visit for them.

They arrived at the Hôtel de Normandie, near the Maison du Vin, in dribs and drabs. Four had driven from Paris and another two from Bordeaux airport. Henry had arrived a day earlier to help with collecting the vehicule, etc.

We had 4 days of visiting Medoc, St Emilion, Sauternes and even Bergerac! Every evening we met in the hotel foyer to go out to dinner in one of the many restaurants in Le Vieux Quartier – which was a stone's throw from the hotel. One night, we visited the Restaurant of 'Ploucs' [country peasants]. We started off with soup then a wooden basket of raw vegetables was put on the table – with a couple of loaves of bread! After this, another wooden basket arrived – with loads pieces of meat, various sausages, ham, etc. By this time, we were roaring with laughter as we *did* look like a group of peasants who had stopped by the wayside for lunch, brought out a little knife to cut the sausage and veg, then wash it down with a glass or two of red wine.

This was when the accordionist arrived. He sang some of my favourite French 'street songs' as I call them, then when he found out we spoke English, we had a rendering of 'It's a long way to Tipperary'. The evening was hilarious, tears were running from our eyes – and I can't remember what the main course was!

The Americans loved the history related to the wine trade of Bordeaux – they couldn't get enough of it and I was still talking about it over dinner!

They were leaving Bordeaux on the Saturday, and the ladies asked if they could do some shopping on the Friday [Henry had told them all about the *Mephisto* shoes]. Henry had suffered with his back pain in the States and had surgery. The surgeon had advised him to wear Mephisto – which are very expensive in America. When Henry came over to France, he bought several pairs and swears by them.... .

On Friday morning, we set off shopping and the first stop was *Aigle*, as the group decided they needed good 'rain jackets'. We walked into the shop where there were several assistants behind the counter – who didn't say a word. Tom was at the front of the group; he opened his mouth and in a true Texan accent, burst forth with 'We want to see your best rain jackets'.

To my amusement, I watched a sudden dash of the staff to our aid … and they spoke perfect English! Different styles of jackets were shown, fleecy linings, hats and gloves. The Americans bought one of each! Neil and his wife said that they wanted to buy a jacket for their daughter – who was about my size, so doing my duty I tried the selected jacket on – with a fleece underneath. Yes it fitted very well – and then Neil announced that this was a present for me because they had enjoyed themselves so much!

The 'presents' didn't stop there – I was also treated to a pair of Mephisto walking shoes. Such comfort – it's like walking on clouds!

This was certainly a trip to remember!

Chapter 32
Closing

After writing all this, I am beginning to wonder why I did what I did. As someone who led quite a different life, sheltered in many ways as military life is; one spent one's days looking after children, going to cocktail parties, giving and attending dinners, etc., etc. I enjoyed giving dinner parties because I enjoyed cooking. My daughter also enjoyed the dinner parties. In fact, one of the few compliments I received from her was that 'I was good at organising dinners'.

I made a point of not getting too involved with the coffee mornings and the curry lunches and *'drinky poohs'*. I found the repetition of the same small talk rather boring. Always having worked during my married life, the escape was easy – except when we went abroad. The social life was tremendous in the Far East but even there I found voluntary work in the Cheshire Homes – this was a heartbreaking experience!

Working both in and outside military life was a great advantage to me when we finally started our new life in France, I was able to cope with the change.

But, something obviously went wrong, my brain cells derived no satisfaction from building walls, mixing cement, carrying water from the well to the house, cooking from morning to night…. . Yes, I needed more, so, with the declining marriage, plus my insatiable thirst to know more about wine and necessity to work, the truth is – I was *driven* into a world I knew absolutely nothing about.

From the start, I didn't like the coach travel. After a couple of trips on the same route it became boring. Previous to this, the only coach I had been on was for transfers in airports! The only pleasure I derived from coach travel was meeting up with people who had become my friends.

The coaches supplied by the tour operators were often of poor standards – some hadn't been through a MOT inspection for several years. I was quite shocked when I read in the papers that one of the companies being prosecuted was actually a company used for my wine tours! This all changed when I started organising my own tours. Roger Garrett and his son made sure that the coach and the driver were suitable for my type of tour.

Trying to cope with all the rules and regulations of coaches became unbearable in the end. I didn't feel it necessary to be included under such stringent laws for carrying a maximum of 16 people – but rules have to be obeyed. The biggest crunch was when fuel prices started soaring and also the cost of coach hire. I just couldn't cope with it and there was no way I was going to increase the price of the tours or the number of passengers to cut down costs – my wine tours were like house parties – and 16 guests were quite enough!

I was relieved when I changed direction and starting teaching and advising. I have visited nearly every wine region in France, Northern Spain, Mosel and Rhine in Germany, Piedmont, Tuscany and other small wine regions in Italy, which is of great benefit when teaching.

Since becoming a wine educator, I have educated in many diverse ways, e.g., teaching passengers on tour, wine presentations, clubs and societies, organising dinner parties, hotel management colleges and in hotels where staff were lacking in knowledge. If you are a wine drinker or associated with the trade – there is nothing more satisfying than knowing something about the subject.

I remember one time when I was giving a tasting and I went to a local wine shop for a couple of bottles of wine I wanted to add to the presentation. I asked the girl if she had this wine in stock – the reply was 'Do you know the code bar?' Another perfect candidate for wine education!

I look upon this book as my 'Phase two' in life and I hope I have succeeded in doing what I aimed to do, amuse you, interest you and, most importantly, educate you.

At the beginning of the Phase, it was a time when I have never felt so low – and so alone – in my life, but it is absolutely amazing what strength you acquire in such circumstances and my goal was certainly to survive.

Now, of course, I have entered Phase three – still immersed in the world of wine but in a quite different facet, sharing the managment of a 33-hectare vineyard property in the heart of the Dordogne.

The wine tours are finished but I still take small private parties to Burgundy and Bordeaux. The Burgundy weekend is very special and about 12 of us meet up each year to celebrate. Celia and Ian Markey are two of the group and they have travelled with me for several years.

Celia is the Registrar I refer to in one of the chapters; she is a Jamaican, tall, vivacious and always laughing. The first tour they took with me was to Burgundy and I shall never forget what happened after our arrival in Beaune, we all met for dinner. Celia walked into the dining room wearing a dress of electric blue with a hint of green, she looked stunning – the colour was perfect for her dark skin. She and Ian sat down and it wasn't long before Ian started chatting and describing something to us. His hands went up in the air and the next thing we saw was his glass of wine in Celia's lap – the dress dripping. Celia laughed, got up, left the room and within minutes returned wearing yet another glamorous dress – still laughing!

Behind this very happy person is also a sad one because, as she told us, one morning after saying goodbye to her first husband as he left for work, 20 minutes later she received a telephone call to say he had died in a car accident. Ian was a friend of the family and comforted her during the difficult period. A few years later, they married.

These few private visits can be made to fit in with my new life which is a very busy one – helping my husband manage the 33-hectare estate of vineyards and plum orchard in which we have 1500 plum trees; we dry the plums on the estate, in huge ovens – converting them into prunes.

There are problems, such as the trials and tribulations of dealing with Frenchmen who resent women who know more about wine than they do, the French bureaucracy and dealing with *les fonctionnèrs* who come to check on the workers. It was only 2 weeks ago that a plum producer in a village nearby got so fed up with these visits that, when the two civil servants arrived on his property, he shot them both – they died immediately. The producer tried to kill himself – but failed. Now all such inspectors in the Dordogne have to be accompanied by policemen.

Yes, it could drive you insane, not to mention the hunting and shooting rights, village fêtes and organising a pit stop for the annual activity day in the Dordorgne – as well as running a wine school in Bergerac. Well that's another story…

Chapter 33
The Glossary

Bernard and Noreen travelled with me many times. He was a retired teacher and Noreen spent as much time as possible with her children and riding horses.

Bernard and I spent a lot of chatting about wine because he had a real interest in the subject and I watched his reactions when tasting or visiting a winery – he really appreciated learning. I think his subject was biology, so this was probably the reason why. They both enjoyed the company – in fact, even now they keep in touch with a few of the travellers.

I think Noreen's favourite holiday was the wine tour to the Loire Valley. I arranged for us to stay at a very nice hotel in Saumur and time was arranged for a visit to the Cadre Noir. We saw the old building in the town where they were originally and did a tour of the new establishment just out of town. It was most interesting – even for someone like me who has been on a horse only once – fallen off and decided horse riding wasn't for me.

They would occasionally come to my office in Devon and invite me out to lunch. We spent our time talking about previous tours and what was being planned for the future.

Bernard was another of those passengers who thanked me in a very special way. It wasn't a cushion, painting or pottery. One winter he phoned to say that he had been keeping himself busy during the cold months by compiling a glossary of wine terms he had learned since joining the wine tours. He said he would like to give it to me. He had typed it but unfortunately not on a computer. When I read through it, I felt very proud that I had given him the incentive to do this.

The glossary has now been 'computerised' and additions made. It is with great pleasure that I include it in my book.

French wines
A vocabulary and glossary of terms with some general addenda

appellations – The Institut National Des Appellations D'Origine (INAO) has differentiated among three main types of wine:-
1. Vins d'Appellation d'Origine Controlée (AOC).
2. Vins Delimites de Qualité Supérieur (VDQS).
3. Vins de Pays.
(for further details refer to the appendix)

appellation communale – the appellation covering a commune (e.g. Pauillac), where there are different crus from different vineyards.

appellation controlée – the system controlling which varieties of grapes may be planted, how and which wine may be made from them, and what the wine will be called. (c.f. appendix)

appellation regionale – the appellation covering a sub-region of a main type of wine. e.g. Beaujolais – Beaujolais Villages; Moulin-Vent.

assemblage – the blending of wines to produce a specific wine.

barrique – a 225-litre barrel, usually made of French Oak. In it, white wines are sometimes fermented and red and white wines may be matured. They are normally replaced every 2 to 3 years as new Barriques have more effect on the taste of the maturing wine.

Blanc de blancs – white wines made exclusively from black grapes. The term is usually reserved for Champagne made from Pinot Noir grapes. The grapes are vinified without skin contact since the juice of most black grapes is colourless. All the colouring matter is found in the skins.

Blanquette de Limoux – sparkling wine made in the region of Limoux, south of Carcassonne, in the departement of the AUDE. The name comes from the covering of white dust found on the undersides of the leaves of the Mauzac Blanc vine, from the grapes of which the wine is mainly made. The Mauzac must be planted to a minimum of 80%, with the rest made up of Chenin Blanc and Chardonnay. It is made sparkling by either the *méthode rurale* (q.v)
or the *méthode champenoise (traditionelle) (q.v)*

B*otrytis cinerea* – noble rot or *pourriture noble*. It is a fungus that attacks ripe white grapes in specific vineyards in the Loire Valley and south-west France. It may arise under certain conditions of humidity and temperature if the harvesting of the grapes is delayed. The grapes shrivel and their sugar becomes concentrated. The fungus will not appear if it is too cold or if it is sunny and dry when the grapes become roasted (roti) instead of *pourri*. The bunches, or even single grapes, are individually picked in a succession of pickings or *tries*. Their juice is used for the production of sweet, white wines known as *vins liquoreux*.
e.g. Bordeaux – Sauternes, Barsac, Cadillac, etc.

Wines made from the Sauvignon grape for finesse and body; the Semillon grape for flavour and richness; the Muscadelle grape for the heady, slightly muscat aroma.

Loire Valley – Bonnezeaux, Quarts de chaume, etc.
Made from the Chenin Blanc grape.

Bergerac – Monbazillac.
Made from the same grapes as the Bordeaux wines.

bottles – French wines are contained in bottles of many different sizes and shapes. In AC areas, only certain bottles may be used. The EC now rules that all wines must be contained in 75 cl (750 ml) bottles. Bottles of Champagne, however, contain about 80 cl and Champagne bottles increase in size as: MAGNUM: 2 bottles; JEROBOAM: 4 bottles; REHOBOAM: 6 bottles; METHUSELAH: 8 bottles; SALMANAZAR: 12 bottles; BALTHAZAR: 16 bottles; NEBUCHADNEZZAR: 20 bottles.

bottle age – an unpleasant smell that comes from a bottle of wine as soon as the cork has been withdrawn. In most cases this vanishes as the musty air which causes it escapes and the wine can be drunk. This is not the same as bad wine or corked wine.

brut – the name generally given to the driest versions of Champagne and other sparkling wines. Wines without any *dosage* (q.v) are known as *brut zero/brut de brut/brut integral.*

buttage – when you 'buttage', you push the soil up to the roots of the vines in order to protect them from the frost in winter. The time to do this is in November.

cave – an underground cellar in which wine is stored and /or matured.

cave co-operative – A wine-growers' co-operative winery. Co-operatives are currently responsible for 50% of French wine.

carbonic maceration – whole bunches of grapes are placed in a fermenting vat without being pressed. They begin to ferment internally and the carbon dioxide produced ruptures the grapes and the fermentation continues in an atmosphere of carbon dioxide. After a few days the grapes are pressed and the juice placed in other vats where fermentation continues. All this produces lighter, fruity wines with low tannin and malic acid, e.g. Beaujolais.

cep – the vine

cep de vigne – the vine stock

cépage – *either* the variety of vine, e.g. Chardonnay, Pinot Noir
or the different varieties of wine used in a blend.

cépages traditionnels – the traditional varieties of vines grown in a region.

cépages aromatiques – better flavour-producing vines.

cépage noble – one of the few grape varieties that consistently give fine wine. e.g. Chardonnay, Sauvignon, Cabernet Sauvignon, Pinot Noir.

chai – an above-ground 'cellar' for storing wine or spirits, usually while further maturing takes place. It is also used for the production of wine.

chambre – describes wine which has been taken from the cellar and allowed to reach room temperature. This is not necessarily the best temperature for drinking the wine.

Champagne – the region and the sparkling wine produced in that region. To have the AOC, the wines must be made from Chardonnay, Pinot Noir or Pinot Meunier grapes grown in the departements of the AISNE, AUBE, HAUT-MARNE, MARNE and SEINE-ET-MARNE. The still wines known as the *méthode champenoise* (refer to the appendix) and the whole process must be carried out in the Champagne Region. It is the only appellation permitted to omit the *appellation controlee* from its label.

champenise – describes wine made sparkling by the *méthode champenoise*.

chaptalisation – the legal addition of sugar to the *must* (q.v.) to assist fermentation and increase the final alcohol content of the wine. This does not sweeten the wine and there are strict rules governing its addition. [See Burgundy for origin.]

climat – an individual, specific vineyard, generally in Burgundy, not classified as Grand or Premier Cru (q.v.).

clos – a vineyard site that was walled in the past and may still be. Particularly in Burgundy.

commune (or finnage) – a village or parish, producing wine.

consumé – the wine or spirit lost from barrels or vats by evaporation. In Cognac it is known as 'La part des anges' or 'angels' share. The black stain found in the houses or buildings is a black fungus that lives off the alcohol vapour.

corked – a fault in a bottle of wine caused either by a bad cork or by air getting inside and oxidising the wine. With varying degrees of unpleasantness, the wine smells 'off' and is discarded. Small, broken-off pieces of cork floating on the wine do not necessarily mean it is corked.

côte (or coteaux) – a hill, slope or hillside. Grapes grown on such sites are usually better than those from valleys or the tops of hills.

en coteaux – describes the vines grown on such slopes.

cremant – sparkling wine that is less sparkling than *Champagne* or *vin mousseux* (q.v.) but more sparkling than *vin petillant* (q.v.) The best is usually produced by the *méthode champenoise* (q.v.) but may not be labelled as such but usually as *méthode traditionelle*. The wine is bottled with between 3 and 4 atmospheres of pressure.

cru(s) – vineyards classified geographically or by reputation. The term may also be applied to the wines produced from them. The term can be applied to a distinguished single property in Bordeaux or a distinguished vineyard area in Burgundy (c.f. Grand and Premier crus).

cru bourgeois – Bordeaux – a wine from the bottom tier of the secondary classification system of the Medoc Region. *Cru grand bourgeois* and *Cru grand Bourgeois Exceptionnel* indicate better wines from this secondary classification system.

cru classe – Bordeaux – a wine from the primary classification system of the Medoc Region. This system is divided into *premier, deuxième, troisième, quatrième* and *cinquième Crus Classes*. It is also used in the classification systems of the Graves, Sauternes and St. Emilion areas.

cuve – a vat or tank in which wine is stored.

cuvée 1. The contents of a single vat of wine after blending.
or 2. A wine from a selected barrel or vat, generally superior to the norm.
or 3. In Champagne it means the juice of the first pressing of grapes.
The term is often found printed on labels but it has no legal status.

cuve clos – a method of making sparkling wine by producing the secondary fermentation inside a closed tank, generally stainless steel. The resultant wine is pumped under pressure for bottling and its quality is not as good as that produced by the *méthode s champenoise, traditionelle* or *rurale* (q.v.).

cuverie – the place where wine (must) ferments (from the French verb *cuver* – to ferment).

dégorgement – the expulsion of a small block of frozen wine and sediment from the neck of a bottle of sparkling wine (refer to appendix).

demi-muid – a large oak barrel, generally of 660 litres capacity.

demi-sec – the taste of a wine (usually sparkling) between sweet and dry. The sweetness is due to either residual sugar or to *dosage* (q.v).

deposit – the sediment or deposit at the bottom of a bottle of wine. Most old wines leave a sediment so they must be carefully poured or decanted. The latter is particularly important with old claret (and port). In sparkling wines, the sediment produced after secondary fermentation in the bottle is removed by the process of *dégorgement* (q.v.).

domaine – an estate (particularly in Burgundy), meaning the total vineyards owned by a grower (éleveur) or négociant (q.v.).

dosage – the process of adding a solution of wine and cane sugar (le liqueur de dosage) to sparkling wines after *dégorgement* (q.v.). The amount added dictated the degree of sweetness of the wine (refer to the appendix).

douve – the stave of a barrel.

élevage – the 'rearing' or 'bringing-up' of a wine, usually in barrels, before it is bottled.

encépagement – the make-up of grapes in a given wine.

en primeur – used of a wine which is drunk or sold very young.

en sec – a method of vinification used to make dry wines from wines that are traditionally sweet.

esters – compounds found in wine resulting from the interaction of normal acids and alcohols present. They typically have a fruity odour and contribute to the odour of the wine.

extra-brut (extra dry) – (refer to the appendix – *'Méthode Champenoise').*

établissement vinicole/viticole – a wine making establishment.

faire le vendange – to harvest or pick grapes.

fermentation – the conversion of the sugars in *must* (q.v.) into ethyl alcohol and carbon dioxide. It is performed by natural and/or cultivated yeasts working in anaerobic (oxygen-free) conditions. This is known as primary fermentation. Normally it continues until all the sugar is converted into alcohol or until the alcohol content is about 15%, which kills the yeasts. In both cases the result is a dry wine. Sweeter wines are due to residual sugar after the yeasts are killed or the artificial stopping of fermentation by fine filtration or the addition of sulphur. A second or malo-lactic (q.v.) fermentation may follow this primary fermentation.

filtration – 1. The mechanical removal of deposits from wine before bottling. This improves the colour and prevents tainting.
2. Very fine filtration to remove yeasts and so stop primary fermentation.

fining – the technique of adding a fining agent (e.g. egg white, bentonite) to a barrel, vat or tank of wine. The agent attracts the suspended deposits in the wine and sinks to the bottom so that clear wine can be drawn off.

flute – 1. The tall elegant bottle used in Alsace or Château Grillet (Rhône, Viognier, one of the smallest ACs in France).
2. The elegant glass recommended for Champagne.

fortified wine – v*ins doux naturels* (q.v.).

foudre – a large, immobile wooden cask used for fermenting or storing wine.

fûts de chêne – an oak barrel.

garrigue – tough, arid soil in the southern Rhône valley.

générique – a regional AOC wine without a *cru* or *communale* appellation.

gouleyant – used to describe a wine that is easy to drink.

goût de terroir – a distinctive taste and style given to a wine by a combination of the variety of grape from which it is produced and the soil in which the vines are grown.

gras – used to mean a rich and full-bodied wine.

gravier – gravelly soil, always found near a river.

gros rouge – a heavy and uninteresting red wine.

grand cru – Alsace – a classified vineyard site.
Burgundy – the finest category of named vineyard site. The term is also used to describe the wine produced from it.

grand vin – the top wine of a Bordeaux Château, blended only from selected *cuvées* (q.v.). The next quality is 'second wine' (q.v.).

l'industrie vinicole/viticole – the wine industry.

lees (la lie) – the sediment left in a barrel or vat after the wine has been drawn off. The best Muscadet is bottled 'sur lie', straight from the barrel without racking (q.v.). The Lees are considered to contribute a 'zest' to the wine.

lieu-dit – a named, but unclassified, vineyard in Burgundy (c.f. climat).

liqueur d'expedition – another name for *liqueur de dosage*.

liqueur de tirage – the solution of old wine, cane sugar and selected yeasts added to a bottle of future sparkling wine to produce the second fermentation (la prisse de mousse – frothing) in the bottle and hence the required degree of sparkle in the wine.

maceration – the process of leaving whole grapes to 'stew' on their skins before, during and after fermentation.

maceration carbonique – carbonic maceration (q.v.).

malolactic fermentation – after the first alcoholic fermentation has ceased, a second non-alcoholic, malolactic fermentation may occur quite naturally. It is caused by bacteria which convert malic (apple) acid in the wine to lactic (milk) acid which softens the sharpness of the wine. (This is because the malic acid contains two acidic or carboxyl groups (–COOH) and the lactic acid contains only one.)

marc – 1. The 4000 kilos of grapes in a Champagne press.

or 2. An 'eau-de-vie' made by macerating spirit with the grape skins left after pressing.

mas – a vineyard or *climat* (q.v.) in the northern Rhône Valley.

méthode champenoise – the method used to make Champagne by inducing a secondary fermentation in the bottle rather than in a cask or vat (refer to appendix).

méthode dioise – (refer to *méthode rurale).*

méthode gaillacose – (refer to *méthode rurale).*

méthode rurale – an old method of making sparkling wine that is still used in some regions, e.g. Limoux. No *liqueur de tirage* (q.v.) is added and the second fermentation takes place in the bottle using sugar still present in the wine due to retarded alcoholic fermentation.

méthode traditionelle – the making of sparkling wine by the Champagne method but outside of that region. It is used for many *cremant* wines, particularly *cremant de Loire,* and for some of the *Blanquette de Limoux* (q.v).

mis en bouteille – bottled by... .

mis en bouteille du(au) domaine/a la propriéte – bottled at the property where the wine was made.

mis dans nos caves – bottled in our cellars (which are not necessarily those of the grower).

mis par la proprietaire – bottled by the grower.

moelleux – medium sweet to sweet, luscious white wine, somewhere between *vin doux* and *vin liquoreux* (q.v.).

monopole – indicates that the whole of a named vineyard belongs to the same proprietor.

mousse – describes the effervescence or bubbles in a sparkling wine.

mousseux – sparkling.

must – the grape juice or crushed grapes before fermentation.

mutage – (refer to *vins doux naturels).*

négociant – a wholesale merchant and wine trader who buys, stores and sells wine and acts as a middleman between the growers and retailers.

négociant-eleveur – a merchant who buys wine from a grower in its first year and 'raises' it in his own cellars.

noble rot – *Botrytis cinerea* (q.v.) or *pourriture noble* (q.v.)

non-vintage – a wine or Champagne made from a blend of wines of different years.

nose – the smell or bouquet of a wine. Basically it tells one if it is drinkable but many other interpretations are possible (refer to 'The Aroma Wheel' developed by The Department of Viticulture and Enology of the University of California).

nouveau – a new wine, particularly Beaujolais.

oeil de perdrix – (Literally 'partridge eye') Describes a pale rosé wine. Used particularly to describe a very rare Champagne Rosé.

oidium – powdery mildew that affects vines.

oillage – the regular topping-up of barrels while they lie in a *chai* or cellar.

oxidation – the action of atmospheric oxygen on the wine in a bottle with a bad cork. The wine develops a bad smell and eventually turns to vinegar.

passerilage – leaving grapes to dehydrate and dry on the vine in order to produce a dessert wine from them.

pasteurisation – the process of treating wine to kill off yeast and/or bacteria.

perlant – wine which produces a slight number of small bubbles on the side of the glass.

perle – a very slightly sparkling wine, often only identifiable on the palate.

petillant – a slightly sparkling wine with not more that 3 atmospheres of pressure inside the bottle.

Phylloxera vastatrix – the louse that attacks vine roots and kills the plant. It came from America and devastated most of the European vineyards between 1870 and 1890. Almost all vines in Europe had to be dug up and replaced by a European cutting that was grafted to a resistant American root stock. It is now very prevalent again in California and New Zealand.

piece – a general word for a barrel, usually of a 215- or 225-litre size.

Plafond Limite de Classement (PLC) – the quantity of wine allowed to be declared above the permitted yield in a specific *appellation*.

pourriture noble – the French name for the *botyris* (q.v.) or *noble rot* (q.v.)

premier cru – the second class of named, Burgundy vineyard *or* the wine made from it. If the wine is so described, but no vineyard is named, then it is a blend of the wines made from a number of Premier Cru sites.

premier grand cru classe – a 'first fine classed growth' from the top level of the St Emilion classification system.

propriétaire – a vineyard owner.

propriétaire-recoltant – an owner manager.

racking – the process of moving wine from one barrel to another, leaving the sediment or lees behind.

rape – the percentage of wine discarded in Châteauneuf-du-Pape and Gigondas (lower Rhône Valley) to maintain quality.

recoltant – a wine grower.

récolte – the harvest or vintage *or* the harvesting or gathering in.

region vinicole/viticole – a wine/growing/producing region.

remontage – the process of pumping up the fermenting wine in a vat and spraying it over the floating layer of skins at the top.

reserve – the term 'reserve' is indicative of certain qualities of wine in other countries but in France it has no legal status on the label.

rosé – a pink wine usually made from black grapes, the intensity of colour and flavour being derived by leaving the juice in contact with the grape skins for varying lengths of time.

rosé de noirs – rosé wines made from black grapes only.

saignée – the process of drawing off the fermenting juice of black grapes to make rosé.

sec – the French word for 'dry' and it means less than dry, e.g. extra sec, sec, demi sec (refer to *Brut* and the appendix: '*Méthode Champenoise*').

second wine – the next quality of wine after the *Grand Vin* (q.v.) of a Bordeaux Château. It is usually blended from less successful cuvées (q.v.) and the wine from younger vines. e.g. *Papillon* (Château Margaux; *Les Fortes de latour* (Château Latour); *Reserve de L'Amiral* (Château Beychevelle).

selection de grains nobles – the term used in Alsace for the very late picking of selected grapes from *Botrytis*-affected bunches. The resultant sweet wine may also be so called.

sève – ('sap') the inherent style and impact of a wine.

sous-marque – a wine sold or labelled under a secondary, possibly fictional, name.

sur-lie – a term used of white wine, particularly of Muscadet de Loire, which is bottled from above the fine lees (q.v.) in the barrel or vat, within the year following the vintage. It may contain some carbon dioxide. (The term is often used in a lax manner so it is best believed in conjunction with an indication of Domaine bottling.)

superieur – indicative of wine with a higher alcohol content than usual.

tannin – the element in wine that assists longevity and is particularly noticeable in young red wines. It comes from the grape skins and stems and the oak of barrels. In young wines it is astringent and makes the mouth pucker. As wine ages, the astringency is lost.

tartrates – the salts of tartaric acid. They may be found in red and white wines in the form of small crystals, often on the inner surface of the cork. They cause no ill-effects and are often indicative of quite a good wine.

teinturier grapes – black grapes with coloured juice.

tendre – wine that is light, delicate, soft and non-acidic and usually slighlty sweet.

terroir – the combination of soil and climate that affects vines and their grapes and the taste of the wine made from them.

tête-de-cuvée – the finest casks or cuves (q.v.) of a particular vintage.

tonneau – a wooden cask or barrel of any size. The word is also used for quoting the prices of Bordeaux wines:-

e.g. 1 tonneau = 4 pieces = 1200 bottles

tonnelet – a keg or small barrel.

tonnelier – a cooper or barrel maker.

tonnelerie – a cooperage.

tout court – the simple *appellation* in Beaujolais, as opposed to the *Villages appellation*.

tries – the successive pickings of a vineyard to harvest only the ripest or *Botrytis*-affected grapes.

tuffeau – the Limestone rock in the Loire valley, which forms the tuffeau-based (chalk and clay) soils on which the vines thrive, particularly in the region of Saumur and Touraine.

vendange – the grape harvest or vintage.

vendanger – the French verb meaning to harvest/pick grapes.

vendangeur(-euse) – a male/female grape picker.

vendange-tardive – the late picking of very ripe grapes.

vigne – the vine plant.

vieilles-vignes – old vines.

vignoble – a vineyard.

vigneron (-onne) – a male/female wine grower.

village – wine with the simple *appellation communale* (q.v.) of the commune named (refer to the appendix).

villages – wine from selected parishes within the region named.

viticulture – wine growing or production.

viticulteur(-euse) – a male/female wine grower.

vinification – wine making.

vintage – *either* the harvest of each year *or* the wine made from the grapes of a designated year.

vintage champagne/cremant – sparkling wine made from blends of the wines of a single year and sold after at least 3 years of ageing.

vin de base – denotes the still wine(s) from which a sparkling wine is made.

vin blanc – white wine.

vin de café – a red wine, light in colour and alcohol.

vin de carafe – pleasant wine for everyday drinking.

vins de cépage – wines where the grape variety takes precedence over the region of origin. Most common for branded wines or '*vins de pays*'.

vin de comptoir – a pleasant everyday wine served in French câfés.

Vin Délimité de Qualité Supérieure (VDQS) – this term covers the much smaller category of below AOC and with similar regulations (refer to the appendix).

Vins Doux Naturels (VDNs) – naturally sweet, fortified red or white wines produced by stopping fermentation early, by the addition of alcohol, before all the sugar in the must has been fermented out. The alcohol is in the form of a neutral grape brandy of at least 90%, added when the must contains about 7% of natural alcohol. The operation is called '*mutage*'. The residual natural sugar gives the wines their sweetness. The finest examples come from Languedoc-Roussillon, e.g. Banyuls (red and tawny); Maury (red and rose); Rivesaltes (red and rose); Muscat-de-Beaumes-de-Venise (white); Muscat-de-Frontignan (white); Muscat-de-Mireval (white); Rasteau (white and tawny).

vin de garde – a wine that should be kept for a long time in order to develop.

vin de grand cru – a vintage wine.

vin gris – a very pale rosé wine, always light and fresh.

vin liquoreux – a very sweet white wine made from grapes affected by *'pourriture noble'* (q.v.), e.g. Sauternes, Monbazillac.

vin mousseux – all sparkling wine apart from Champagne. It may be made *either* by secondary fermentation in a bottle or tank *or*, for cheaper wines, by the addition of carbon dioxide.

vin ordinaire – plain wine with no regional or varietal origin.

vin de pays – literally means 'country wine'. It is wine from a specified region with some regional characteristics. It is usually determined by administrative geography with more flexible regulations than for AOC and VDQS wines (refer to the appendix).

vin de presse – after fermentation and the free run-off of the young wine the residue of skins is re-pressed to extract the remaining (about 1/5th) wine. This is the 'vin de presse', which is kept separate from the rest until the final *'assemblage'* (q.v.).

vin rosé – pink rosé wine.

vin rouge – red wine.

vin de table – the most basic category of French wine with no provenance other than the country of origin printed on the label.

vin tranquille – non-sparkling wine.

Appendix

Appellations

The *Institut National des Appellations d'Origine (INAO)* has differentiated between three main types of French wine:

1. Vins d'Appellation d'Origine Controlée (AOC)
2. Vins Délimité de Qualité Supérieure (VDQS)
3. Vin de Pays.

AOC

What is controlled is:

(a) The area of production.

(b) The variety of grape
- sometimes only a single variety.
- sometimes several complementary varieties.
- grapes from newly planted vines may only be used from *'la quatrième feuille'* or their fourth vintage.

(c) The degree of alcohol
- there must always be a minimum and sometimes a maximum.

(d) The yield per hectare
- there is a maximum permitted yield termed *'le rendement de base'*, which is fixed by the INAO.
- local *'syndicats'* can apply for an augmentation or reduction (never yet applied for) in the basic yield, depending on the quality of the crop. This is known as *'le rendement annuel'*.
- on top of this, each appellation can apply (but it was refused for Grand Cru wines) for a further increase of up to 20% of *'le rendement annuel'* known as *'le plafond limite de classement'* (PLC).
- in Bordeaux this may result in the basic yield being increased by up to 60%.
- any producer declaring wine in excess of *'le rendement annuel'* + PLC loses the appelation.

(e) The methods of viticulture
- controlling the number of vines per hectare.
- the type of pruning.
- sometimes the method of picking e.g. by successive *'tries'* for Sauternes. Hence *'trie sur le volet'* or hand-picked.
- whether or not the grapes may be destalked before fermentation.

(f) The methods of vinification
- prohibition of the use of concentrated musts in most appellations and of *'vinage'* (addition of alcohol to the musts) in all wines.

– acidification and de-acidification are permitted under the control of the local *'station oenologique'*.

(g) Analysis and tasting
– all AOC wines must be submitted to a tasting panel made up of members of the local *'syndicat'* and representatives of the INAO. Those not passing are declassified but may be represented. A second declassification is final.

(h) Bottling
– obligatory bottling in the region of the appellation. Wines shipped out in bulk lose the appellation.

The higher appellations of Premier and Grand Cru are, with the exception of the Crus Classes of Bordeaux, based on geographical *'climates'* (vineyards) within the appellations, with stricter controls on the yields and alcohol contents.

VDQS
The same basic rules apply as for AOC wines but the range of grapes is wider and the degrees of alcohol sometimes lower. All wines must be submitted to a tasting panel to obtain the VDQS label. Without this they are declassified to Vin de Pays or Vins de Table. In recent years many VDQS wines have been raised to AOC status and some Vin de Pays to VDQS. This is particularly so in the Midi.

Vins de Pays
These present an ever-changing scene. They came into being in 1968 with a decree authorising certain Vins de Table to indicate their regional origins.
In 1973 a further decree fixed precisely the conditions of production for a Vin de Pays:-
e.g. (a) The region
(b) The grape variety(-ies).
(c) The yield
(d) The alcohol content
(e) The level of SO_2.
(f) The level of volatile acidity.

In 1979 these conditions were refined and particular rules established for individual Vins de Pays, corresponding to different geographical interpretations:-
1. *Vins de Pays Régionaux* – these may come from several grouped Départements as long as they correspond to an accepted style of wine,
e.g. Vins de Pays d'Oc – for the whole of the Languedoc-Roussillon.
Vins de Pays du Jardin de La France – for the Loire valley.

2. Vins de Pays Départmentaux – these must carry the name of the Département where they are produced,
e.g. Vins de Pays du Gard.
Vins de Pays de L'Ardèche.

3. Vins de Pays de Zone – these may state the name of the individual commune where they are produced,

e.g. Vins de Pays du Val d'Orbieu (Aude département)
Vins de Pays des Coteaux du Salaves (Gard département)

Group 3 can be sold as 2 and 1. Group 2 can be sold as 1, if so desired.

La méthode champenoise

The process of making still wine into sparkling wine by a secondary fermentation in the bottle. The method is used in France, and other parts of the world, but the term *'Méthode champenoise'* may not be used outside of the Champagne region where it is more elaborate and disciplined. Outside of the Champagne region the methods used in France are named *'Méthode rurale'* (*Méthode dioise/Méthode gaillacose*) or *'Méthode traditionelle'* (refer to the glossary of terms).

1. The grapes are sorted by only picking the best and taking care not to damage the skins (particularly for Blanc de Noirs wines (q.v.)).

2. The grapes are pressed as quickly as possible in units of 4000 kilograms.
From this unit or *'marc'* (q.v.), a maximum of 2666 litres of must may be extracted by three separate pressings:

1st *'La cuvée'*	–	2050 litres.
2nd *'La taille'*	–	410 litres.
3rd *'La deuxieme taille'*	–	206 litres.

The best Champagne houses only use the 'cuvée' for their wines.

3. The impurities in the must are allowed to settle – *'la débourage'*.

4. The now clearer must is fermented in stainless steel vats, the alcoholic fermentation being followed by a malo-lactic fermentation (q.v.) to lower the total acidity.

5. The resultant still white wine is then blended with still wines from the same year (for vintage Champagne) or other years (for non-vintage Champagne), the process being known as *'assemblage'*.

6. The 'champenisation' then starts by bottling the still wine blend (*'le tirage'*) with the addition of a *'liqueur de tirage'*, which is a solution of cane sugar in old wine with selected yeasts (*'les levures'*) added.

7. A second fermentation (*'la prisse de mousse'*) then takes place in the bottles, which are laid horizontally in the cellar. This process must take place slowly over many months in order to produce the very small bubbles of gas when the wine is eventually poured. The gas pressure produced is between 5 and 6 atmospheres for a full Champagne and 3 to 4 for a cremant.

8. This secondary fermentation also leaves a deposit made up mainly of dead yeasts along the side of the bottle. This is eliminated by placing the bottles in specially designed racks (*'pupitres'*) at an almost horizontal level. They are turned daily (*'le remuage'*) by a quarter turn over several weeks. At each turn the bottle is also tilted slightly so that it eventually arrives at an almost vertical position (*'sur*